By the same author

★

STAGE-SETTING: FOR AMATEURS AND
PROFESSIONALS

PROSCENIUM AND SIGHT-LINES

CHANGEABLE SCENERY: ITS ORIGIN
AND DEVELOPMENT IN THE
BRITISH THEATRE

THE OPEN STAGE

THE SEVEN AGES OF THE THEATRE

THE STAGING OF PLAYS BEFORE SHAKESPEARE

★

THE GEORGIAN PLAYHOUSE
(*Pleiades Books*)

THE ESSENTIALS OF STAGE PLANNING
in collaboration with Stanley Bell and Norman Marshall
(*Muller*)

THE VICTORIAN THEATRE

PLATE I. A Circular Theatre about 1400. Showing a 'scaffold' and actors, with the audience surrounding them. *From the* Térence des Ducs *manuscript, Bibliothèque de l'Arsenal, Paris*

THE
MEDIEVAL THEATRE
IN THE ROUND

A STUDY OF THE STAGING OF
THE CASTLE OF PERSEVERANCE
AND RELATED MATTERS

Revised and Expanded Edition

by

RICHARD SOUTHERN

THEATRE ARTS BOOKS
NEW YORK

First published in 1958
Second edition 1975
by Theatre Arts Books
333 Sixth Avenue New York 10014
Printed in Great Britain
by Butler & Tanner Ltd
Frome and London

ISBN 0-87830-085-6

I should like to dedicate this book
to the memory of Bertolt Brecht
and to the Berliner Ensemble
in recognition of a theatrical experience
among the greatest of our time

LIST OF CONTENTS

LIST OF CONTENTS

PART THREE

The Scaffolds round the 'Place'

PART FOUR

The Performance of The Castle of Perseverance

APPENDIX ONE

APPENDIX TWO

ILLUSTRATIONS

PLATES

FIGURES IN THE TEXT

ACKNOWLEDGEMENT

I HAVE to make grateful acknowledgement to the Early English Text Society, and to the Oxford University Press who afforded me permission to quote extensively from *The Macro Plays* (E.E.T.S. extra series No. 91, reprinted 1924). Also we acknowledge the detailed work in Edwin Norris' *The Ancient Cornish Drama* (1859).

FOREWORD TO THE SECOND EDITION

THE first edition of this book in 1957 offered evidence about the medieval technique of presenting plays in Rounds. This second edition includes some further evidence from a different play, set out in a new Foreword and an Appendix. The new Foreword is concerned with a particular problem in interpreting a plan diagram in this play, which is the Cornish mystery *Origo Mundi* (*The Creation of the World*), being part one of the three-part *Ordinalia* whose other two parts are *The Passion* and *The Resurrection*.

Since my first edition an occasion offered to present a full performance of this *Ordinalia* in an actual Cornish Round (the presentation by students of the Drama Department of Bristol University at Piran Round in July, 1969). The present writer made a complete scheme for the action based on the information gained earlier from the study of *The Castle of Perseverance* as set out in the first edition; but because the full details of this scheme could not then be taken up, there seemed reason to make a summary of them and offer it as an Appendix to the new edition of the book from which they originally derived, and to which they add certain significant extensions. This new Appendix duly follows at the end of the book, but for the present Foreword I have picked out one particular feature of the plan diagram to discuss separately—and this for a special reason as will appear.

The plan for *The Creation* in Fig. A consists of two concentric circles with eight Latin names or titles written in the ring between them. From the study of *The Castle* which follows, these names can be taken to be the names of 'scaffolds' or stages of a particular kind, and all—with one exception—can be readily identified. They are, reading anti-clockwise from the top; coelum (heaven), tortores (tormentors in the sense of professional strong-arm men or bullies), infernum (hell), Rex pharao (King Pharaoh), Rex david (King David), Rex sal (King Solomon), Abraham (Abraham), and finally—and this is the cause of the present Preface—an obscure word that looks like epi or ept or epc or (as one authority has said) ort. There is a line over the last two letters indicating that the word is an abbreviation.

FIG. A. The plan diagram for the *Origo Mundi* from the Cornish *Ordinalia* cycle.

The two views of the interpretation of this word have been; (1) by Pollard who expands it to *episcopus* (that is to say 'bishop', see his 'Afterwords' in the Early English Text Society's edition of *The Macro Plays*, Extra Series XCI, 1924) and (2) by Chambers who expands it to *ortus* or *hortus* (that is to say 'garden', see his *The Medieval Stage*, vol. II, p. 135). Which of these somewhat remarkably dissimilar readings is the more likely?

It is especially important to decide this question because if 'garden' is right then it must be admitted as a matter of course that this *Creation* plan is shaped simply on the lines of *The Castle* plan and has little to add to it. But if 'bishop' is right the *Creation* plan can be shown to throw a certain new light on medieval technique of which there is no, or little, hint in *The Castle*. The reason for this perhaps surprising assertion is interesting. The whole question of how the Earthly Paradise (that is, the Garden of Eden) was represented in the play depends on it. What is involved is as follows:

Three localities are presented in the opening passages of *The*

Creation: Heaven, Paradise, and a less clearly specified place which can be considered simply as 'outside Paradise'. Heaven is clearly shown in the text of the play to be raised up in some way because characters have to *ascend* to go to it, and *descend* to leave it. It must therefore resemble more or less what are called 'scaffolds' in the *Castle* plan. And the third locality 'outside paradise' is, on the other hand, equally clearly shown *not* to be raised up and therefore to be presumably at ground level, because characters *descend* from Heaven to enter it and *ascend* to Heaven from it.

But the second locality, Paradise Garden, creates a problem. On the one hand God is clearly directed to *descend* to it when going to it from Heaven, but to *enter* it (not *ascend*) when going into it from the Place outside Paradise. And yet—according to Norris's translation (referred to below)—*on one occasion one of Adam's sons, Seth, seems to be directed to go* up *when he approaches it from the Place outside.*

I believe it is so important to get this uncertainty cleared away before going on to study the problems of *The Castle* plan that I have chosen to lift out the relevant passage from the script to discuss here.

The script is in the ancient Cornish language, today an almost forgotten tongue. A translation with lengthy notes was published in 1859 by Edwin Norris in two volumes under the title *The Ancient Cornish Drama.* As to the date of the play, E. H. Pedler (see Norris, II, p. 506) believes it cannot be 'much later than the last quarter of the thirteenth century'; while Norris himself states (II, p. 437) 'certainly it cannot be assigned to a period earlier than the fourteenth century'. It might be placed, then, a clear century before *The Castle* of *c.* 1425. I have chosen to use Norris's edition for what I think are good reasons despite certain criticisms of it by some of the few students of this obscure language, and despite some more recent attempts to English it which are less complete or seem unwarrantably modernized. I accept the fact that Norris's English verse is stilted, but to me this appears as a conventionalism strangely sympathetic to the prim- itive nature of the drama itself. But chief of all I find his edition valuable because he gives the original Cornish version and the English translation on facing pages, and (particularly where the acting directions, which are in Latin, occur) this helps occasionally to make possible some check on the theatrical accuracy of Norris's interpretation. And it should be emphasized that Norris was not, and did not pretend to be, a theatre man or even a student of medieval theatre technique. He was concerned simply with the ancient text and devoted himself to it. Thus there are some renderings now and then of what are purely technical matters where he is clearly at loss and offers, quite frankly, an approximation. Some of these renderings can I think be amended, particularly after a detailed study of *The Castle of Perseverance*, and certain others which Norris perhaps felt puzzling can now be read with somewhat more confidence. (Norris himself says of this very plan, 'I do not know the meaning of the following Diagram, unless it be a rude representation of the stage or amphitheatre on which the drama was exhibited; shewing the locality of heaven and hell, and the places where some of the chief actors remained when not actually engaged in repeating their parts.' See Norris, II, p. 218.)

In the quotations which here follow I give only the English translation so far as the dialogue proper is concerned, but I give the acting directions both in the Latin of the original text and also in Norris's English translation. Both are as in Norris printed in italics but I have, for distinction's sake, put my insertions of the original Latin in inverted commas. The reason for including both Latin and English will be seen later.

The passage containing the problem about the presentation of Paradise which I want to consider comes after the episode of Cain and Abel when the expelled Adam has grown old. Near death, he calls his third son, Seth, and asks him to go to the gate of Paradise to ask of the 'Cherubin' who guards it 'if there will be for me / Oil of mercy at the last, / From the Father . . .' (ll. 693–5).

The query about whether Seth now has to 'go up' to reach the gate of Paradise comes in the last of the three occasions on which he approaches the gate with his question. I give the whole passage in some detail.

To begin, Seth has the following direction at l. 732,

'Et tunc iet ad paradisum [et dt cherubin]'

(Norris explains that the passages he encloses in square brackets are written in a later hand than the rest of the manuscript. There is thus a possibility that such passages are in the nature of added clarifications inserted in the light of experience gained from previous performances. Norris translates this direction as:)

> *And then he shall go to Paradise; [and the*
> *Cherub says:——]*

(I now abbreviate the dialogue to essentials.)

CHERUB.
Seth, what is thy errand, [. . .]?

SETH.
My father is old and weary, [. . .]
And through me he prayed thee
To tell the truth
Of the oil promised to him
Of mercy on the last day.

CHERUB.
Within the gate put thy head, [. . .]
And look on all sides; [. . .]

(The angel is inviting Seth for the first time to look in through the gate of Paradise but not to enter it. Seth agrees and says:)

SETH.
Very joyfully I will do it: [. . .]
To tell it to my father. [. . .]

(The first of the three directions now follows, l.752:)

> '[*et respicit et vertit se dicens*]'
> [*And he looks, and turns round, saying:—*]

Fair field is this; [. . .]
But the tree [. . .] it is dry.

CHERUB.
Look yet again within, [. . .]

SETH.
I will go to the gate immediately,
That I may see further good.

(The second direction now follows, l. 794:)

'[*vadit et respicit et revertit*]'
[*He goes, and looks, and returns.*]

SETH.
There is a serpent in the tree; [. . .]

CHERUB.
Go yet the third time to it,
    And look better at the tree.
Look, what you can see in it,
    Besides roots and branches.

(There now follows the third and significant direction, l. 802:)

'[*iterum vadit in sup*$^{(erum)}$]'
[*Again he goes up.*]

SETH.
In the tree I saw, [. . .]
A little child newly born;
[. . .] swathed in clothes, [. . .]

CHERUB.
The Son of God it was whom thou sawest, [. . .]
He will redeem Adam, thy father,

What is the original intention behind the wording of this third direction?

Nowhere else in the whole cycle is the phrasing *vadit in sup:* to be found. Always, when a character has to go up to some scaffold, the verb *ascendit*, 'he goes up', is used, for example at ll. 330, 605, 1284, 1478, 1882, etc. But if *vadit in sup:* is held to mean the same thing as *ascendit* then it follows that Paradise must be raised, presumably on a scaffold. And since no other scaffold on the plan can be assigned to Paradise there is only the *epc.* scaffold available, and Chambers would be justified in reading its title as *ort.*, or *hortus*, that is 'Garden'.

But there is evidence against this; namely, that God has to ascend when he goes from Paradise to Heaven (e.g. at l. 330). Also, at no point when any character leaves Paradise is he directed to descend—the sort of expression used is *recedunt de paradiso*, 'they go away from Paradise'. Furthermore, to go into Paradise is expressed by such a direction as *iet ad paradisum*, 'he goes to

Paradise' (l. 208)—not *ascendit ad*, or 'ascends to'. However, all these counter arguments can have little weight unless a new reading can be found for the direction that Norris records as *vadit in sup (erum)* and translates as 'he goes up'. Can such a new reading be legitimately offered? The crux of the matter is that this Latin direction is a contraction in the original—*vadit in sup:*—and that the termination *erum* is (as his brackets show) Norris's expansion. But it is not the only possible expansion.

It can equally be argued that the expression *in sup:* refers to time, and means *in supremo*, that is to say 'for the last time', on the analogy of *in praesentia* which is a phrase meaning 'at the present time'. Or it might not even be two words at all but merely the single adverb *insuper*, meaning 'moreover' or 'an additional time', 'once more'.

At the very least these possible alternative readings would weaken the case for a raised Garden of Paradise; taken with the distinct statement that a character has to *descend* to go from Heaven to Paradise but never to *ascend* when entering Paradise from any direction whatever, I believe they justify a final decision that Paradise was *not* elevated on a scaffold, and that *epc:* should be read as *episcopus* and not as *hortus*.

How in fact The Garden might have been presented I prefer to consider together with other details of the presentation of the *Ordinalia* cycle after examining in detail the information which lies in the script of *The Castle of Perseverance*, and in the light of all that can be learned from it about presentation in medieval Rounds. The study of *The Castle* therefore now follows.

The Castle of Perseverance

The medieval theatre in Britain is chiefly pictured as a system practised by amateur players, in which they employed a succession of wagons pulled about the streets of a city. But we understand that system only very vaguely; it presents many problems in working. There was another system that, I believe, was of wider use and possibly belonged to a more consciously theatrical tradition. Of this we can create a much fuller picture, and to this system the great epic play, *The Castle of Perseverance*, belonged.

I use the term 'epic play' with due regard to the connotation that has been given to it in the illuminating writings of Bertolt Brecht.

To anyone who has appreciated the epoch-making performances of the Berliner Ensemble, *The Castle of Perseverance* will speak with a familiar theatrical language. It too is a 'social' play; it is a play belonging to that form of society 'where the smallest social unit is not one man but two men'—in their interplay upon each other, or in the interplay of the dual man inside each individual. Moreover it is a social play in its shrewd complicating of morality by an economic factor. . . .

It is a play of this age as well as of that; and the system of staging it which that age invented is strikingly stimulating to our modern mind in so far as we too have come upon an 'epic' form of theatre that is intended to be at once direct in its appeal to people, and yet will no more be limited to that fashion of naturalism that clings to the picture-frame stage.

The Castle of Perseverance is a Morality Play of about 1425, of which there survives not only a manuscript of the dialogue with certain stage directions but, what is very much more to our present purpose, a sketch plan showing how the show was arranged—one of the first, if not the very first, plan of a theatrical presentation in English history.

It is not an easy plan to understand at first sight, nor is the play, in the original, easy to read. But with some care certain interpretations can be made with confidence and others with a little more temerity. In seeking to explain these interpretations it seems only fair to the reader to offer him the exact evidence of the original. Properly, this would involve his reading the whole manuscript itself, but to save him this I have reproduced certain relevant sections of it in two ways; first, as they appear in the original (that is, as far as modern type-setting can manage to do such a thing); and second (immediately after), in a modified form so as to be more familiar to a modern reader's eye.

One notable result of this is that it soon becomes apparent that we are dealing with a playwright of remarkable quality, and with poetry which can be highly evocative and dramatic and is savoured with just that sense of acidity that gives a tang of tastiness to the whole—both verbally and philosophically.

But the course of a modernizer is never smooth. In this work I have, to the best of my ability, held to the following ideal:

When a quoted passage is brief (that is, in the nature of a word or two, or a sentence) I have quoted it *either* in the original form *or* in a modernized version, according as it seemed to me most informative in the context. But I have seldom given the quotation in both forms together.

When, however, the passage is of a substantial length, I have given it in *both* forms, first in its original and then, in brackets, in its modernized form. The result of this is that a reader may, if he wishes, when he reaches such a longer quotation cut right through it till his eye lights on the bracket, and then read steadily on from there, taking in the modernization and ignoring the original. His progress through the ideas expounded in the book will thus be uninterrupted by the hindrance of unfamiliar language and spelling. He may then on second reading, or at such time as he wishes, be able to refer to the original and make judgement himself of my interpretation and of the precise significance of the evidence it contains.

In my modernization I am well aware that I have laid myself open to criticism in my alteration of certain words. I have altered them, however, with two intentions in mind. The first is to make the text intelligible to a general reader, the other, equally important, is to make it intelligible as spoken verse to a potential spectator. Verse that is spoken in the theatre may well contain words which, apart or read by eye, a spectator might not understand, but which in the current emotion of a speech he accepts without a quaver because the *intention* of the sentence is clear. Thus I have retained many of the original rich words when (though they are odd in themselves) the meaning of the sentence they belong to, when spoken as a whole, would in my opinion be clear, significant and vivid.

I have done all I could to retain the poetry of the original.

A final point for readers unfamiliar with medieval scripts. Many words in such a script are written not in full but in abbreviation. When these words are expanded to their full by the editor of a modern text, it is the custom to print any added letters in *italics*, to show they they are not in the original and to deal fairly with you if you should incline to another reading of the original.

So much in introduction to *The Castle of Perseverance* before we take up our main task of the study of the staging in detail.

R. S.

London 1956
Swanage 1973

PART ONE

THE CASTLE OF
PERSEVERANCE

1

THE PLOT AND THE CHARACTERS

The Banns ✷ *Nomina Ludorum*

THE manuscript of *The Castle of Perseverance* consists of four things; a prologue in the form of 'Banns', the play itself, a list of the characters and, on the last page, a plan. I propose to study first the Banns, second the Characters, third the Plan and fourth the Script. This seems a logical order because by it we begin with an ordinary citizen's introduction to a hitherto unknown play, as he stood on the grass near his home to hear two decorated figures read the announcement of its coming performance and a description of the plot; next we turn for a moment to see how the unknown, medieval poet-playwright's intention, when he framed that plot, is foreshadowed by his choice and grouping of the characters that were to play his parts; following upon this we turn to the very long and knotty problem of what preparations were made for the performance itself, and what kind of theatre and what method of presentation were developed to allow the show to be put over to the watching audience. After such a beginning we shall come to the performance itself of *The Castle of Perseverance* with a knowledge which will enable us to appreciate a system of medieval staging which has been up till now almost unexplained.

The Banns

The manuscript begins with a piece of introductory matter in the nature of an announcement or advertisement. This is a feature of several medieval plays, and it is called the Banns. The banns were read at large to the populace in some public spot near the place of the production, some days (in this case, a week) in advance. The banns of *The Castle* contain twelve stanzas or 156 lines. They are written for delivery by two *vexillatores*, or flag-bearers, speaking alternate stanzas. They begin with a greeting; it is in a

3

broad and dignified style and can well serve as a pattern of the character of the whole play. The opening nine lines of the First Flag-bearer's speech are as follows:

Glorious God! *in* all degres, lord most of myth,
  þat heuene & erthe made of nowth, boþe se & lond*e*,
þe aun3elys *in* heuene, hy*m* to serue bryth,
  & [man] -kynde *in* mydylerd he made w*ith* hys hond*e*,
& [our lo]fly lady, þat lanterne is of lyth,
  Save our lege lord, þe kynge, þe leder of þis londe,
& all þe ryall*is* of þis revme, & rede hem þe ryth,
    & all þe goode comowns of þis towne þat be-forn us stonde
      In þis place! . . .

(Glorious God! In all degrees Lord of most might—
  That heaven and earth made of nought, both sea and land,
The angels in heaven him to serve bright,
  And mankind in middle-earth he made with his hand,
And our Lovely Lady, that lantern is of light—
  Save our liege lord, the King, the leader of this land,
And all the nobles of this realm, and rede them the right,
    And all the good commons of this town that before us stand
      In this place! . . .)

Thus we get, already, some picture of the occasion—the two Flag-bearers, probably clad with some pomp, on a town-green, and the 'good commons' of that town assembled in a crowd to hear this announcement. The Flag-bearers now go on to outline the argument of the play, and since in fact they give one of the best and clearest summaries of the story that we can find, we will follow the thread.

The Second Flag-bearer begins (ll. 14–26) with a reference to Man's bareness of all goods as he enters and leaves the world, and alludes to the two angels—the Good and the Bad—that pull Man this way and that.

The First then picks up again (ll. 27–39) with mention of Man's three enemies—the World, the Fiend and the Flesh—then lists the Deadly Sins; Pride and Covetyse (that is, Covetousness or Avarice) lure him to the World; the Devil lends him Anger and Envy; and the foul Flesh, homeliest of all, calls to him through Sloth, Lechery, Gluttony and other sins both great and small. And thus Man's soul is soiled with more sins than seven!

The Second Flag-bearer goes on to say (ll. 40–52) that when

4

these sins assail Man, the Good Angel, mourning that the lovely likeness of God should be lost, sends conscience and confession with penance-doing to call Man to good living. And then Meekness, Patience, Charity, Soberness, Busyness, Chastity, and Largity (or Generosity) bring him to refuge in 'the Castel of good Persév-eraunce'.

(ll. 53–65) After this, the Bad Angel urges the Three Evils and the Seven Sins to regain Mankind, pitting Pride against Meekness, Anger against Patience, Envy against Charity—but the battle be-tween Covetyse and Generosity will be the longest.

(ll. 66–78) Covetyse encourages Gluttony against Soberness, Lechery against Chastity and Sloth against Busyness. The Good Angel strives to hold Man in the Castle. The Bad would bring him out.

(ll. 79–91) When Man shows loathness to leave, the Bad Angel sets Covetyse to offer him goods, and the World teaches him to ask for 'more and more'.

(ll. 92–104) As Man inevitably grows older, this last sin now gains more and more might, until the Good Angel is cast behind and the Bad comes in the ascendant and

> . . . Man to him taketh,
> That wringeth him wrenches to his last end
> Till Death cometh foul dolefully, . . .

Then Man becomes concerned over the destination of all his great possessions, and inquires who shall be his heir—and learns it is someone called 'I-wot-not-Who'.

(ll. 105–17) This is sore news, and just as poor Man wishes that his goods 'were sifted among his nigh kin', 'there shall come a lyther lad with a torn hood', bearing the hated, mysterious name, and he shall take all that was Mankind's just at that moment when

> all his life is lighted upon a little pin
> At the last . . .

(ll. 118–30) Man's spirit fled, the Bad Angel contends with the Good whether Heaven or Hell shall be its destination; but Mercy shall save it in the end, through Our Lovely Lady.

(ll. 131–43) The last stanza but one opens:

> Grace, if God wyl graunte us, of hys mykyl myth,
> þese parcellis in propyrtes we purpose us to playe
> þis day seuenenyt, be-fore ȝou in syth,

At .... on þe grene, in ryall a-ray.
3e haste 3ou þanne þedyrward, syr*is*, hendly *in* hyth,
  All goode neybor*is*, ful specyaly we 3ou pray,
& loke þat 3e be þere be-tyme, luffely & lyth,
  for we schul be onward be vnderne of þe day.
      dere Frendys,
    we thanke 3ou of all good dalyau*n*ce
    & of all 3our*e* specyal sportaunce,
    & preye 3ou of good contynnau*n*ce
      to our*e* lyuys endys.

(Grace if God will grant us, of his mickle might,
  These parcels in properties we purpose us to play
This day seven-night, before you in sight
  At ...., on the green, in royal array.
Ye haste you then thitherwards, sirs, hendly in height [courteous ex-
  ceedingly].
  All good neighbours, full specially we you pray,
And look that ye be there betimes, lovely and light,
  For we shall be onward by undern of the day.
      Dear Friends,
    We thank you for all good dalliance,
    And for all your special sportaunce [entertainment],
    And pray you of good countenance
      To our lives' ends.)

And the First Flag-bearer then concludes (ll. 144–56):

    D*eus*, oure lyuys we loue 3ou, þus takande our*e* leue.
    3e manly me*n* of ...., þus C*ri*st saue 3ou all!
    he maynten 3our*e* myrth*is*, & kepe 3ou fro greve,
      þ*at* born was of Mary myld in an ox stall.
    Now, mercy be all.................., & wel mote 3e cheve!
      All our*e* feythful frendys, þus fayre mote 3e fall!
    3a, & welcu*m* be 3e wha*n*ne 3e com, prys for to p*r*eve,
      & worthyi to be worchepyd *in* boure, & in hall,
        & in eu*er*y place.
      fare-wel, fayr*e* frendys,
      þ*at* lofly wyl lystyn & lend*is*!
      Cryste kepe 3ou fro fend*is*!
        tru*m*pe up, & lete vs pace!

(As our lives we love you, thus taking our leave.
  Ye manly men of.................., thus Christ save you all!
He maintain your mirths and keep you from grief
  That born was of Mary mild in an ox stall.

6

Now mercy be all................, and well might ye [move]!
  All our faithful friends, thus fair you befall.
Yes, and welcome be ye when ye come, price [prowess?] for to prove,
  And worthy to be worshipped in bower and in hall,
        And in every place.
    Farewell, fair friends,
    That lovely will listen and [stay];
    Christ keep you from fiends!
        Trump up! And let us pace.)

And so they go on their way.

We are now, therefore, informed not only of the picture of these heralds announcing the performance a week ahead, but also of something of the character of the poetry we are later to savour.

Keeping in mind this sketch of what the spectators are promised as the subject of the coming play, let us next turn to the List of Characters and see how much it has to tell us of the way the playwright will embody this subject in his drama.

Nomina Ludorum

The characters are all given Latin names in the List, but in the dialogue of the play they are always called by translated English names, and so to save confusion—and because some most interesting reflections can be made upon the names and their arrangement—I here give the Latin list together with a parallel list of the English names of the characters as used in the play, beside it.

Hec sunt nomina ludorum

In primis, ij Vexillatores	First, 2 Flag-bearers
Mundus & cum eo	World, and with him
Voluptas	Lust-liking
Stulticia	Folly
& Garcio	and Boy
Belyal & cum eo	Satan, and with him
Superbia	Pride
Ira	Wrath (or Anger)
& Invidia	and Envy
Caro & cum eo	Flesh, and with him
Gula	Gluttony
Luxuria	Lechery
& Accidi[a]	and Sloth

7

Humanum Genus & cum eo	Mankind, and with him
Bonus Angelus	The Good Angel
& Malus Angelus	and The Bad Angel
Auaricia	Covetyse
Detraccio	Backbiter
Confessio	Shrift
Penitentia	Penance
Humilitas	Humility (Meekness)
Paciencia	Patience
Caritas	Charity
Abstinencia	Abstinence (Soberness)
Castitas	Chastity
Solicitudo	Industry (Busyness)
& Largitas	and Generosity (Largity)
Mors	Death
Anima	The Soul (of Mankind)
Misericordia	Mercy
Veritas	Truth
Justicia	Righteousness (Justice)
& Pax	and Peace
Pater sedens in trono	The Father enthroned
Summa, xxxvj ludores	Total, 36 players

The List is set out in a way that has particular significance for the understanding of the action; the parts are grouped, and each group deserves some comment. The List begins:

In primis, ij Vexillatores.

These are the two Flag-bearers who have nothing to do with the action of the play itself, but whose function it was to read the banns as we have seen. The next group is:

Mundus & cum eo Voluptas, Stulticia & Garcio.

Here the grouping catches our attention. We have World, and *with him* Lust-liking, Folly and a Boy—and this 'with him' is important. World is one of the trio of evil characters who each have a scaffold to themselves among the five marked on the Plan (which we shall soon consider). He is the first of the Three Scriptural Temptations, or Instruments of Evil, who are in fact The World, The Flesh and the Devil. Under him are specifically grouped (*cum eo*) three servants or followers, two of them characteristic of worldly

8

leanings (first, Lust-liking; second, Folly), and the third a mysterious and—as we shall find—extremely malignant figure, cryptically named *Garcio* or Boy.

With regard to the two principal followers of World, it is useful to note that there are clearly specified here only two. We shall find later that confusion may arise because one of these two, Lust-liking, has a double name, and is sometimes called Lust and sometimes called Liking and sometimes called by the combination Lust-liking. Because of this it may appear on first reading the relevant lines in the play that World has three followers beside the Boy; to avoid this mistake it is valuable to note that clearly only two are here specified—*Voluptas* (Lust-liking) and *Stulticia* (Folly).

These two particular characters cause, from the point of view of the construction of the play, a bit of a puzzle. As we shall see, there is a sort of symmetry in the disposition of the parts generally; each Major Evil (World, Flesh and Devil) has three followers, and at this point we cannot do better than consider the next two groups in the List, in order to see the curiosity of the patterning. The two are:

> Belyal & cum eo Superbia, Ira & Invidia.
> Caro & cum eo Gula, Luxuria & Accidi[a].

The pattern appears to be developing smoothly; here are the other two Major Evils, *Belial* (the Devil) and *Caro* (the Flesh). The Devil has under him Pride, Wrath and Envy; while Flesh has Gluttony, Lechery and Sloth.

In these two trios, then, we have in fact six of the Seven Deadly Sins, but there is one Sin unaccounted for and, as we shall show, there is an immense significance in the separation of the Seventh Sin. But for the moment we have to notice something in what has gone before; the second and third Major Evils, the Devil and Flesh, are neatly served by dividing six relevant Sins between them—three each. But the first Major Evil, the World, though he has three servitors, has an oddly different group. He has a boy, he has Folly, and he has Lust-liking who would appear at first sight indistinguishable from Lechery among the Seven Sins. There is perhaps something in the idea that Lust-liking in medieval connotation signifies any inordinate desire for material things, while Lechery represents only that desire directed towards sexual things (incidentally, as the script will show beyond possibility of doubt,

9

Lechery *is* limited to this particular field of desire—and moreover she alone of all the Seven Sins is intended to be played as a woman; the rest are all men). For all that, the similarity of Lust-liking to a Deadly Sin is so great that one pauses to ask: Why should not the six Sins alone have been divided among the three Major Evils, two and two, and why invent these two further sinful figures (beside the Boy) for World? Or if they were not invented, where do they come from?

The point of all these queries is brought out in the play, where we see that, after their business in the earlier part, the playwright abandons Lust-liking and Folly and they (having helped to make the symmetry of the three trios) are dropped out of the action as soon as all the Sins appear. It may be that exigencies of casting and doubling come in here, and that the two players had to change into the parts of Shrift and Penance a little later in the play.

Whatever may be the reason for them, the three trios are quite clearly specified—three Sins under the Devil, three Sins under Flesh, and a more oddly assorted trio of two and a boy under World. The Devil and his are apportioned the Scaffold to the North; Flesh with his trio have the Scaffold to the South—and thus opposite the Devil—while World and those under him are half-way between, to the West.

The List of characters now continues:

Hu*m*anu*m* Gen*us* & c*um* eo Bon*us* Angel*us* & Mal*us* Angel*us*.

This is Mankind, the central character, with his Good Angel and his Bad Angel. Here is the first character on the list who has no trio, and who is not specifically related to his own special scaffold, but who forms a sort of floating, homeless being with his contrary genii—now staying in one place, now in another, but to none constant long.

The next group on the List breaks still farther from the pattern; so far the *cum eo*, inserted, has shown that in each group the subsequent figures were always in some particular relation to the leading figure of that group. Here there is no *cum eo*, and the four in this group are independent of each other. They are:

Auaricia, Detrac*c*io, Confessio, Penitentia,

that is to say, Covetousness (or Covetyse, for the metre of the play makes it a trisyllable), Backbiter, Shrift and Penance—two evil and two good characters.

We have now uncovered the Seventh Deadly Sin in the person of Covetyse. We notice that he is abstracted from the subordinate trios of the others. We shall notice on the Plan that he is promoted to the distinction of a scaffold to himself, as if he were an equal of the Major Evils (we shall see, however, that he has no servants under him as they had; and we shall see that nominally he is himself the servant of World, acting as his treasurer). Lastly, when we read the script we shall see the significance of all this; for the rather quiet (though very positive) figure of Covetyse turns out to be the most effective material factor in the shaping of the whole play at its climax.

It is, indeed, partly for this reason that we have so minutely examined the list of characters up to this point. For we have here an outstanding feature of the play, as I see it. It is this: From the point of view of the contemporary moralist, it is unusual to see the particular Spirit here demonstrated to be the prime cause of the downfall of Man—it is not the Spirit of Pride, as is commonly preached, but that of Covetousness. As we shall see, the be-all and end-all of the play's action rests upon this figure alone. It is Covetyse only who at the great siege of Mankind's Castle transcends the powers of all the Seven Virtues and, after all his fellow Sins have been vanquished in battle, quietly strides forward and, with no violence but only a smooth offer of financial security, achieves the whole tragic action of the play—the fall of Mankind.

We see how original and effective a stroke this is; original in being a reading of the cause of Man's fall which is not the traditional theological cause; effective in that when the moment occurs in the play its impact is considerable and its conviction unquestionable and at the same time deeply touching.

The remarkable singling out of this one figure to be the ultimate evil power governs the whole shape of the play. Not only does it account for the climax of the central action—that is to say, the victory in the siege of the Castle—but it forms part of the motive for the plan of the staging.

The latter influence may be seen in this way. The crucial action is the battle between the Virtues and the Sins. The Virtues belong to the Castle in the centre. The Sins are divided; three of them belong to the Devil and three to Flesh, and as such they are associated with their particular scaffolds in the North and South respectively. But the Seventh Sin, Covetyse, breaks the symmetry of the rest, and comes neither from the scaffold of the Devil nor of Flesh—nor even that of World. Neither does he come from any of the four cardinal points of the compass where the chief scaffolds are, but he comes, unaccompanied and secure in his own unaided power, from his own scaffold and his own unique point of the compass—the North-East.

This is part of the reason for that strange quintet of scaffolds, not arranged symmetrically round the circle, but with one of them placed at odds in an otherwise even arrangement.

Later, when we study the sight-lines of the 'theatre' itself as it was set up, we shall find another, and very cogent, reason for one out of five scaffolds always being placed odd—but the choice here of the odd scaffold for Covetyse particularly is, I think, made for a deeper reason.

The next figure in this group is of a different nature. He is Backbiter, a sort of scandalmongering messenger, who is sent on errands by his master, the World. One wonders if there were any purpose in his being displaced in the List from his master, and being set in another group; he would seem to have made a better third to World's trio than the Boy. But thus he is grouped.

The last two figures of this group form a pair—Shrift and Penance. For some reason which I do not understand, Sir Edmund Chambers, in his *English Literature at the Close of the Middle Ages*, 1945, p. 56, appears to reduce these to one character, since he says, describing the plot: 'But now Shrift, apparently called both *Penitentia* and *Confessio* in the rubrics . . . leads Mankind to repentance.' I can see no justification for this, since both here in the List of Characters, and again in the script, the names appear separately, separate speeches being assigned to either character as we shall see. The parts are small ones.

There are two more groups and one individual. The first of these groups is a major one in that it contains all the Seven Cardinal Virtues together. It reads:

Humilitas, Paciencia, Caritas, Abstinencia, Castitas, Solicitudo, Largitas

—that is, to use the names spoken in the play, Meekness, Patience, Charity, Soberness, Chastity, Busyness and Generosity (or Largity). Now, in contrast to the Seven Deadly Sins (each of which is more or less orthodox in name according to the exposition of

Gregory), these Seven Virtues are an oddly assorted choice. The orthodox Seven are the Three Christian Virtues—Faith, Hope and Charity—plus the Four Platonic Virtues—who are, approximately, Prudence, Justice, Fortitude and Temperance. Our playwright again seems to have forsaken orthodoxy here. Save for Charity, and perhaps Temperance under the name of Soberness, we have in the Seven Virtues of *The Castle* none of the accepted Seven.

The final group is miscellaneous. It contains Death, the Soul of Mankind and the Four Daughters of God. It reads:

Mors, Anima, Misericordia, Veritas, Justicia & Pax

—that is, Death, the Soul, Mercy (or Pity), Truth, Righteousness (or Justice) and Peace.

Some confusion may arise in the text over the names of the Four Daughters of God, and Furnivall, the editor, inserts a stage-direction at the head of their scene, reading '[*enter* Mercy, Righteousness, Truth, Justice, *and* Peace]'. But the Daughters are distinctly stated in more than one place to be four in number, and it appears in the lines of the play that Righteousness and Justice are equated in the same person.

The final character is the Occupant of the fifth and last scaffold—the one (significantly) on the East. It is:

Pater sedens in trono. (God the Father, enthroned.)

At the end of the list is the line '*Summa* xxxvj lud*ores*'—though in actual fact the list appears to total thirty-five, not thirty-six.

We may then perceive by the List of parts alone that we are about to deal with a relatively forceful and original thinker in this playwright, and one who is likely to animate these characters to some particular purpose and according to a view of life that is his own. And this, I think, we shall find confirmed when we have examined the play.

PART TWO

THE 'PLACE'
IN 'THE CASTLE OF
PERSEVERANCE'

2

THE REFERENCES TO 'PLACE' ON
THE PLAN

A Description of the Plan ∗ *The Place, first reference (the water round it)* ∗ *Second reference (the stytelers in it)* ∗ *Third reference (the Castle in its midst)* ∗ *Fourth reference (the act of playing in it)* ∗ *Summary*

So far, this approach to *The Castle of Perseverance*, through the Banns and the Characters, has been simple and pleasant-going. Now we have to turn to the Plan whereon are set out the arrangements for the performance—and here we enter a forest of problems of every sort.

The Plan has been very frequently reproduced, but less frequently studied in any detail. Interpretations—and even plain descriptions—have been conflicting. Yet this is possibly the most important document of its sort surviving from English medieval theatre. Sometimes it has been discussed with certain preconceptions in the writer's mind (such as, for instance, that all English medieval theatre took place on wheeled pageant-wagons, or that it involved a large, raised stage, something like the one we have today), and it is important, therefore, that we should be prepared to put previous comments and conceptions aside if we wish to understand the Plan, and that we should examine it with a completely fresh eye.

When, now, with such an intention, we try to describe what the Plan shows (referring to the reproduction in Fig. 1), we may do it as follows:

A Description of the Plan

Two concentric circles form a border round a main area. In the centre of this area is the representation of a battlemented Castle-tower; the thick black lines representing the slightly concave sides of the tower reach somewhat below the area where the pattern of stones is represented—thus suggesting that the tower is on legs.

In the space between the legs, under the lines of stones, is a small bench-like object on four legs that we shall find is a bed.

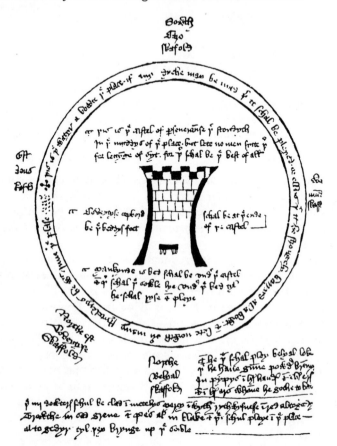

FIG. 1. The plan of the theatre for *The Castle of Perseverance*, about 1425, from the manuscript. In this plan the South is at the top. Reproduced by courtesy of the Council of the Early English Text Society.

There are various legends, as follows:

Written round between the two circles: þis is þe watyr a-bowte þe place if any dyche may be mad þer it schal be pleyed; or ellys þat it be strongely barryd al a-bowt; & lete nowth ou*er* many stytelerys be wi*th*-Inne þe plase.

Above the tower: þis is þe Castle of Perseuerau*n*se þat stondyth In þe myddys of þe place; but lete no men sytte þer, for lettynge of syt; for þer schal be þe best of all.

Either side of tower: (*left*) Coveytyse cepbord / be þe beddys feet. (*right*) schal be at þe ende / of þe Castel.

Below tower: Mankynde is bed schal be vnder þe Castel & þer schal þe sowle lye vnder þe bed tyl he schal ryse & pleye.

Outside the circles: (*above*) Sowth Caro skafold.
                    (*right*) Wes[t] Mund[us] skaffo[ld].
                    (*below*) Northe Belyal skaffold.
        (*below left*) Northe-est Coveytyse Skaffold.
                    (*left*) Est Deus [s]kafold.

Below right: he þat schal pleye Belyal loke þat he haue gunne-powder brennyn[ge] In pypys in his handis & in his eris & in his ars whanne he gothe to bat[tel].

Below: þe iiij dowteris schul be clad in mentelys; Merci in wyth, Rythwysnesse in red al togedyr; Trewthe in sad grene & Pes al in blake; & þei schal playe in þe place alto gedyr tyl þey brynge up þe sowle.

There are only three items which are in any sense graphically represented on the Plan, so as to give us any idea of what they may have looked like. They are: the ditch of water which, we are shown, was circular; the castle tower, which was in the centre of the circle; and the bed below the tower.

Associated with these are five scaffolds, but we have no indication of what they looked like, or what they were for, or even of exactly where they were built, save that we do know at which point of the compass each of them was.

Further, we have no indication whatever of where the people of the audience were situated; nor in what area, or areas, the action of the play occurred.

I want now to take up the task of deciphering this Plan sufficiently to form an idea of how it and the performance fitted together, and then of what the performance must have looked like to the people who watched it.

To do this has required the collection and study of different pieces of evidence, but one clue began early to stand out as offering a master key to all the rest—and indeed to one complete aspect of the theatre of the Middle Ages. I am aware that this clue must seem an oddly unpromising one at first, and that some readers may need to be convinced of its importance, for it is simply that the area shown in the middle of the Plan and embraced by the circles is called *the place*.

I want to show that this is a fact; that it is a significant fact; and what the significance of it is. I begin by remarking that the name *place* is mentioned in four different places on the Plan. Rendered in more familiar English the four mentions are:

(1) This is the water about the *place*. . . .
(2) . . . let not over many 'stytelerys' be within the *place*.
(3) This is the Castle of Perseverance that stands in the midst of the *place*.
(4) The four daughters . . . shall play in the *place* altogether till they bring up the soul.

In the fourth reference there is as I hope to show some proof of the theory I have begun to formulate. But even without this, I claim that already by the assembly and comparison of these four short passages it can be appreciated that the word *place* may be used here in a particular sense. It is either used so pointlessly that these passages have little real significance, or else it is used with more than its ordinary meaning, and the passages intend something distinct and particular. It is with the latter possibility in mind that I want to examine the four references in detail.

The Place, first reference (*the water round it*)

Taking the first reference in full, we may render the legend written round the circular ditch as follows:

This is the water about the place if any ditch may be made where [?] it shall be played, or else [see] that it be strongly barred all about; and let not over many *stytelerys* be within the place.

Let us leave till later the curious reference to 'stytelerys' and consider the first reference to the *place*. We are shown that this *place* around which the water lies is a circular area. We are told that this area can be surrounded by one of two, apparently alternative, methods—by a ditch and water, or by being 'strongly barred all about'. Why are we offered an alternative?

It is worth while drawing especial attention to the implication possible here. What the legend tells us is roughly as follows: 'If the ground in the particular spot where you perform this play will allow, you should dig a ditch round the area you select; if the ground will not allow this, you must arrange for that area to be "barred about", that is, enclosed in some other way.' This certainly suggests that the writer did not know where the play would be played; that he knew that various localities were possible, and that the procedure would have to vary with the locality.

But it may mean more than this. Is the writer thinking of the play not as being performed once only and in one place, but as a show that was 'toured' and played at various places? In other words, did he offer the alternative because he had in mind performances in different localities, some where ditch-digging would be possible and some where it would not?

The important point is that if the above were so, we may be dealing with a play that was to some extent a professional show as against the amateur, single performances by trade guilds of some of the Mysteries. If it were professional then admission-charge must be levied and thus the audience must be prevented from seeing unless they paid. So some enclosure of the area becomes vital.

This idea of a travelling play is perhaps confirmed in the Banns since the name of the town or village is, as we have seen, left unspecified in the lines, e.g.

> . . . we purpose us to play
> This day week before you in sight
> At (So-and-so), on the green, in royal array.

This play, then, may have been one that had various performances in separate localities, at each of which particular preparation had to be made in the way of reserving a special circular area, either with a ditch or with 'bars'.

What we now have to set ourselves to find is how much can be discovered about this preparing of a *place*. What in particular did it involve? How were the play and the audience situated with regard to the *place* when at length it was prepared?

The reference we have just considered has informed us that there were at least two different methods of enclosing a *place*. What can be learnt from the other references?

The Place, second reference (*the stytelers in it*)

We encounter here a special difficulty in that reference 2 contains a word that is entirely unfamiliar and at first incomprehensible:

> . . . and let not over many *stytelerys* be within the place.

We learn from it that there were likely to be, within the circular area of the *place*, a number of 'stytelerys', that is to say 'stytelers', or people who 'stytel', but that it was desirable for some unspecified reason to keep their number fairly small—to see that there should not be too many of them. I will anticipate enough to say that it is possible after further study to suggest what the stytelers' job might have been and why they were there—though in strictly limited numbers—in the *place*, but it will be far easier to understand the matter when we have gathered a little more information about the organization of the audience and the movement of the performance. Part of the required information is latent in the next reference to which I wish to go on straight away. For the moment I will content myself with one remark about the present reference; when it says that the stytelers must not be over-numerous *within the place*, it clearly means more than that they are to be kept few in the locality or place where the play was performed—it means they must be kept few in the arena itself where the performance occurred, that is (and again we see the word used with a particular meaning) in the *place*.

The Place, third reference (*the Castle in its midst*)

Reference 3, rendered in full, is:

This is the Castle of Perseverance that stands in the midst of the place, but let no men sit there for letting of sight [i.e. obstructing the view], for there shall be the best [position] of all.

Let us take this in detail. In the circle of the *place* the Castle-tower stood, in this play, as a centre-piece. But we notice that a certain precaution had to be observed—namely, that where the tower was, no persons should be permitted to sit because they would hinder the view of others. This is important, and we must make our inference especially clear here, or a particular confusion may arise. The precaution immediately brings to mind that curious suggestion of legs under the Castle, and with it an idea that the whole superstructure of the tower might have been raised up so as to leave a clear view-through underneath it at ground level. This idea is confirmed by the existence of a bench or bed between these 'legs' under the Castle, whence, as we shall see, there is to enter the central character of the play, Mankind, as a newly-born child.

The point made in the legend is that *men* must not *sytte ther*; what does this mean?

The first thing is to decide what 'men' means in this context—and I think it means people of the audience. It is unlikely to mean the actors, because actors would have to be in this area anyway from time to time during the ordinary business of the play. And I think some other phrase than 'no *men*' would have been used had it been intended to refer to players.

Secondly, the provision is distinctly against their *sitting*—which has two bearings; first it strengthens my belief that audience, not actors, are the people referred to, and second, it suggests that some at least of the audience were seated.

Now the third point I want to make about this passage is more controversial. As I see it the prohibition is against any people sitting *'ther'*, that is, not merely in the *place* but particularly in the *myddys of* the place—the 'middle of' the place, below and around where the Castle-tower was. The inference is very important and, I think, inescapable—that members of the audience could and did sit in *other* parts of the place, but it had to be seen that they left the centre clear. The presence of audience in the *place* is denied by some authorities but I hope to show there is ample further evidence for it. The reason for leaving the centre empty is not only obvious to one's mind but, happily, is stated here—that is to say 'for lettynge of syt'; for obstructing of vision; because people there would block the view of what was going on. When we are in a position to offer an opinion on where certain actions of the show took place, and on where the audience was normally situated to watch those actions, we shall be able to appreciate this restriction more fully.

Finally, this passage ends with the statement that 'here' (that is again, as I see it, in the *middle* of the place) 'shall be the best [position] of all'—best for what? I suggest: for any action to happen so as to be best seen by the greatest number of people. That would be a fair and obvious enough statement; yet it has an interesting implication—namely, that *all* action did not take place in the centre of the *place* (although the 'best' may have done) and that other parts of the area were used on occasion, though of these parts not quite so many people were able to get so close or unobstructed a view as they could of the middle of the *place* itself.

The Place, fourth reference (*the act of playing in it*)

Reference 4, rendered in full is:

The Four Daughters [of God] shall be clad in mantles; Mercy in white, Righteousness altogether in red, Truth in sad green, and Peace all in black; and they shall play in the place altogether (?) till they bring up the soul.

Here first of all is the chief reason to believe that the employment of the word *place* in a specific and technical sense is a fact; for we are clearly told in this reference that a group of players, after acting for a space of time in the *place*, could proceed with their action in a place which was *not* the *place* but which must still have been visible to the audience (for the Daughters have to go on acting there), and must therefore have been within the 'theatre' as a whole. This needs to be enlarged upon.

The full meaning of this reference will admittedly not be clear till we have established more in detail what was the procedure in such plays, but we are told that these four characters shall

> pleye *in* þe place alto gedyr tyl þey brynge up þe soule.

The 'soule' is easy to understand after reading the play—it is one of the later characters, the Soul of Mankind.

To 'brynge up' the soul can again be interpreted with some confidence; it means that the Four Daughters of God bring up the Soul of Mankind from the Devil's clutches to the high throne of the Father. (All this is clearly proved in a study of the script.)

We are left now with a phrase that presents something more of a puzzle; what can be the significance of playing 'in the place alto-gether'?

We are in a position even at this early stage to make some guess at what playing 'in the place' means—it means playing upon the area within the circle. True we have not yet been led to suppose that there was any other place in which to play except this area—though we shall soon see that we must extend this idea—but for the moment what seems to me chiefly obscure is whether we should read the last phrase as 'all together'.

Were we content to suppose the meaning is that the Four Daughters act in a close group (not separately from each other but *together*) up to a certain cue, namely, the bringing up of the Soul, then we would expect that *after* this cue it would be found that for some reason they dispersed or had cause no longer to act together—that in other words they become separated.

But the script does not for a moment allow this. On the contrary, once the Four Daughters have brought the Soul to the Throne of God they find themselves restricted in a smaller area than before, as we shall later understand.

We cannot therefore accept the interpretation: 'They shall play in the place *in a close group* until they bring the Soul up to the Throne.'

An alternative meaning is offered if the original is rendered: 'they shall play in the place *altogether* . . .' (that is to say, 'in the place exclusively, and nowhere else') 'till they bring up the Soul'. What now would be implied is that they play only in the *place* until their cue, and then afterwards they are permitted to leave the *place* and go on with their action somewhere else. Of the two interpretations we believe the first is entirely ruled out by the script.

The very important question that now follows in regard to the nature of the *place* arises in this way; we found earlier that acting could take place in 'the midst of the place', and that in fact this was the 'best of all'. Hence we deduced that other scenes of acting might occur in other parts of the *place*. Thus we had to picture the *place* as an arena in which acting might concentrate first in one part and then in another. But now, to all the above we have to add a further idea, namely that, on occasion, the acting might be removed from the arena altogether and occur somewhere which was *not* the arena. And this we shall find, when we have been able to gain more evidence, is in fact true—puzzling as it may be at the moment.

Let us, however, remember our purpose just now; it is simply to make sure that, when the writer alludes to the *place* he alludes with a specific meaning to a particular part of the theatre.

We can summarize our discoveries so far as follows:

Summary

We have learnt from a preliminary examination of these four references in the Plan of *The Castle* the following things about the *place*:

First, that the *place* was round and, to be suitable, had to be encircled by a ditch filled with water, or by 'bars'.

Second, that within the area of the *place* certain functionaries called stytelers could be found, but that there ought not to be 'over many' of them.

Third, we believe we may deduce that both 'scenery' and audience were within this enclosed *place*, but that care had to be taken against obstructing the vision of the spectators. Also that the *best* position for acting was in the middle of the *place*—whence we deduce that acting could occur in other parts of the *place* than the middle.

Fourth, we make the further deduction (though at present we need other evidence to support it) that not only could the acting occur in different parts of this arena called the *place*, but that some acting might even occur in a spot, or spots, which were not in the arena at all and to reach which an actor had to leave the arena, or at any rate be no longer in the *place*.

What such spots might be we have still to discover.

A final conclusion to be drawn, as I see it, from these four references is perhaps the most significant of all. It is that this *place* was an area of very considerable and specific importance in the presentation of a show—a vital element in the technique; an essential part of a 'theatre'—in short a technical matter in the full sense, and one deserving a proper technical term to name it. Such a name I believe it had, and I hope to show in what follows that *the place* was an understood, particular, theatrical term in the Middle Ages, and bore specific and important dramatic implications. I think it will appear that *the place* was in more senses than one the basis of a system of presentation in the medieval theatre.

This, then, concludes the references to the *place* in the Plan of *The Castle*. We shall soon go on to study other evidence about the *place*, but before we leave this Plan, readers will probably wish to have a word about the other legends. Besides the brief references to the scaffolds there are three further legends.

First: the lines to left and right of the tower. These are so obscure that just now even to suggest an equivalent in modern English is difficult, let alone to establish a meaning. We will put this legend aside till we reach a point in our review of the performance where I believe it might be applicable (see p. 204).

Second: the legend below the tower. This is straightforward enough: 'Mankind's bed shall be under the Castle; and there shall

26

the Soul lie under the bed till he shall rise and play.' This, as we shall see later, is going to offer us a puzzle in that apparently some three hours of the play have to elapse before the Soul of Mankind is due to rise and take part. His wait under the bed must have been pretty cramping if he really had to stay under it all that time. We shall touch on this matter again later.

Third: below the circle and to the right is a note about the Devil using fireworks in the war scene: 'He that shall play Belial, look that he have gunpowder burning in pipes, in his hands, and in his ears, and in his arse, when he goeth to battle.' This conjures a curious picture. One has little comment to make—it says so, and so it must be true. But how the squibs were ignited, how long they burned, and just at what cue in the play they were set off we do not know. We will recall this note later, on p. 198.

I wish to turn now to inquire whether any references, direct or indirect, to this *place*, which is referred to four times in the Plan, are to be found in the lines of the play itself among the speeches of the players.

3

THE ALLUSIONS TO 'PLACE' IN THE DIALOGUE

What the Characters tell us about the Place ✴ *The Tradition of the Green*

HAVING established some details of the nature of the *place* in a medieval theatre, as afforded by the Plan of *The Castle*, and having shown them to offer us some justification for regarding the term 'the Place' as a technical expression with particular implications, we now turn to the text of the dialogue of the play to see how often any word or idea of this nature is used and whether the references contain any information which will help to make clearer for us what the Place was, what it looked like, and how it served the show.

What the Characters tell us about the Place

I have found twelve such references, as follows:

(1) ll. 157–60, Worthy wyt*is* . . .
þorwe þis pr*o*pyr pleyn place . . .

(2) l. 163, 3e, syrys semly, all same syttyth on syde . . .

(3) l. 227, gadyr 3ou to-gedyr, 3e boyis on þis grene!

(4) l. 271, . . . þer-for, on hylle
syttyth all stylle . . .

(5) l. 1147, I clymbe fro þis crofte
with Mankynde, o, to sytty*n* on lofte.

(6) l. 1765, . . . & all 3ene maydnys on 3one playn,

(7) l. 1893, Sche schal dey up-on þis grene,

(8) l. 1908, . . . up-on 3one grene grese.

(9) l. 1915, to 3one feld lete us fle,

(10) l. 2144, if þou fonde to comy*n* a-lofte
I schal þee cache fro þis crofte.

(11) l. 2633, . . . wi*th* Coueytyse goth on þis grene.

(12) l. 2911, I go glad up-on þis grou*n*de,

The first reference may very likely employ the word simply in its general sense of 'spot'—as 'this proper, plain spot'. It might well be that the theatrical sense is so technical that the writer would not expect it to be understood by the spectators. But, while taking this view, I certainly would not hold it beyond the bounds of possibility that the poet was conscious of a half-sly pun on the two senses. In any case, whatever the shade of meaning, it is to the Place that the reference alludes, and thus the particular adjectives are interesting. The reference is in the opening lines of the play where World is greeting the audience with a sweeping rhetorical gesture by which he brings in all assembled before him as they watch the drama begin. He says:

> Worthy wights . . .
> Through this proper, plain place, in peace be ye bent!

The adjectives 'propyr' and 'pleyn' are clearly chosen for their alliteration but, despite this, there is no reason to doubt that the spot which was chosen as the Place of a play was meant to be in fact *proper* (or arranged fittingly for the occasion) and also *plain* (or unobstructed).

(This idea of *plain* is one found elsewhere in a similar connexion. For example, in our present play the word is used, this time as a full noun, in reference to the Place when, at l. 1765, a character talking to his master at the North side, points to the Seven Virtues who are grouped together in the centre near the Castle-tower, and calls them:

> all ȝene maydnys on ȝone playn

—which is as much as to say 'all those maidens out on the plain there'. And we can find other examples in other plays of this usage of the word 'plain'.)

The second example on the list is closely associated with the first; taking the two speeches in their context we see they are addressed to two sections of the audience—the first to those worthy wights throughout the proper, plain Place, and the second to those Seemly Sirs *who sit at the sides.*

We learn on the one hand, then, that spectators were thronged, watching, through the Place, and on the other that further spectators were provided with a means for sitting 'at the sides' of the Place—which suggests round its perimeter.

Furthermore, there is a very slight hint that (as we might

expect) those who had the privilege of *seats* at the sides of the throng were in some sort of superior position, for they are distinguished as 'sirs seemly', while those in the Place proper are merely 'worthy wights'.

The third indirect reference in the list can be classed with the seventh, eighth, ninth, eleventh and twelfth as all exemplifying one particular characteristic of the Place, and this group it will be convenient to deal with all together in a moment. This postponement gives us a chance to associate the remarkable fourth reference with what we have just discussed about the audience at the sides of the *place*, to which it adds a cardinally important detail.

When Flesh calls for quiet his injunction is:

> Therefore, on hill
> Sit you all still!

This direct reference to a *hill* in a speech particularly addressed to the audience must have had some significance—it cannot, as a word, have had no application at all in the speech. When we couple our allusion to those that sit on the side, with this suggestion that some seats at least were on a hill or mound, we have the germs of an idea with which to construct the picture which we shall attempt in later pages.

(One is perhaps to be forgiven for a mental digression to The Hill at the cricket-ground at Sydney so well known, at least by hearsay, to followers of test matches, which is exactly parallel as an accommodation for spectators. The Sydney 'Hill' has a reputation for barrackers; how often to a batsman might the lines 'Therefore on Hill, sit you all still' have expressed at moments his deepest wish!)

The fifth reference on the list brings another aspect of the Place before us, and it can be taken with the tenth as they both illustrate the same point. To appreciate its significance fully we must retain the impression of the thronged 'hill' round the perimeter of the Place, and of the embracing and enclosing sensation it would create. This realized, it will readily be seen that we are well on the way to regarding the Place not only as a flat, demarked arena, but as a regular, built-up saucer or enclosure. Thus it is of some significance to us to find (l. 1147) that, when Envy decides to climb up to Mankind where he is throned aloft (that is, above the level of the plain, in a way we shall discuss later), Envy says:

> I climb from this croft
> With Mankind, o, to sit up aloft.

The word 'croft' is interesting in this sense of 'an enclosed place', for other similar uses of it can be found. One is at l. 2144 in the present play when Patience, one of the Virtues defending the Castle against the attack of her opposing Vice, Wrath, cries:

> If you're fond enough to come aloft,
> I shall drag you from this croft!

The particular meaning of 'cache' (rendered here as 'drag') is perhaps open, but the use of 'croft' is indisputable.

Again, Chambers quotes a Bassingbourne play as being 'in a croft', and a Chelmsford play that was 'in a "pightell" ' (*The Mediaeval Stage*, ii, 135), which word implies an enclosure in the same way that 'croft' does.

Moreover, Creizenach, in referring to a discovered fragment of a fourteenth-century Miracle Play including a certain Dux Moraud, says that 'the play was produced for payment, within an enclosed space ("fold")'. (*The Cambridge History of English Literature*, 1932 ed., vol. v, p. 41.) Thus, the idea of the Place as definitely an enclosure is to be met with more than once.

A final and especially picturesque feature of the Place is contained in the last group of references which we promised to take together.

At l. 227 the Devil threatens the young fellows of his audience with intent to make their flesh creep, and warns them to

> gather you together, you boys on this green!

Again at l. 1893, World threatens Meekness that

> she shall die upon this green,

and at l. 1908, the Devil blackguards some character who happens to be

> upon yon green grass.

Then at l. 2633 we have Industry reporting that Mankind

> with Covetousness goeth on this green.

31

All these references to the green and the grass are of considerable use in touching-in colourfulness to our picture. To be classed with them are the two remaining ones in which there is a reference to the Place as 'yon field' (l. 1915), and as 'this ground' (l. 2911).

I want to make one further observation about these last six indirect references to the Place. It is based on the following six facts:

In 'gather you together, you boys on this green' (l. 227), the Devil is speaking about the youngsters sitting on the grass before him; we believe that this grass was the grass of the Place and that the boys on the green are the boys in the Place. Thus we conclude that 'this green' means the Place.

In 'all those maidens on the plain there' (l. 1765), Backbiter is pointing across to a group of maidens who are, for certain, in the centre of the Place. Thus the Place is alluded to as 'yon plain'.

In 'she shall die upon this green' (l. 1893), World is threatening the death of Meekness (one of the above maidens) upon the green grass of the Place. Thus, again, the Place is 'green'.

In 'upon yon green grass' (l. 1908) the Devil is urging his forces to scare these same maidens, whom he calls 'skallyd skoutis', and again they are upon 'yon green grass'. We believe the maidens were in the Place at this point, and thus we have an added reference to the Place as 'green grass'.

In 'with Covetousness goeth on this green' (l. 2633), Industry is complaining of Mankind's shortsightedness in ignoring his future life, and in having gone with Covetousness from the Castle and into the Place; therefore Industry is alluding to the Place when she says Mankind has gone with Covetousness 'on this green'.

In 'I go glad upon this ground' (l. 2911), Garcio, the boy, is admittedly using an expression lightly and for the sake of rhyme, but he is in fact in the Place when he speaks this line, and he does allude to where he is standing as 'this ground'. Thus the Place is the 'ground'.

The observation I wish to make over these six points is that here is an accumulation of evidence that the Place was *not* any sort of raised stage, but was in fact the 'green', the 'plain', the 'grass', the 'ground' itself on which the whole assembly of actors and specta-tors, seats and scaffolds, was arranged and established.

It is necessary to have proved that the Place was not a raised stage but the grass or plain or ground where the show took place, because some authorities define 'Place' as 'stage', and this may be confusing if we understand them to mean a *raised or built-up* stage.

The Tradition of the Green

The phrase 'on the green', used of what we should today call the 'acting-area', may strike a theatre-man with a sense of surprise, not as a strange expression but as a familiar one, because exactly this phrase can be heard in the theatre today. Whether our modern term is relatively new (e.g. rhyming slang: stage—greengage—green), or whether it really dates back to medieval times I am not prepared to say. But I do certainly know that if a modern producer at a rehearsal on the stage calls from the stalls to his stage-manager, and asks him if he will summon, say, one of the fly-men so that he may be given an instruction, the stage-manager may very well shout up to the flys—'Bill, come down on the green a minute; the guv'nor wants you'.

He means 'come down on to the acting-area'. He is without doubt using a phrase that dates back to the days of the old green baize stage-cloth used to cover the stage in Restoration times; and we may go still farther back, and find that a green covering for the stage was also used in the masques at Court. But why was green used? Had it any distant origin in the green of the grass on the medieval Place? If so it might be one of the oldest stage terms in English theatre history. At present, however, we can say no more than that the acting-area was called 'the green' over five hundred years ago, and is called 'the green' today.

We are already beginning to have enough suggestive impressions to tempt us to try building the elements of the Place into a three-dimensional shape. I would, however, ask for the opportunity to include one more group of evidential material before we begin reconstructing. That further group of evidence is not an easy one to sift; but an indisputable part of our picture will come from it, without which we could only proceed lamely.

Let us leave the dialogue of the play and turn to the remaining component that so far we have overlooked—the stage directions, which are going to offer us the stiffest exercise of all.

4

THE LATIN STAGE DIRECTIONS
AND THEIR REFERENCES
TO THE 'PLACE'

*The Problem of the Stage Directions * General Observations on Descending into the Place * Placea; the First Stage Direction * Placea; the Second Stage Direction * Placea; the Third Stage Direction*

W HEN we come to examine the stage directions in *The Castle* we are confronted with some special difficulties. Firstly, they are mostly written in Latin. Secondly, they are written by a fifteenth-century scribe who was presumably an Englishman and thus one to whom the Latin language was not a living tongue, and whose knowledge of its syntax may have been imperfect. Thirdly, the Latin words of the stage directions are rarely written in full, but have abbreviations which we today must expand by more or less inspired guesswork. Lastly, the handwriting in which they are written is such that certain letters are almost exactly the same in form as other letters or pairs of letters—thus 'u' and 'n', 'm' and 'in', etc., are practically indistinguishable.

These are, to be sure, common difficulties in a medieval manuscript, but they present especially tricky problems in the edition of *The Castle* from which it is most convenient to work—namely The Early English Text Society's publication, Extra Series, No. 91 (1904, reprinted 1924). Before pointing to these problems, perhaps the following should be stated about this edition: the original manuscript was at the time the private property of Mr. J. H. Gurney and is carefully described in the Introduction to the above edition. A transcript was made from this original by Miss Eleanor Marx at the instance of Dr. F. J. Furnivall. Professor Alfred W. Pollard was prevented by other work from editing this, and Dr. Furnivall took on the task, requesting Professor Pollard to write the Introduction and certain notes but—'the summons came at a very inconvenient time' (op. cit., p. x). These facts may account for certain fairly serious inadequacies in the presentation of the stage directions in the printed edition—inadequacies which bring up the problems mentioned above, and which caused a good deal of puzzlement during the early stages of the writing of the present notes. It has, therefore, seemed best to take these Latin stage directions with particular care, and refer them letter by letter to the original before basing any conclusions upon them—and also in order to clear the path somewhat for other readers.

The matter seemed to call for study of the original script, but fortunately the need to worry the owner to the extent of a visit was made unnecessary by the existence of a complete facsimile reproduction of the manuscript issued in 1908 by The Tudor Text Society. It is upon this work that the present chapter is based.

Since, however, medieval Latin is a highly specialized subject (to say nothing of medieval handwriting), it was clear that expert assistance was needed, and Dr. James Willis of University College, London, most courteously answered an inquiry for help. He also brought to his knowledge of medieval Latin the co-operation of Prof. G. P. Goold and Dr. O. J. L. Szemerényi.

The result was material for the following analysis; for the conclusion based upon it the present writer is responsible.

The Problem of the Stage Directions

There are thirty-two stage directions in the original script of *The Castle*. Of these there are in fact only three which bear direct evidence on the nature of the Place, but they are almost impossible to understand as they are, because of the obscurity which distorts them and many of the other directions as well. This we shall have to try to clear before we can turn to those three particular directions with, it is to be hoped, a better understanding.

In the E.E.T.S. edition the editors have not only presented the original stage directions in a way that sometimes obscures the meaning, but they have added a great many modern directions of their own. These we must weed away as a preliminary, and even this task needs care, for though these modern directions are faithfully printed in italics and enclosed in square brackets to show that they are editorial interpolations; yet in the case of the original Latin directions, the letters added by the editor to expand the

contractions are also printed in italics (and are very numerous)—
and, further, these original directions are sometimes also preceded by a square bracket (though they are not concluded with
such a bracket), so it will be evident that distinction between
original directions and interpolated directions is often not immediately clear! In discussing the subject here, then, we begin by
ignoring all the interpolated, modern directions.

The remaining thirty-two original stage directions (including
three very brief instructions in English, possibly somewhat later
in date) are here set down in order as they appear in the script, and
the reader will immediately see what a cryptic problem is offered.

(1) After l. 457, pipe vp mu
(2)   „   492, tūc descend^t in plac' parit'
(3)   „   578, Trūpe vp. tūc ibūt voluptas & stulticia mal' angel'
              & humanū gen' ad mūdū & dic'
(4)   „   618, tūc ascend' hūanū ge' ad mūdū
(5)   „   650, trūpe vp
(6)   „   1012, tūc ibūt suƥbia ira inuidia gula luxuria & accidia ad
              avaric' & d; suƥbia
(7)   „   1339, tūc ibūt ad hūanū gen' et d; cōfessio
(8)   „   1449, tūc descendit ad cōfessionē
(9)   „   1699, tūc int^{a}bit
(10)   „   1708, tūc cātabūt eterne rex altissiē &c.
(11)   „   1748, tūc ibit ad Belial
(12)   „   1767, tūc vtan^t sƥbia īuida & ira
(13)   „   1778, & verberab^t eos sr̄ terrā
(14)   „   1791, ad carnē
(15)   „   1812, tūc Caro clamab^t ad gul' accid; & lux'
(16)   „   1823, tūc úberau^t eos ī placeā
(17)   „   1836, ad mūdū
(18)   „   1853, tūc buccinab^t cornio [?] ad auariciā
(19)   „   1864, tūc úberau^t eū
(20)   „   1899, tūc mūd' cupiditas & stultic' ibt̄ ad castellū c
              vexillo et d; demon
(21)   „   1969, tūc descend; in plac'
(22)   „   1971, d; ad belyal
(23)   „   1982, ad Carnē
(24)   „   1991, ad Mundū
(25)   „   2199, tūc pugnabt̄ diu
(26)   „   2378, tūc pugnabt̄ diu
(27)   „   2410, ad mūdū
(28)   „   2557, tunc descendit ad auaric'

(29) After l. 2921, tūc iet ad hmanū [?] gen'
(30)   „   3229, tūc ascendet ad prem ōēš pit' & dix^t verita[s]
(31)   „   3586, tūc ascendent ad malū angelū ōēš pit' & dic;
(32)   „   3594, tūc ascēd; ad tronū

The expansions of these original Latin stage directions, with their translations, now follow together with certain notes on particular problems. The author is deeply indebted to Dr. Willis for leading help throughout in this matter; any passages given in quotation marks in the accompanying notes are in Dr. Willis's own words.

(A brief account by Dr. Willis of his interpretations of these stage directions was made at the time and can be referred to in the *Modern Language Review* of July 1956 (vol. li, p. 404).)

(1) After l.   457,   Pipe up music
                       (Pipe up, music.)

(2)   „   492,   Tunc descendunt [*or* descendent] in placeam pariter.
                       (Then they descend [*or* shall descend] into the place together.)

(3)   „   578,   Trumpe up. Tunc ibunt Voluptas et Stulticia, Malus Angelus et Humanum Genus ad Mundum et dicet [*or* dicit]:
                       (Trump up. Then Lust-liking and Folly, the Bad Angel and Mankind shall go to World and [Lust-liking] shall say [*or* says]:)

(*'The subjunctive mood is not used in these directions except in one case, which seems to be corrupt.'* See No. 12.)

(4) After l.   618,   Tunc ascendet Humanum Genus ad Mundum.
                       (Then Mankind shall ascend to World.)

(5)   „   650,   Trumpe up.
                       (Trump up.)

(6)   „   1012,   Tunc ibunt Superbia, Ira, Invidia, Gula, Luxuria et Accidia ad Avariciam et dicet Superbia:
                       (Then Pride, Wrath, Envy, Gluttony, Lechery and Sloth shall go to Covetyse, and Pride shall say:)

(7)   „   1339,   Tunc ibunt ad Humanum Genus et dicet Confessio:
                       (Then they shall go to Mankind and Shrift shall say:)

37

(8) After l. 1449, Tunc descendit ad Confessionem.
(Then he descends to Shrift.)

(9) „ 1699, Tunc intrabit.
(Then he shall enter.)

(10) „ 1708, Tunc cantabunt 'Eterne rex altissime', etc.
(Then they shall sing 'Eterne rex altissime', etc.)

(11) „ 1748, Tunc ibit ad Belial.
(Then he shall go to Belial.)

(12) „ 1767, Tunc intrant [?] Superbia, Invidia et Ira.
(Then Pride, Envy and Wrath enter.)

(*Furnivall renders the verb as* vertunt. '*This is very difficult. No satis-factory interpretation has been offered of* vertunt. *The word is hard to read, but certainly ends in* -ant, *not* -unt, *and thus, if it comes from* verto, *is the unique example of a subjunctive in the stage directions. It seems likely that we should read* intrant.')

(13) After l. 1778, Et verberabit [?] eos super terram.
(And he shall [?] beat them over [?] the ground.)
(*See note on No. 16.*)

(14) After l. 1791, Ad Carnem.
(To Flesh.)

(15) „ 1812, Tunc Caro clamabit ad Gulam, Accidiam et Luxuriam.
(Then Flesh shall call to Gluttony, Sloth and Lechery.)

(16) „ l. 1823, Tunc verberabit [?] eos in placeam.
(Then he shall [?] beat them into the place.)

(*Furnivall gives* verberant. '*The plural is inexplicable, since it is Flesh alone who thrashes Gluttony, Sloth and Lechery. The manuscript has* úberauᵗ, "*n*" *and* "*u*" *being indistinguishable in this hand. If the scribe meant* verberant *he saved neither time nor space by writing his* "*t*" *above the line. Probably we should read* verberabit. *Confusion of* "*b*" *and* "*v*" *is well known, and when we are dealing with a script like the present one the two letters might resemble each other in sight no less than in sound.*')

(17) After l. 1836, Ad Mundum.
(To World.)

(18) „ 1853, Tunc buccinabit cornio ad Avariciam.
(Then he shall blow on a trumpet [?] to Covetyse.)

(*Manuscript apparently* cornio. Cornuo *would be equally strange.* '*No doubt* cornu *was intended.*')

(19) After l. 1864, Tunc verberabit [?] eum.
(Then he shall beat him.)
(*On the expansion of* úberau^t *see No. 16.*)

(20) After l. 1899, Tunc Mundus, Cupiditas et Stulticia ibunt ad castellum cum vexillo, et dicet demon;
(Then World, Cupidity and Folly shall go to the castle with a flag, and the Devil shall say:)

(*Furnivall reads* domino Demon. 'Domino *is a ludicrous blunder, and is the first of three by which various* domini *are foisted into the text. The manuscript simply has* "d;", *which means* dicit *or* dicet.')

(21) After l. 1969, Tunc descendunt [*or* descendent, *or* descendit, *or* descendet] in placeam.
(Then they [*or* he] descend [*or* shall descend] into the place.)

(*There are two points here. Is* descend; *singular or plural? This, of course, depends entirely on who* descends, *and the matter is one we shall discuss in detail when we come to study the script as it was probably presented. (Suffice now to say that it might be only Flesh who descends, or it might be that Flesh and his three minions, Gluttony, Sloth and Lechery are together and all descend at once—but let us reserve the question till we can see the situation in the play itself and realize the curiously interesting theatrical situation that is involved.) The second point lies in the expansion of* in plac'. *Furnivall renders it,* in placea, *and raises insoluble problems. We prefer to read,* in placeam, *which is normal and completely consistent with the system of presentation which arises of its own accord out of the evidence we shall offer about medieval staging of this particular sort. Let us reserve the question till we have recorded all the stage directions, and then let us return to those three which refer to what is (as I would remind the reader) our main concern in this present chapter, namely the elucidation of the nature of the Place.)*

(22) After l. 1971, Dicit [*or* dicet] ad Belyal;
(He says [*or* shall say] to Belial;)

(23)   ,,   1982, Ad Carnem.
(To Flesh.)

(24)   ,,   1991, Ad Mundum.
(To World.)

(25)   ,,   2199, Tunc pugnabunt diu.
(Then they shall fight for a long time.)

(*Furnivall renders the last word* domini, *and Pollard adds a marginal note* '[They assault the Castle].' *In fact, they do not assault the castle; only one person, Pride (Superbia), outside assaults Meekness (Humilitas) in the Castle. He is beaten, and then Envy (Invidia) assaults and is beaten by*

39

Charity (Caritas), and then Wrath (Ira) assaults and is beaten by Patience (Patientia). But these are single combats as we shall see when we come to analyse the progress of the presentation incident by incident. Thus, we claim it is not they but he (in a series of separate cases) who attacks. But this is not all the matter: we do not read the last word of the direction as domini, *and therefore we do not believe that* They assault the castle *is the correct translation. The transcriber must have read,* diu *as* dñi, *but there seems no reason not to read it just as it is—namely,* diu, *'for a long time'. Thus we take the whole direction as meaning* not They—*that is Pride, Envy and Wrath—* assault the castle, *but* They—*that is Pride and Meekness—engage in a lengthy combat. The same error occurs below at l. 2378 (No. 26)—given erroneously as l. 2478 in Furnivall's 1924 reprint.)*

NOTE. At l. 2334 in the 1924 reprinted edition of the E.E.T.S. (but not in the first edition) an error of numbering in the lines begins, so that this line is numbered 2434, and all lines until l. 2739 are similarly advanced in error by 100. In the next three references we keep to the correct numbering, and readers referring to the 1924 reprint should remember that in their edition the directions mentioned will be found at ll. 2478, 2510 and 2657, respectively. After l. 2739 the reprint resumes correct numbering.

(26) After l. 2378, Tunc pugnabunt diu.
                     (Then they shall fight for a long time.)

(27) „   2410, Ad Mundum.
                   (To World.)

(28) „   2557, Tunc descendit ad Avariciam.
                   (Then he descends to Covetyse.)

(29) „   2921, Tunc iet ad Humanum Genus.
                   (Then he shall go [for *ibit*] to Mankind.)

(30) „   3229, Tunc ascende[n]t ad Patrem omnes pariter et
                   dicet [dixit *in MS.*] Veritas.
                   (Then they shall ascend together to the Father
                   and Truth shall say:)

('This is very corrupt. The editor rightly alters ascendet *to* ascendent, *but says* dix[t] *is for* dicat. *We have seen above how little reason there is for reading* dicat *anywhere in these directions. The scribe apparently has been copying from a manuscript using suspensions, and he has wrongly expanded* ascend *into* ascendet *and* d *into* dixit. *But his sins stop there*; paritores [*which Furnivall gives for* pariter] *is a mere chimaera. The manuscript reads* pariter—"*then all together shall go up to the Father*".')*

40

(31) After l. 3586,   Tunc ascendent ad Malum Angelum omnes pariter
et dicet:
(Then they shall all ascend together to the Bad
Angel, and [Peace] shall say:)

(32)   „   3594,   Tunc ascendent ad tronum.
(Then they shall ascend to the throne.)

Here—as the reader will see—is a pretty pile of problems. But
fortunately we can take them separately and we are only concerned
now with one of the problems—namely, what is there to be found
in these stage directions which has a direct bearing upon the nature
of the Place?

If we are to find any reference to the Place under a Latin name,
it is interesting to ask beforehand what Latin word we expect to
find used to denominate it. We may well discover something to
assist our inquiry whether the word Place has a theatrical or an
ordinary significance, for if it is used in its ordinary significance
the Latin equivalent is likely to be the one obvious word *locus*
which, as every schoolboy knows, is the commonest equivalent.
In fact, however, we do not find the word *locus* used at all throughout the stage directions of *The Castle*. (Though it is not uninteresting to see that we find *locus* used occasionally in reference to other
plays, and there it probably has a meaning different from what we
understand by Place in our present study, see Appendix, p. 230.)

We do instead find, in the *Castle* directions, one word which
corresponds exactly with our particular theatrical meaning of
Place; it is the term *placea*.

This word *placea* (spoken as a trisyllable and with the *e* pronounced as accented) is a corrupt word as far as classical Latin
goes. It is not usually to be found in a Latin dictionary (though
Du Cange records it, but with no theatrical meaning). The word
that is, however, found in dictionaries is *platea*. This form we
shall also find in the stage directions of certain foreign medieval
plays, and it is the form in general use by writers in English on the
medieval theatre. I have not, however, found the word *platea* as
such used in the stage directions of any English play at all; in
English plays the forms found are *placea* or *place*, according as the
particular play has Latin or English stage directions. In contra-
distinction to the above: in the Latin directions of certain Cornish
plays (that is with text in the Cornish language) *platea* is found,

and it is found also, as I have indicated, in plays from the Continent. (All the same, all Cornish plays do not stick to this form, for *placea* is used throughout *The Life of St. Meriasek* in its Latin stage directions.) One Cornish play has stage directions in English; here *place* is found and also the interesting variant 'playne'—but both are rare.

Once we slip from *place*, through *placea*, and arrive at *platea*, we find a word that has some claim to be in wide use by students of the medieval theatre, and we shall have to make some study of it and try to clear up, if possible, something of the uncertainty that hangs about it (though for this purpose we shall have to add an Appendix to our study of *The Castle*). It is then that we shall, I think, find that we are here touching the whole kernel of the principle of staging in the Middle Ages.

Let us, however, go on with the study by listing the uses of the word *placea* in the *Castle* directions. The task is not a long one since there are only three such references, but they are of considerable significance. We will number them in the same sequence as our earlier references to *place*. They are:

(5) l. 492, Tunc descendunt in placeam pariter (No. 2 on p. 36).
   (Then they descend into the place together.)
(6) l. 1823, Tunc verberabit eos in placeam (No. 16 on p. 36).
   (Then he shall beat them into the place.)
(7) l. 1969, Tunc descendunt in placeam (No. 21 on p. 36).
   (Then they descend into the place.)

Before we look at each of these separately on p. 45, there are some general observations on all of them as a whole.

Furnivall's edition has, in my opinion, confused the problem immensely by reading sometimes *in placea*, and sometimes *in placeam*, when the ending in the original is never more than a mere abbreviation, because he thus leads one to suppose that the playwright had two different sorts of action in his mind with regard to the Place. What Furnivall makes of the three directions is as follows:

l. 492, tu*nc* descend*at* in plac*ea* parit*a*.
l. 1823, tu*nc* u*er*berant eos in placea*m*.
l. 1969, tu*nc* descend*unt* in plac*ea*.

I believe that there is no justification at all in the script for these (as it seems to me) extremely puzzling variations in the case-ending of *placea* used after *in*. As we have pointed out above, p. 36, the actual rendering in the original is *plac'* and *placeā* and *plac'* respectively (as far as modern type-setting can represent it). But each of these can be quite justifiably interpreted as *placeam*, in the accusative. No ablative need be brought in. Thus *in plac'* means *in placeam* or 'into the Place' just as much as *in placeā* does. To introduce the ablative in the first and third examples suggests that they differ in their meaning of *in* from the second example—which would then read '. . . beat them *into* the Place', while the others would read '. . . descend *in* the Place', thus hinting rather at some mysterious business involving an action begun and ended *in* the Place as against the straightforward action from somewhere else *into* the Place, given in the second example.

If now we accept the same expansion—*placeam*—in all three examples, we have now to come to the main question of this part of our consideration: though a descent *into the Place* may be straightforward in intention as a phrase, whatever does it mean as an actual theatrical fact?

General Observations on descending into the Place

Let us take the first of the above stage directions: we begin by making quite clear that our reader escapes the confusion raised by Furnivall's rendering. The direction does not mean: 'Then let him descend within the prepared [?] place.'—which is all that can be made of his *Tunc descendat in placea parita*. Instead it means: 'Then they descend together into the place.'—which clearly has different implications.

But, though we have chopped away some dead wood, we have not yet made a noticeable clearing in the jungle; the meaning of a 'descent into the Place' has to be established, and established so as to be intelligible in relation to the conception of the Place which we are beginning to build.

Picture the Place as we have tentatively arranged it. Now, how can an actor or a group of actors *descend* into it? Where can they descend from?

One quick way to answer this may be found as follows: we have here three stage directions instructing actors to descend, but not indicating where they should descend from. Are there, in contrast, any 'reverse' directions, instructing actors to *ascend* and, if so, are these more communicative and do they suggest where they ascend to? If so, then the elevated spot may be the same in both cases.

In fact we can find more than a hint. There are four directions indicating ascent—Nos. 4, 30, 31 and 32. In No. 4 Mankind ascends to World. In No. 30 all (i.e. the four Daughters of God) ascend to the Father. In No. 31 they ascend to the Bad Angel. In No. 32 they ascend to the Throne (of the Father).

Now both World (in No. 4) and God (in Nos. 30 and 32) have—as we are informed by the Plan—separate *scaffolds* marked in their name, the World's in the West, and God's in the East. If we can next discover where the Bad Angel was at the moment of the Daughters' ascent to him, and that he was similarly on a scaffold, then we might have a suggested explanation of all four ascents.

In point of fact the situation at stage direction No. 31 is this: God has instructed his Four Daughters to go from him to Hell to fetch back the Soul of Mankind (l. 3577)—

> goo to ȝone fende,
> & fro hym take Mankynde!
> > brynge hym to me,
> > & set hym here be my kne,
> > In heuene to be. . . .

> (Go to yon fiend,
> And from him take Mankind.
> > Bring him to me,
> > And set him here by my knee,
> > In heaven to be. . . .)

The Devil also has his own scaffold, that on the North. It is to this scaffold, we shall hope to show, that the Bad Angel has led Mankind's Soul earlier when, at l. 3078, he says to him:

> In hye helle schal be þyne hous;

> (In high hell shall be thine house;)

(Notice the unusual adjective 'high' applied to Hell—unusual but consistent, if by Hell is meant the Devil's high scaffold.) His lines later suggest a walk across the Place to this Hell, for he says (l. 3100):

> Now dagge we hens a dogge trot;

Therefore, this also of the four stage directions relating to ascent may be pretty confidently held to mean that 'ascend' means

'go up on to a scaffold'. It is true that in the direction last discussed there are uncertainties in the text as regards the precise
details; these we shall state in their place, but the general reading
of what happened is, I think, fair enough to justify our forming a
theory (to be confirmed if we find further evidence) that a direction
to *ascend* means that the player is to go up from the Place to a
scaffold; and conversely, therefore, that a direction to *descend* means
that the actor is to go down from a scaffold into the Place.

These scaffolds are clearly going to be very important indeed in
our reconstruction of the method of presentation, and we shall
have to discuss them in detail in a separate section. For the present, however, we must leave them as shadowy elevations at five
points round the Place and turn to the three stage directions referring to the *placea*.

Placea; the First Stage Direction

Resuming now our examination of the first stage direction referring to *placea* (see p. 42). It ran: 'Then they descend into the
place together.' We now have some provisional conception of
where they descended from—namely, from a *scaffold*, whose nature we must study separately. Now we have to see *who* descended
and on what occasion, and what that particular descent has to tell
us about the nature of the Place.

This stage direction, we would remind the reader, is the first
significant stage direction in the play. Nothing (except a note to
Pipe up music) is to be found in the first 492 lines which precede it.
These lines have contained introductory speeches from, first, the
World; second, the Devil; and third, Flesh. Next Mankind has
spoken and held a longish exchange with his Good and Bad
Angels and then, at l. 458, the plot begins. We return to World;
he makes a speech beginning:

> Now I sytte in my semly sale . . .

—thus, he is seated, and in some situation that does duty for his
'seemly salle'—his fitting palace. We may guess (and we shall find
confirmation later) that he is enthroned aloft on his high scaffold.
He calls two servants, named respectively Lust-liking and Folly
(*Voluptas* and *Stulticia* in Latin), and orders them to cry all about
in tower and town to see if there be any man, far or near, who will

give himself to the World's service. Lust-liking replies that they are ready to go forth, in a speech of two stanzas that is highly significant to us, and must be studied in full:

VOLUPTAS. lo, me, here! redy, lord, to faryn & to fle,
 to sekyn þee a servaunt dyngë & dere.
Who-so wyl with foly rewlyd be,
 he is worthy to be a seruaunt here,
  þat drawyth to synnys seuene.
Who-so wyl be fals & covetouse,
With þis werld he schal haue lond & house;
þis werldys wysdom ȝeuyth no[t] a louse
 Of God, nyn of hye heuene.
       [tunc descendunt in placeam pariter.

Pes, pepyl! of pes we ȝou pray.
 syth & sethe wel to my sawe!
Who-so wyl be ryche & in gret aray,
 to-ward þe werld he schal drawe.
Who-so wyl be fals, al þat he may,
 of God hym-self he hath non awe,
& lyuyn in lustis, nyth & day,
 þe werld of hym wyl be ryth fawe,
  to [?] dwelle in his howse.
  who-so wyl with þe werld haue his dwellynge,
  & ben a lord of his clothynge,
  he muste nedys, ouyr al þynge,
   euere-more be couetowse:

(Lo me, here ready Lord, to faren and to flee,
 To seeken thee a servant, dingë and dear.
Whoso will with Folly rulëd be,
 He is worthy to be a servant here,
  That draweth to sinnës seven.
Whoso will be false and covetous,
With this world he shall have land and house.
This world's wisdom giveth not a louse
 For God nor for high heaven.
      [Then they descend into the place together.

Peace, people! Of peace we you pray.
 Syth and sethe well to my saw;
Whoso will be rich and in great array,
 Toward the world he shall draw.
Whoso will be false all that he may,

Of God himself he hath no awe,
And liven in lustës night and day;
  The world of him will be right fawe
    To dwell in his house.
Whoso will with the world have his dwelling,
And be a lord of his clothing,
He must needs, over all thing,
    Evermore be covetous.)

The greatest interest lies at this moment in the interpolation of the stage direction in the middle of this speech and *at a point where the whole tenor of the speech changes*. In its opening stanza, before the stage direction, the speech is unmistakably addressed to World, and the speaker, Lust-liking, is talking to World on World's scaffold. But in the middle of the speech, Lust-liking and Folly, having taken leave of World, turn to obey his behest and *descend together into the Place*. Now, immediately, the address of the speech is altered; Lust-liking goes on speaking, but he speaks now not to World but *to the audience*; he says, 'Peace, people! . . .' and (possibly implying that they are not to be dismayed at this descent into their midst of two supernatural figures from the scaffold—and there must have been a stir at that moment!) he goes on by asking them to be still and listen well to what he has to say.

Pollard adds a marginal note here that is, I think, confusing. He writes, '*Pleasure leaves World's Scaffold and goes inside the Castleditch.*' We query much of this. We believe that there is no evidence that the scaffold was *outside* the ditch; that it would be inconsistent to suppose it were; and that there is no shadow of hint of any bridge across the ditch whose purpose was to allow an actor to cross to the Place. Further, as we have seen, it is most likely that the audience itself was within the ditch. Lastly, both 'Pleasure' (i.e. Lust-liking) *and* Folly descend together—not Lust-liking alone.

But it is still too early in our study to go much into detail about the action here involved. For the present let us be content just to glimpse the picture afforded of a moment in the action when two figures could leave a high scaffold and go down to the green of the Place below, and there address the people of the audience directly.

This much we may legitimately deduce from the stage direction, and by so much is our conception of the Place extended.

Placea; the Second Stage Direction

In the second of these three directions referring directly to the Place, our conception is again slightly widened. The direction is at l. 1823 and runs: 'Then he shall beat them into the place.'

The general action here is that Flesh, having been told by Backbiter that the three servants, Gluttony, Sloth and Lechery, have let Mankind slip through their fingers to the temporary safety of the Castle of Perseverance, turns savagely on them and thrashes them. The particular action is less certain, and raises problems which will be discussed at the relevant place in our description of the action of the whole play, but this at least is clear: the three cringing figures are beaten and end by retreating over the grass of the Place in disorder. Whether they are beaten down from the scaffold, or whether they are in the Place to begin with and Flesh violently descends from his scaffold to beat them farther off, is not clear, but beaten they are, and beaten away into the Place.

Thus, to our conception of the Place we may add that it is the scene, on occasion, of violent and widespreading action, and is also the region to which characters hounded by the lordly occupant of a scaffold retreat.

Placea; the Third Stage Direction

The third and last stage direction referring directly to the Place is at l. 1969 and reads: 'Then they [or he] descend into the place.' Here, the occasion is the going forth of Flesh from his scaffold (with or without his three servants?) to join in an attack on the central Castle. It adds, I believe, nothing to our present knowledge of the Place except the pretty obvious fact that a character, being on one of the scaffolds at the rim of the circle, has to descend into the Place and walk across to reach a spot in the centre of the circle. The action here (with a minor puzzle concerning the number of people involved) will be discussed in more detail in the full description of the presentation of the play.

So much for the evidence of the stage directions specifically referring to the Place. Having now drawn as much as we can from direct references to the Place (and incidentally discovered how important its relation was with the Scaffolds) we have to review what we have found and point out that there is, lying implicit in it, a curious but inescapable factor which we have but lightly glanced at so far, and which will do much to make our picture of the Place clearer.

5

THE DITCH AND THE HILL ROUND
THE 'PLACE'

The Mound and its Relation with the Audience * *A Terence
Miniature* * *The Size of the Place*

THE plan of *The Castle* has in fact an important omission. The
omission may not strike our attention until we have examined
it for some time, but sooner or later we recognize that something, which is a quite inevitable consequence of things as they are
shown, is not there. It concerns the ditch.

In parenthesis, the ditch itself offers us a puzzle. In the first
place, why was it there? In the second place, what an enormous
and apparently disproportionate amount of labour it must have
involved, just for (as we understand it) one day's performance!
Furnivall notices this; he says of the plan: 'Our first impression is
that it looks very ambitious, and that if an itinerant company thus
dug ditches or raised palisades they must have done business on a
very large scale.' (See his 'Introduction', p. xxvii.)

These two thoughts go together. Assuming that the ditch was
there in order to keep people away from the show who had not
paid for admission, and that it thus helped in gathering a revenue
—what, now, did it cost to dig? Even given suitable ground it must
have taken several men some days. Was the labour supplied by the
players? Or was it derived from the local populace? In either case
did it not involve payment? What was the economical balance
between the income and the cost? Had the ditch to be drained and
filled in again after the show?

An examination of this matter appears likely to lead me into
lines of inquiry that I feel myself very unfitted to take. I am familiar
neither with the relation between man-power and earthwork construction, nor with labour-costs in the Middle Ages; and there
exists one consideration in all this that makes me feel not unjusti-

fied in handing these problems to those better qualified for them than I—that consideration is that, whatever the answer may be, this ditch was in fact (on some occasions at least) dug.

The Mound and its Relation with the Audience

We return to the fact that the players, having chosen a stretch of suitable open grassland, began by getting a circular ditch dug. And now we face our essential omission in the Plan. What did they do with the earth that came out of the ditch? It must have made a big mound. This is what the plan does not show.

I must make this point with emphasis. It is perhaps too easy for a reader to suppose that the opening statement on the plan—that is, the words *This is the water about the place if any ditch may be made*—simply means that what he has to visualize is a flat area with a circular trench cut out of it but otherwise *all flat*.

This is inevitably not correct. If the trench is dug out, the earth from it must go somewhere. Speaking in diagrammatic terms, when you dig a ditch in a plain you do not do this—

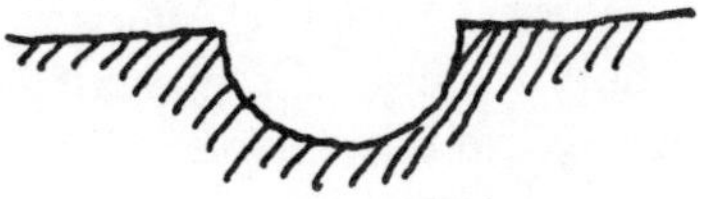

FIG. 2

but this—

FIG. 3

The distinction is important for what follows.

To dig a ditch in a plain is to provide two things—a hollow and a hill.

Following this we now have to make a decision. In the above diagrams we showed only a section of the ditch. If now we think

51

of a full circular ditch, we have to ask—on what side would the hill, thrown up by the excavated earth, have been disposed by the workmen? On the outside bank, or on the inside bank?

I think that if we examine this question clearly we may come nearer to solving the problem of where the audience was situated with regard to the Place. Let us, therefore, now couple this hill of earth (plus the ditch) around the circular Place, with the idea of a crowd of people settling in position to watch a show. Where could the people be?

We have now posed the question in such a way that there are only two possible answers, and of these it will be very clear which we must reject. The two possible positions for the audience are:

1. Outside the ring-ditch, leaving the central plain free for the performers (which many authorities accept).
2. Inside the ring-ditch.

But now what about the great mound of earth round the bank of the ditch?

The audience *could not have sat outside that because it would have come between them and the show*!

This entirely disposes of the picture created by Furnivall, in the passage that I have italicized from his 'Afterwords' on p. xxxiii of *The Castle*, where he visualizes 'the gathering of the audience round the outer circle of scaffolds . . . *leaving the inner circle free for the performance itself*, as I suppose'.

In the same way it as completely disposes of Chambers's picture in *Literature*, where he says of *The Castle* at p. 55: 'A circular place is to be *kept free of spectators*, and surrounded, if possible, by a ditch filled with water, but, if not, barred about.'

In fact it disposes of all views which hold that the spectators were not *in* the Place.

It is with a sense of some responsibility that one finds one's conclusions so gravely traversing accepted opinions, so let us look into the question as closely as we may to see if there is any justification for those opinions.

If we suppose the audience round the outer bank of the ditch, and the hill *on the inner bank*, we are clearly supposing an absurdity, for we get what is shown in Fig. 4. But do not let us give up—let us try all other possible arrangements.

Keeping next the audience still outside the ditch, but now throwing up the earth hill on the *outside* also, we have an arrangement as shown in Fig. 5—and it is obvious that in this arrangement the audience will no longer allow the hill of earth to intervene and obstruct their view, for there is no doubt that they would climb it and sit on its inner side! This may be all very well for viewing, but it is very bad for business, for it means, of course, that you must give your show free. You cannot control entrance; anyone may get in who can scramble up the mound.

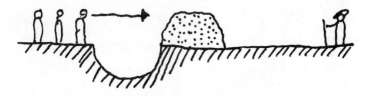

FIG. 4. Section showing the Hill inside the ditch and the audience outside. The actor is hidden

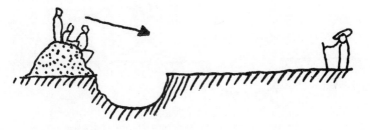

FIG. 5. Showing the Hill and the audience both outside the ditch. Audience entirely separated from action

An alternative to Fig. 5 may perhaps be claimed—that the mound of earth might have been carted some way away so as to leave a space between it and the ditch inside, wherein the audience could assemble. But this idea is clearly going to work out as something more laborious and expensive still.

Now let us abandon the authorities and their empty plain, and try the opposite alternative of keeping the audience *inside* the ditch. Where now is our hill of earth? Clearly, either as in Fig. 6 or in Fig. 7. Fig. 6 is quite profitless, and wastes a commercially valuable vantage point—it is also against the evidence, for we know that some at least of the audience *sat* on the hill ('on hylle syttyth all stylle'). Thus we are left with Fig. 7.

This is not only a sound and sane use of the material offered (in itself a recommendation, for none of the other arrangements can be called this), but it is also, on every point, consistent with the evidence that we have assembled up to the present about the Place. When we add that the other arrangements are *not* consistent with these items of evidence—it seems to me that we have come as near as may be to establishing a case for the arrangement shown in

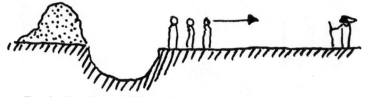

FIG. 6. Showing the Hill outside the ditch and the audience inside. The audience cannot now sit on the hill

FIG. 7. Showing both Hill and audience inside the ditch. This is the arrangement which conforms with the evidence

Fig. 7 being the right one. And thus I claim (*a*) that the hill was thrown up on the inside of the ditch; (*b*) that the audience were inside the ditch also; and (*c*) that part of them were in the Place itself and part sat on the hill.

There is another way of looking at this matter, now that our vision of the Place is growing clearer, and it will bring further evidence in favour of our conclusion that the audience were all inside the ditch. We may demonstrate it in this way:

We have agreed that Figs. 4 and 6 are proved unacceptable arrangements, for Fig. 4 presents a hill between the audience and the play, and Fig. 6 does not provide for the spectators sitting on the hill, and we know from the script of the play that they did so. We have chosen Fig. 7 in preference to Fig. 5 on slightly less certain ground—namely, because Fig. 5 appears to forbid any system of checking the audience's entrance at a 'gate', and thus of collecting a revenue. But we have not positively established that there was a revenue. It is only a possibility which we have rather arbitrarily decided to favour. Is there then a better basis of choice between Fig. 5 and Fig. 7?

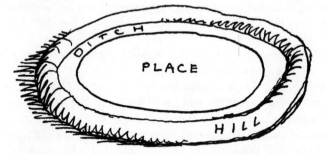

FIG. 8. Bird's-eye view of Place with the Hill outside the ditch according to the arrangement in Figs. 5 and 6. An inconsistent arrangement

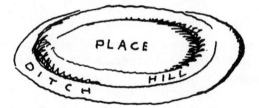

FIG. 9. Bird's-eye view of theatre the same size as Fig. 8 but with the Hill inside the ditch, corresponding with Fig. 7. A consistent arrangement

I think such a thing is offered by the following consideration. (At this point we are in a position to develop our diagrams a little farther, and we may replace them with a drawing of the whole circle in bird's-eye view.)

In Fig. 8 I show a circular Place with a ditch round it and the hill of earth thrown up outside the ditch. This corresponds with our diagram Fig. 5, an arrangement which we think unacceptable; but this drawing now brings to our attention a new disadvantage which was not apparent before. Let us compare it with Fig. 9. Here we have a central Place and ditch of the same size as before— but with the earthen hill thrown up on the inner bank of the ditch;

55

that is to say, round the perimeter of the Place itself as in Fig. 7. We can now see at once how very much nearer the audience is to the action in Fig. 9 than in Fig. 8, how much more compact it all is, and what an amount of space is wasted by the intrusive ditch in Fig. 8—an important consideration when one remembers that the show took place in the open air where the problem of ensuring that the actors' voices might carry is a serious one.

We are, then, further confirmed in our opinion that Fig. 9 is the likely arrangement.

Having constructed these two views, we may venture to tender an answer to one of our earlier questions, namely—what was the ditch dug for? Was it to separate audience from players, to keep, as it were, the spectators from walking on to the 'stage'? Or was it to surround the whole theatre, in the manner of a moat, to prevent unauthorized persons from getting in to see the show? It now looks as if the latter (on this evidence) was far more likely— even though we must remain very much aware that we have not been able to establish independently that admission was, in fact, charged.

A Terence Miniature of c. 1400

I want here to make a small interpolation that is very relevant to our subject. After the above discussion, we have come to the conclusion that the audience and the players must both have been together in the circular Place. Is there to be found any picture in the whole history of theatrical iconography that shows such a thing? If so, then clearly it is going to strengthen our case.

In fact we have such a picture, and one that has never, to my knowledge, received much notice or any special comment. It is to be found in a manuscript of Terence called the *Térence des Ducs*, possibly made for Charles VI, and now in the Bibliothèque de l'Arsenal, Paris. It belongs to about the year 1400. Here there is a miniature in the lower part of which two figures are seen advancing through medieval houses to receive a book from 'Terentius'. But in the upper part of the panel (see Frontispiece) is clearly represented a circular enclosure arranged so that we can see, not only two doors in the wall with spectators issuing from them, but beyond into the interior of the circle itself. The wall round the enclosure twice bears the name *Theatrum*. Within is a closely milling throng of people in the centre of whom is a sort of draped and roofed pulpit, or scaffold, where a figure (inscribed *Calliopius*) is reading from a book. This scaffold, or *pulpitum*, is marked with the word *scena* (and thus offers us an interesting variant of the application of this word). Near the *scena* two figures can be sorted out from the rest of the throng by means of the instruments they are playing as being musicians. The rest at first sight may seem a motley and undifferentiated crowd.

But examination shows that some individuals in this crowd, between the *scena* and the side of the enclosure nearest the front, are wearing masks, and gesticulating and dancing; there is no doubt that they are, in fact, actors because, along the top of the encircling wall just below where they are grouped is the legend *joculatores*. There are possibly four of these actors—with a fifth shown (rather interestingly) as stepping out, with a very vigorous gesture, through an opening in the side of the central *scena* into the crowded ring—'making an entrance' in fact.

There remain a considerable number of further figures, shown in whole or in part, filling the rest of the circle. These are well displayed at the sides, partially displayed at the back where only their heads and shoulders are visible above the *scena*, and they are also present (thus making a full circle) round the near side of the enclosure between the actors and the near wall, but these nearest spectators (whose position is so important to our present point) are not easy to see because the painter, wishing not to confuse over-much his portrayal of the actors, has represented these onlookers only by three little bobs above the top of the wall, simulating the backs of their heads. But he has given us sufficient. The audience is *inside* the Place, and it is *all round* the Place. It might perhaps have been difficult to prove these were audience and not actors on the score of their appearance or position alone (and the miniature would then have been meaningless for our purpose), but we most fortunately have an illuminating inscription in two words written in the spaces at either top corner of the panel; on our left is *populus*, and on our right *romanus*.

There is then no doubt that they are audience. We can now say this: in the lower part of the panel we have a representation of (?) the Roman people honouring Terence at a presentation; above we see them being entertained in a theatre at one of his performances.

It is, of course, very likely that a medieval miniaturist representing a Roman theatre would see it with the eyes of his own time. If it is true that he did so here, then this painter of about 1400 has shown us a typical circular Place or *platea*, like that in *The Castle*, strongly 'barred about' with a wall, and containing in its centre a scaffold from which a reader spoke and from which players entered, and also having the remainder of its area filled with audience and actors; and about the audience we can say two important things:

1. they are all enclosed within the Place,
2. they form a complete circle, looking on at the actors from every side.

Thus we have a set-up that is in principle almost exactly like that we have constructed for *The Castle*, save that there are no scaffolds round the outer rim. But since Terence's plays were not written with such scaffolds in mind, there is little reason to have included them in this *theatrum*. We seem justified in supposing that the miniaturist, in leaving them out, considered he was giving a faithful enough picture of a Roman theatre and, safe in that belief, conceived all the rest out of his experience of the theatre of his time. If this be true then our apparently odd miniature is an unusually direct record of one form of medieval theatrical presentation.

However that may be, we offer it at the moment as a crowning piece of evidence that, about 1400, it was not inconsistent to portray an audience as *within the Place*.

The Size of the Place

There is clearly only a very conventional attitude towards scale and proportion in the above miniature. That observation calls up a new question that we must notice before we can proceed much farther with our reconstruction of *The Castle*: What are the sizes of all these things we are discussing? What is the diameter of a Place? And what the typical depth and width of its ditch?

There is, so far as I can see, practically nothing of any real value in *The Castle of Perseverance* to help us to answer directly, and we must eventually look elsewhere. However—though it is pretty certain that the Plan is not drawn with any sense of scale—one observation may be made; the scribe found it not inconsistent to him to represent the width of the ditch as about one-thirteenth of the diameter of the Place. I know that this is only of the slenderest value to us, seeing how arbitrarily a medieval draughtsman might regard proportion, yet it is something; for it begins to lead us into the conception of a reasonably spacious *ensemble*.

In substantiation of this, I may give the following: Let us consider the size of the ditch; it had to prevent persons crossing it with any ease, this means that it cannot have been less than some 10 ft. wide, and cannot have been less than 4 ft. deep—or it could have been leapt or waded by any venturesome lad. It should be realized that for an athletic and determined man, such an obstacle is as nothing at all; but I do not think we have necessarily to complicate our problem with a really effective gap against all comers —since that would lead us into the neighbourhood of 25 feet by modern standards of athletics. But it cannot have been a *little* ditch, if its purpose was to keep people out, and having this in mind one is inclined to imagine that a ten-foot stretch of water would be a sufficient deterrent to the majority. Let us therefore posit 10 ft. by 5 ft. deep.

If this is true we are provided with certain other dimensions— those of the Hill. It must have been 5 ft. high and 10 ft. thick at the base; *or* both higher and thinner, *or* both lower and thicker; but containing the same volume of earth as came out of the ditch. From this one goes on to notice that a Place enclosed by a hill of earth some 10 ft. wide at its base must have been a pretty big circle to begin with, to be able thus to allow some 20 ft. (that is, 10 ft. on either side) of its diameter to be occupied by a mound, and yet leave a sufficiently large plain-area empty in the centre for the performance.

If now, purely for experiment, we suppose a 10-ft. ditch, and multiply this by 13, for a guess at the proportionate size of the circle enclosed on the *Castle* Plan, we get 130 ft. diameter. Cut off a rim of, say, 10 ft. wide all the way round on which the Hill must stand, and we get a central Place of 110 ft. diameter ($130 - (2 \times 10)$ ft.).

It may be useful in visualizing this space to remember that a regulation lawn-tennis-court is 78 ft. from baseline to baseline; allow 8 ft. more at either end for comfortable step-back, and you get a lawn 94 ft long. Thus, our circular Place, imagined on this basis, would be just 16 ft. wider than a good tennis-lawn is long.

That seems to exhaust the very slight sources of information in the Plan itself and, of course, what we have deduced is the purest guesswork so far. We have now to ask whether we can bring any further evidence to confirm or refute these very provisional figures.

6

THE DIMENSIONS OF THE CORNISH ROUNDS

Carew's Earthen Amphitheatre ✳ *Scawen's Theatre 'to contain thousands'* ✳ *The Round at St. Just*

HERE let us turn away from the script of the play, to seek elsewhere for information to help us to a more certain picture of what the size of such a circular theatre might be. A student of theatrical history will most surely be reminded by what I have reconstructed so far of the Cornish 'rounds' or *Plen an Gwary*. How big were they? Certain passages about these rounds have been quoted often, but it seems important to repeat them here and assess their relevant information on our question. A convenient assembly of the main material, together with his own notes, will be found included in Edwin Norris's translation of the great Cornish Mystery trilogy which he published under the title of *The Ancient Cornish Drama* in 1859 (see also p. 237 ff.)

Carew's Earthen Amphitheatre

The earliest source there mentioned is Richard Carew's *The Survey of Cornwall*, 1602, p. 71b. This book was reprinted in 1723, 1769, 1811, and it is included, with modernizations of spelling in F. E. Halliday's study, *Richard Carew of Antony, 1550–1620* (1953). The relevant passage comes in a description by Carew of the pastimes and exercises of the Cornish men, embracing guary miracles, 'three men's songs', hunting, hawking, wrestling and hurling. It reads:

The Guary miracle, in English, a miracle-play, is a kinde of Enterlude, compiled in *Cornish* out of some Scripture history, with that grosseness which accompanied the Romanes *vetus Comoedia*. For representing it, they raise an earthen Amphitheatre, in some open field, hauing the Diameter of his enclosed playne some 40. or 50. foot.

60

We have here two facts. First, a noticeable resemblance to the picture we have created out of the *Castle* Plan, and one with a welcome clarity, now, about the eminence of the hill, for the words are: 'they *raise* an earthen Amphitheatre.' There is no mention of a ditch, but by a parity of reasoning the earth of the 'raised amphitheatre' must have come *from* somewhere, just as the earth out of the *Castle* ditch must have gone *to* somewhere. Thus we may deduce the ditch from the Cornish mention of the raised amphitheatre, as we can deduce the hill from the mention of the *Castle* ditch. We have no indication on which side this ditch the hill was thrown up, but we do advance a step forward with our second fact in this reference; we have the diameter of the 'playne enclosed'—our Place—as some 40 or 50 feet.

This size, we remark, is considerably less than we had begun to visualize on the slender basis of our reading of the *Castle* Plan, but it presents us with the idea of a very compact little circle that, given good weather-conditions, might probably have been pleasant both to speak in and to see in. It might be worth reminding the reader that such a circle is just about as broad as half the length of our comfortable tennis-lawn.

One other idea emerges, though less distinctly, from the reference; the phrasing is such that we seem to be offered a suggestion that these amphitheatres were quite normally thrown up in preparation for a show despite the hesitation we felt in supposing so big an undertaking when the notion first came to us concerning *The Castle*.

Upon these figures let us now offer a small mathematical calculation. We will suppose a play is being performed in a circular theatre of this kind with a Place of the diameter of 50 ft., then, outside this, a circular hill, and outside again a 10 ft.-wide ditch. The hill came out of the ditch and will therefore compare with it in volume—let us accept the simple figure of 10 ft. wide for the hill at its base. We have now a total circle within the ditch of 70 ft. diameter (50+10+10).

Take now the inner circle or Place; the circumference of a 50 ft. circle is (by the formula $2\pi r$) 157 ft.; this is the perimeter of the Place. Now, five scaffolds impinged on this Place at stated points in the *Castle* Plan. Let us add them (in positions we shall justify later), and let us say that each is 8 ft. wide. Then we have a scale plan as in Fig. 10. This shows us that there are three 31 ft. sections of hill left available for spectators, together with two smaller, 11 ft.-wide sections, either side Covetyse's scaffold (speaking in round figures). Now there does not so far seem to be, at any rate on theoretical grounds, any fatal unlikelihood about these figures and their practicality so far as it goes. We are therefore encouraged to continue and make one further calculation.

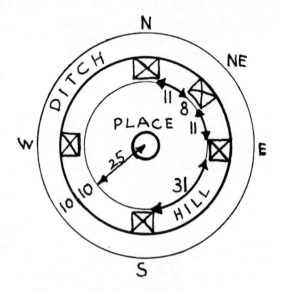

FIG. 10. Diagram of the dimensions of a small theatre such as described by Carew, with a Place 50 ft. in diameter

A 50 ft.-diameter circle has an area (by formula πr^2) of some 1,962 sq. ft. If we allow 3 sq. ft. as space for a standing person we could accommodate 654 people in the Place at a pinch. This is a very outside figure because we know that certain parts of the Place (for example, the 'midst') must be kept clear. On the other hand, we have the five sections of the inner slope of the Hill available for seated spectators. Thus, speaking in the most cautious terms, we might feel inclined not to be surprised if we were sometime to find verification for a figure of between 500 and 700 people as representing the size of an audience in one of Carew's amphitheatres.

(A small note in parenthesis before we leave Carew is of some slight interest—though not directly connected with theatrical presentations. He tells us (on p. 75*b* of the 1602 ·edition) that the Cornish men have among their pastimes (as we well know) the play of wrestling, and states that 'For performing this play, the beholders cast themselves in a ring, which they call, making a place'. A display of wrestling makes a spectacle of a very different nature from the performance of a theatrical show, but all the same, the division is not so great that we need disregard a sort of chiming in our minds at that description of the beholders casting themselves in a ring and calling it *making a place.*

'Making a place' was, then, a recognized conception as part of an audience's behaviour, at this period.)

Now with our approximate 500–700 audience in mind let us proceed to the next example.

Scawen's Theatre 'to contain Thousands'

The next example quoted by Norris is ill documented by him. He gives it as a passage from a manuscript by one Scawen, belonging to soon after the Restoration. But its content is a little surprising. Scawen remarks on:

The play-shows or spectacles . . . solemnized not without shew of devotion in open and spacious downs, of great capacity, encompassed about with earthen banks, and in some part stonework of largeness to contain thousands, the shapes of which remain in many places at this day, though the use of them long since gone.

Here is a new conception!

'Open and spacious downs of great capacity . . . of largeness to contain thousands.' Admittedly the passage is such as to be more in the nature of an impression than a statement of fact—but the impression it does convey is undoubtedly of something far bigger than Carew's 50-ft. circles containing at most 700.

The impression, let us also note, is of something much closer to the size we guessed for the *Castle* Plan.

But there is another, and very useful, piece of information in this note of Scawen's. He speaks of 'open . . . downs encompassed about with earthen banks . . . of largeness to *contain* thousands'. There is surely no possible way of reading this word 'contain' but to take it as stating beyond all denial that the audience was not outside, but inside—'*contained*' by the earthen banks. No mention is made here, it is true, of any ditch—but the material with which to build an 'earthen bank' must have left a ditch in its place when it was excavated.

We have the slight additional fact that, sometimes, stonework was used to reinforce the earthen mounds. This, curiously, makes their construction an even greater and more expensive task, and indeed suggests that, once built, such reinforced amphitheatres must have been more or less permanent (some of them have lasted to the present day!); and this permanency is in strange contrast with the somewhat casual impression conveyed in the tone of the *Castle* legend: 'if any ditch may be made where it shall be played . . .'.

At this point we are prompted to issue a warning to ourselves: Have we any possible right at all to connect this English play—with, moreover, traces of the Midlands, or even North Midlands, in its dialect—with earthworks in Cornwall wherein were presented plays of a different race and a different language? Was there anything in the performance of *The Castle of Perseverance* that was related in any way at all with the technique of the Cornish *gwaries*?

There are points for and against any such resemblance. Among those *against* seems to be this inclusion of stonework into the Cornish rounds. It gives us the idea of something distinctly more permanent, and thus—whether correctly or incorrectly—of something more pretentious and on an altogether greater scale and more organized than the 'strolling' quality which we have been inclined to ascribe to *The Castle*.

Among the points *for* is one which might at first sight appear conclusively *against*. For we talk of the *Cornish* rounds—they are always *Cornish*. There is an implication that such rounds—and hence such a system of playing in rounds—are to be found nowhere else but in Cornwall. We shall I think find, however, that this is not true. There *are* similar circular earthworks in other parts of the country, and there are signs of playing in circular theatres of this kind, not only in other parts of Medieval Britain than Cornwall, but in other countries of Medieval Europe than Britain. So, different race and different language are no bar to the existence of a common technique. I believe it is not that the 'Cornish rounds' and the circular system of presentation they imply are unique—or deserve the distinctive name 'Cornish'—but that the system was widespread and that the Cornish examples have simply attracted more attention.

The Round at St. Just

The next example Norris quotes is more fully documented. Here, at last, we have reference to a surviving (though now much defaced) example.

William Borlase was an antiquary who published, in 1745, his *Observations on the Antiquities Historical and Monumental of Cornwall*. Here, after examination of certain rings of standing stones, he goes on to discuss unbroken earthen circles, and gives the following interesting passage (pp. 195 et seq.):

In these continued Rounds, or Amphitheatres of stone (not broken as the Cirques of Stones-erect) the Britans did usually assemble to hear plays acted . . . these are call'd with us in Cornwall (where we have great numbers of them) *Plân an guare*; viz. the level place, or Plain of sport and pastime. The benches round were generally of Turf. . . . We have one whose benches are of Stone, and the most remarkable Monument of this kind which I have yet seen; it is near the church of St. Just, Penwith; now somewhat disfigured by the injudicious repairs of later years, but by the remains it seems to have been a work of more than usual labour, and correctness (See Plate XVI. Fig. i & ii.). It was an exact circle of 126 feet diameter; the perpendicular height of the bank, from the area within, now, seven feet; but the height from the bottom of the ditch without, ten feet at present, formerly more. The seats consist of six steps, fourteen inches wide, and one foot high, with one on the top of all, where the Rampart is about seven feet wide.

The plate, referred to by Borlase, is in fact rather a hindrance than a help to picturing the Round. It shows a plan of the circle and what purports to be a section, to a different scale, through the Hill. But though the six stone steps are clear in both, there is no slightest indication in either of the 7-ft. rampart. (Nor of the presence of a stone *outer* wall to the Hill which will be referred to below on p. 66.) One is therefore inclined to hesitate before placing much faith in the plate as a record.

From this passage in Borlase we note the following points:

He says, 'the *Britans* did usually assemble to hear plays . . .' (not only the Cornish).

He says that in Cornwall specifically there are 'great numbers' of such rounds.

He calls the mound 'benches . . . of Turf' indicating that there were seats cut in it.

He gives the remarkable figure of 126 ft. as the diameter of the circle at St. Just in Penwith.

He gives the height of the hill above the Place as 'now' 7 ft.—implying perhaps that it had possibly been higher in years gone by.

He gives clear mention of the ditch *outside* the bank of seats (as we expected), and mentions a drop into it of 10 ft., and formerly more.

He concludes by suggesting that in addition to six rows of steps on the inner side of the bank, there was a wide 'rampart' (does he imply a 'promenade'?) round the top, 7 ft. wide.

But the most remarkable fact in all the above for the inquiry we are making at this moment is the size of the arena. It is 126 ft. in diameter. Far from giving us the picture of a smaller Place than we had guessed for *The Castle*, as did Carew's reference, this round at St. Just produces a distinctly larger picture—126 ft. as against our estimated 110 ft. for *The Castle*. Our *Castle* figure was founded on such slight evidence that it would be pointless to build much upon it; what I do want to observe, however, is that we have now proof of some arenas that were definitely smaller than we have envisaged for *The Castle* (Carew's 40 ft. or 50 ft.) and we have proof now also that some were bigger (Scawen's containing 'thousands', and St. Just at 126 ft.). Thus the figure we guessed for the *Castle* Place is not an impossible figure. It is properly within the range of known, existing, or observed, similar structures.

We add that a circle of the dimensions of St. Just might hold something like 4,000 people.

Perhaps at this point it would be useful to include a note given by Norris about the present state of the St. Just round. The Rev. Geo. Hadow (vicar of St. Just) communicated the following to him:

The old structure still remains in St. Just Church-town, close to the principal inn; the clear outline of the circus is quite apparent, being formed externally by a stone wall of about four feet perpendicular height, whilst a green bank slopes inwards; there is now no outside ditch, nor are there any steps . . . a pathway leads right through it from the town to the market place.

In this note we see the mound much reduced, the ditch vanished and also the steps, and we have the addition that a pathway cut through the mounds and across the plain—though whether this was a later feature or had been part of the original, we are not told.

But it is to be remarked that in the illustrative plan given by Borlase one gap only is shown in the circular mound.

What is also interesting as appearing to be a piece of conflicting evidence is the statement that the *external* wall of the Hill was of stone—not the steps on the inner face, as Borlase told us, for indeed these have now disappeared. Further we note that the stone wall in question has a '*perpendicular* height' of 4 ft. This suggests, though not conclusively, that it was a sheer vertical wall. If this were true it would descend into the water of the ditch without leaving any foothold for a leaper to land on, and this might justify the use of a slightly narrower ditch than we have figured; but not, I think, much narrower if the earth of so large a hill had to come out of it.

In a later book of Borlase's, *The Natural History of Cornwall*, 1758, is the description of a further 'round' called The Perran Round. He writes of it with some elation, rather suggesting it is his most important discovery of the sort so far. But about the Perran Round there is today a difference of opinion. To begin with, it is claimed as a much more ancient work, and further, it is claimed that it was built without any theatrical function in mind. It is a large round, 143 ft. across on the north–south axis and 135 ft. on the east–west (which we cannot avoid feeling is on a scale of size that would offer pretty formidable difficulties to an actor with long speeches to deliver in any breeze . . .). It is now a national monument, and a company of local inhabitants has come into existence to look after the monument; Mr. Treve Holman, its chairman, wrote (in *Theatre Notebook*, vol. iv, no. 3, 1950) a disclaimer of Borlase's views. We shall therefore not consider this Round in further detail so far as our present study is concerned.

Some account of the Cornish Rounds was given by R. Morton Nance in a paper called 'The Plen An Gwary or Cornish Playing-place' read in May 1934, and published in *The Journal of the Royal Institution of Cornwall*, vol. xxiv (part 3, 1935), Truro. On many matters we are not able to accept his statements concerning staging, but he offers an interesting list of places connected with Rounds: 'We have place-name or other evidence of the *plen an gwary*, at St. Ives, Ruan Major, Ruan Minor, Landewednack, Newlyn East, St. Columb Major, Redruth, St. Hilary, Sancreed, Sithney, Kea, and Camborne, and this cannot end the list by any means, for in the 15th century scarcely a Cornish-speaking parish could have been without one.'

In addition to this brief note on the Cornish Rounds, we may perhaps add the following which refers to a different part of the country but may possibly prove to be not unrelated to our present subject—though it must be emphasized that, without further study, it cannot be counted as positive evidence. At the end of their edition of *The Castle*, the editors insert this communication from Miss Edith Rickert (p. 188*b*):

As I studied the plan of the Castell, I was reminded of a place near Penrith, in Cumberland, called locally 'King Arthur's Round Table'. It is a circular turf platform about 20 yards in diameter, surrounded by a shallow ditch, and a raised bank that might have been used for spectators. If I remember rightly, there are two earth causeways over the ditch.

In the absence of evidence as to the use of this place, the local guide-book says that it may have been a tilting-ground; but I cannot help thinking that it would have been admirably adapted to the performance of plays in the manner suggested by the 'Castell'. I believe there are various other such 'Round Tables'; but this is the only one I have seen.

We note here mention of both ditch and bank, though we are not unfortunately told whether the bank is inside the ditch or outside. But we do see with especial interest that Miss Rickert here visualizes—I believe for the only time in the whole notes to this edition of *The Castle*—the possibility that the bank might have been used for spectators.

The 'causeways' bring up the question of access to the arena. This matter will claim our attention as our picture of the Place with its encircling mound grows clearer. If we grant that the audience were all on the inside of the ring-mound, how did they get in? Did they scramble up the hill and slither down the inner side? Impossible! Was there a bridge at one point by which they could cross the ditch? If so was the Hill, at the bridge-head, cut through so as to leave a level way into the Place? We have no evidence at all as yet, save that the Hill at St. Just was formerly cut at one point (see Borlase's plan), and is today cut at two points (according to the evidence on p. 66). We have to return to these queries later.

Leaving aside the possibility of the existence outside Cornwall of 'rounds' with a theatrical purpose, we must sum up our evidence about size.

The sizes, then, have been various; they range from Carew's

'40 or 50 foot', through Miss Rickert's 'about 20 yards' to the surviving 126 ft. of St. Just. When into this range we fit our hypothetical 110 ft. for the circle of the *Castle* Plan, we see that it has at least the merit of approximating to dimensions that can be shown to have been used for theatres of this shape in other parts of Britain.

7

ON THE DYNAMICS OF THE PLACE-CROWD AND ON THE STYTELERYS

*The Movement of the Audience * The Lanes and the Sight-Lines * The Movement of the Audience (resumed) * A Definition of Styteler*

I AM aware that the title of this chapter reads like an introduction to a piece of modern science fiction about outer space-time and its denizens, but I decided to leave it. I am also aware of some aversion in myself hitherto to allowing the word *dynamics* to intrude into a discussion of the theatre—or indeed of any art—but I felt I had to get over the aversion in this particular instance. The reason comes from *The Oxford English Dictionary* and from the fact that an understanding of 'force as producing or affecting motion' and of 'moving forces, physical or moral, in any sphere' . . . considered in regard to the audience in the Place is precisely what is needed to round off our present examination, and bring us into a position to see (I think) why there had to be 'stytelerys' within the Place—and why, also, there had to be not over many of them there.

When in sober fact we come to consider in detail the works and the responsibilities that were involved in putting on a performance of *The Castle of Perseverance* before a gathering of medieval Englishmen, upon their native sward and under their accustomed sky, we must admit that it was pretty sure to have been a complicated undertaking.

You had to deal, to begin with, with a crowd. It would be an unsophisticated crowd, upon which you had deliberately to work in an emotional respect—you had to work them up about the brutality of the World, the horror of the Devil, the seductions of Lechery, and the finality of Death. You had to inflame them with the pomp and arrogance of overlords, and with the blood-stirring of slanging-matches and of physical beatings and combat. What you gave them was a strong and heady brew.

There was also the heightened atmosphere created by curiosity and expectation. I do not know how long it would have taken to prepare a Place for a performance, but it would be a time every minute of which must have stirred anticipation in the neighbourhood, in the same way as the irruption of a train of fair-ground vehicles does today.

Your *Vexillatores* gave out their banns. You dug or adapted your ditch (or built your barriers). You dealt with all the many local problems involved in flooding that ditch. You adapted the earthen mound thrown up, so that it both hid the Place within and served for the seats of special spectators. You built your scaffolds and arranged for storage of your costumes and properties—and possibly the stabling and hire of horses. There might be banners involved that would flutter provocatively in the breeze beforehand.

You would make some stir in the locality; and if you were a good showman you would make a particular point of doing so.

On the evening before, we picture the Place with all its accessories. The last night before the show must, above all, have been a time of risk. 'Those kids' were quite likely the bane of your life.

For 'those kids' were probably just as bad in the Middle Ages as they are now. If they saw a ladder, it was 'Here's a ladder! Let's climb up it!' If they saw a throne, it was, 'Here's a throne! Let's sit in it!'—and Heaven help any of the more delicate properties. If you want the usual research-worker's chapter and verse for this propensity (though I'm sorry it is a trifle late in date), please see *Dobsons Drie Bobbes*, 1607 (ed. E. A. Horsman, Oxford, 1955, p. 14): 'The boyes of the Citty . . . in the winter eeuenings enacted many a lewd stratageme about the shoppes . . . as bursting glasen windowes, ouerthrowing Milke maides pailes, pulling downe stalles' (so they might even have had a scaffold down if they'd been given half a chance!) 'and crushing out the linckes which were hung foorth to giue light to the Passengers in the streetes.'

So a playing-place *had* to be strongly barred about.

The point I want to make is that you have to suffer the generation of a force—the force of a stimulated crowd. That force will undoubtedly have expression; the crowd will *move*.

The Movement of the Audience

Let us picture this in some detail. We begin at dawn with our empty theatre. You have bidden your audience be punctual:

Ye haste you then thitherwards, Sirs, hendly in height,
All good neighbours, full specially we you pray,
And look that ye be there betimes, lovely and light . . .

They may, or may not, be already gathering and jostling at your entrance bar. When the time arrives you lift your bar and let them into the arena. They come like a swirling sea, or like a crowd into a football stadium, or like the first rush of galleryites at 'doors-open'. Now what happens?

Always supposing you had a full audience (and it is a strangely miserable picture to conceive such a show being presented to a mere handful!), the people flood into the Place, with its Castle on legs standing fair in the centre, and with its ranges of seats round the edge and, here and there, a high scaffold. The people divide and do one of two things; they either climb the Hill round the side. and settle in the seats there, or they pick a spot on the grass of the Place itself where they think they will see well, and they settle down.

We do not know whether the seat-holders have any token by which they are privileged to ascend to the better positions, or whether all places are open to all. If there is any distinction made, then it will be very clear to us at this point in our investigation that we are faced with the necessity of a new element in our picture—namely, for an official or a system by which the two grades of audience can be separated and kept separate—for it is pointless if the first-come rabble can flood the best seats at will, or seep into them gradually after the play begins.

Now (though we are only too conscious of a multitude of minor matters that escape our knowledge already in the picture) let us go on in order to reach a particular consideration. Where, at this point, are we to imagine the people in the Place to be concentrating?

Here it begins to be quite inescapable that the gay, irresponsible picture of *laissez faire* which we have been playing with is coming more and more under a strong compulsion. We have got to do something in our picture about this audience in the Place. We have got to control it in certain ways.

We already know from our study of the Plan that we must prevent them from settling in the *midst* of the Place—'let no men sit there for letting of sight, for here shall be the best of all' (whatever the exact implication) is likely to mean that people will be most inclined to go towards it.

Apart from this need to keep the centre itself clear, we know that at l. 492 two figures are going to come down from one of the scaffolds and walk through the crowd across the grass to Mankind (who comes from the Castle in the centre), meet him and take him back to World's scaffold. How can it be ensured that they have a way through the crowd?

Much depends upon the size of the circle and upon the density of the crowd. Did the crowd in the Place all stand, or did those spectators near to a scene of action drop to their knees or squat or even (if there were space) lie down with their elbows in the grass and their chins in their hands? But this could not go on for long— and here the 'dynamics' of the crowd begins to work.

Let us picture it in this way; for the sake of argument let us begin by supposing the crowd quite undirected in any way. They occupy any part of the Place they please, standing or sitting. Then the play opens; World speaks from his scaffold. Now there can be no doubt, I believe, that in response the full crowd throughout the Place will turn to the West. World's speech lasts perhaps two minutes, and then the Devil speaks from the North. Now the crowd will turn to the North. And so forth. Not only this, but if the crowd is not too packed there is likely to be more than turning —there is likely to be actual movement across the Place in the direction of the scaffold in question. It might be almost like the tilting of a drum of dried peas.

Now add to this elementary instance of 'dynamics' another factor; it has already been offered to us in the idea of the descent of Lust-liking and Folly into the Place to fetch Mankind. Will there be space in the crowd for them? Let us imagine ourselves at the far side of the Place from the scaffold where they stand. This means that we should be exactly at the East with our backs to God's scaffold. But no! that cannot be quite true. Already dynamics is operating. For, as a glance at Fig. 10 will show, if we stood at the foot of the scaffold on the East and looked across to the scaffold on the West, we should not be able to see it properly because the central tower of the Castle would be in the way.

What are we to do? Most likely we move a little to our right or left, to enable ourselves to see past the tower and bring World's scaffold into uninterrupted view. In fact, anyone standing in front of a scaffold will find the one opposite more or less obscured—and thus people would tend not to take up positions in front of a scaffold. Here, then, is a force at work on their movement—or at least on their position—and before we go on to discover a contrary force which will cause a conflict, let us pause a moment to look at this first force in detail.

The Lanes and the Sight-lines

The above fact obviously has an influence on the disposition of the crowd of spectators through the Place. The matter is worth considering in some detail, for in such a consideration we can see not only how the crowd would dispose itself so as to make a particular production-technique possible—indeed would make such a technique come into existence—but we can also see why the scaffolds were disposed in *The Castle* in the particular positions in which the Plan shows them. Let us take the disposition of the audience first.

To study this disposition I want to suppose a very simple circular theatre with only four scaffolds—one at each cardinal point of the compass, and with a central tower in the middle of the Place as in *The Castle*. This I have diagrammatically represented in Fig. 11.

Let us now consider the sector of the audience in the South-East. We will suppose ourselves standing in the Place anywhere in this sector and looking towards the Castle-tower in the centre. It will be evident that we can move round somewhat to our right— that is towards the East scaffold—but that as we move we shall come to a spot where, in looking across the arena, the tower begins to get in the way of our view of the West scaffold. This spot we have marked C. The East scaffold itself would then be at our right elbow; by turning full right we could see it clearly. By turning only half-right, we could see the North scaffold to the right of the tower; by turning full to the left we could see the South scaffold. Thus all these scaffolds would be in clear and uninterrupted view. Further, we could see, if we looked straight across the arena to the opposite side, the scaffold on the West— but this would be very near to being cut off by the central tower. As long as we went no farther than C, we could keep the West scaffold just in sight. But if we moved a few steps nearer to the East scaffold, the scaffold on the West would progressively slip behind the tower and become hidden from us—until, if we stood full in front of the East scaffold, the scaffold on the West would be lost completely.

Returning to the spot C, we can draw a sight-line past the Castle-tower so as just to include the West scaffold. This sight-line is shown in the diagram.

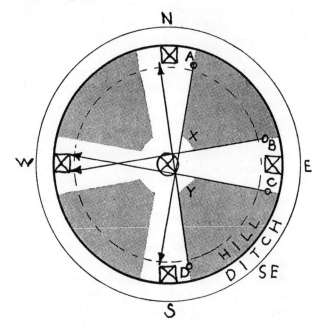

FIG. 11. Diagram of a theatre with a Place 100 ft. in diameter, and set with four scaffolds equidistantly; the shaded portions show audience-areas from which all scaffolds would be visible.

Turning now to our left and walking round the rim of the Place towards the South scaffold with our eye constantly directed in-wards across the arena we find that, as we move, we can still keep all the scaffolds in perfect view till we reach the spot marked D; a step farther than this and the scaffold in the North begins to be hidden from us. So, if we do not wish to be unsighted—that is to have this scaffold masked from us by the tower—we must take a sight-line from the spot D past the tower, to the far corner of the North scaffold, and we must not pass beyond that sight-line.

Now these two sight-lines cross not far from the centre of the

75

Place. Let us mark the point of intersection as Y. It will now be clear that from any position whatever within this sector CDY (which I have shown shaded in diagram 11), you would have an unobstructed view of every scaffold round the Place.

If now we turn to the North-East sector, we can mark an exactly similar area, ABX, from any position in which we find every scaffold is similarly visible. And so for the rest of the circle.

When these areas also are shaded like the first to distinguish them, it becomes clearly seen that we are left with four unshaded spaces like lanes or avenues radiating from the centre in the form of a cross; from anywhere in those lanes the view of one or other of the scaffolds would be inevitably hindered.

Thus the first point that I wanted to make is demonstrated in the case of a simple theatre with only four scaffolds, and we see that, for the best viewing, the audience-disposition would theoretically be in four symmetrical sectors, leaving four lanes clear, one between each scaffold and the centre.

Let us now advance a step and consider for a moment a similar Place with *five* scaffolds, all placed equidistantly round the circle. I show this in Fig. 12.

In Fig. 12 I have shaded the totally unobstructed areas as before, but it will be seen that they are now considerably reduced areas. The siting of the scaffolds now causes a wide lane to cut through the centre of what were the clear sectors in Fig. 11, and from anywhere in these wide lanes the scaffold opposite would be hidden. The narrower lanes before the scaffolds are left as access for the actors. In other words, if five scaffolds are equally placed round our arena there are no wide sectors of vision as before whence they can all be seen, but only a number of narrow sectors. The size of the audience is in effect considerably reduced.

We begin to see now a good reason why the presenters of *The Castle of Perseverance* decided against placing their five scaffolds symmetrically round the Place. What did they do instead? In Fig. 13 I have drawn a similar diagram, but this time so as to show the five scaffolds as they are disposed in the plan of *The Castle*; that is, with four at the four cardinal points, and the fifth asymmetrically at the North-East. I have again shaded the areas (as in Fig. 11) whence an unobstructed view of all scaffolds would be fully obtained.

It is, I think, instructive to compare this with Fig. 12, and see

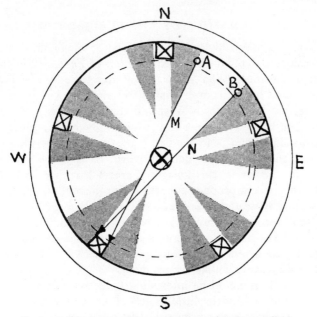

FIG. 12. Diagram as Fig. 11, but set with five scaffolds equidistantly; the shaded portions show reduced areas from which all scaffolds would be visible.

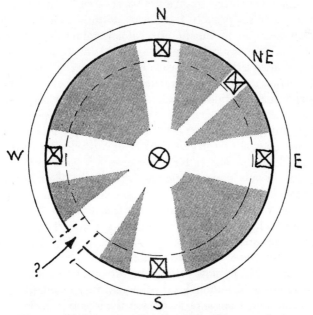

FIG. 13. Diagram of a theatre with a Place 100 ft. in diameter, set with five scaffolds asymmetrically according to *The Castle* Plan; showing increase in the areas from which all scaffolds could be visible.

how Fig. 13 allows a bigger audience. There is no doubt that from the consideration of viewing, the presenters of *The Castle* made the wisest arrangement. What, in fact, they would produce (as Fig. 13 shows) would be two complete large sectors where vision was perfect—sectors in the North-West and the South-East, one sector in the South-West where vision would only be complete from positions along, and near, the two converging sides of the sector, but from the middle of which the North-East scaffold would be hidden by the tower (this unsighted area I have left unshaded); finally, they would produce a fourth sector in front of, and beside, the North-East scaffold itself. Part of this sector could not be used because the scaffold occupied it, and part again could not be used because of the need to preserve a lane from the scaffold to the centre for the actors to walk along. But otherwise the whole becomes a very workmanlike arrangement.

Incidentally it would be interesting to know if we have found here the reason why the little sketch of the Castle-tower in the centre of the Plan has concave sides! It seems a strange characteristic at first, and yet after studying these sight-line diagrams, it must be perfectly obvious that to pare down the width of the tower about its centre—to give it a waist—renders it without any doubt easier to see past. In fact a waist to the Castle-tower might mean an increase in the number of spectators able to see all scaffolds, of as many as 120 people—that is to say a row of 12 in single file down either side of each of the five main lanes!

One further remark may be made on this last diagram. Some few pages ago our attention was called to the need for some kind of entrance into the Place, at a point (or points) where the ring-mound could be cut and where the ditch could be bridged, and presumably some control of entry arranged. This whole matter of entry into the Place remains, as far as my research goes, in fullest obscurity. I can only point to one curiosity: in the diagram we have just been discussing we have, automatically and without any intention of that sort, produced a perfect position for such an entrance which, of itself, is not suitable for any other purpose in the whole performance—in fact is so much dead ground—that is the 'blind' avenue at the South-West.

The reader will by now perhaps be prompted to exclaim—'But these arrangements—though very fine and very ingenious—are so complicated that I am sure no medieval audience could be got to

understand them, or at least to keep to them without either a lot
of experience or somebody to guide them!' True; and it is just this
that brings the need for another factor into our picture before we
can call it complete. To lead up to this factor I want to return to
the sketch of the audience settling into place for a show, which we
had to interrupt in order to consider these diagrams.

The Movement of the Audience (resumed)

We have now established that we should not be standing quite
in front of God's scaffold, but a little to the side of it. Thence we
should look across the Place, with its sea of heads, towards World
on the far side on his scaffold.

At once another feature of our picture that we have frequently
mentioned before drops into place with a reasonableness that one
might have failed to appreciate up to this moment: those scaffolds
had indeed to be very high! A mere 3 or 4 feet would be scarcely
any use at all to make dominant a figure fifty or a hundred feet
away on the far side of the Place beyond such a sea of people. The
scaffolds would have to be at least 7 or 8 feet high! Now we may
appreciate indeed Chaucer's 'joly Absolon' playing Herod 'on a
scaffold hye'.

World, with Lust-liking and Folly, hold our attention across the
mass of people from their elevation, but we may not be able to
hear them too well. Then we shall begin to press forward.

So that against the tendency to leave an empty space in front of
a scaffold, which we noticed earlier, there is an opposing force
which tends to encroach on such spaces as soon as acting begins
on the scaffold above them.

But just as the people start to edge into the attractive sparser
area before one particular scaffold, urged both by their interest
and by the pressure of their fellows behind who can see and hear
less well, the tide of motion suffers a check and meets a reversing
force; for the actors are coming down from that scaffold and need
a lane through the crowd on the grass. How can their artistic need
be satisfied without involving a 'collision of forces'?

One way would be to depend upon the physical or personal
power of the player himself. But it is not a safe way. To jostle one's
path through a crowd wastes one's breath and so endangers one's

vocal delivery—which is an important matter in an open-air arena of this size. Again, some roles of their own character—Sloth, Humility, a Child—must neither be hustling nor dominant.

Another way might be to scare the advancing crowd back with grotesquerie and fireworks. This, no doubt, the Devil did, blowing off squibs from all sorts of unconventional parts of his body. But it would not be a becoming technique for the Good Angel.

How else can you control this crowd? You cannot, I think, leave it to the people themselves, because even if they have the best intentions, they will forget. For instance, let us suppose some sort of lane to have been kept clear from the scaffold's foot by the obliging spectators; as soon as the actor descends and begins to pass along it he becomes less easy to see for the people at a distance (among whom we are included)—he will be lost in the press. Some spectators will rise with us on tiptoe to keep his moving hat in sight. Nearer people flanking the lane will, as he passes them, lean forward and turn their heads after him to look where he has gone, and immediately there will be a tendency (reinforced by the press at the back) to close-in the lane behind him. The whole audience will move. Some unsighted, quick-witted lads may leave their positions altogether and scamper off through the crowd in the direction the player is going, to try and arrive at his destination before him, and maybe get to be in front of the crowd when he stops. And the actor may be cut off.

To appreciate this technique of acting which involves descents into, and crossings of, the Place, we have got to realize the frequent disappearings behind spectators' heads of the moving players, and all the resultant swayings and risings and movings and redistributions and settlings-down-again of the Place-crowd. It will recoil and surge back, it will divide like the Red Sea and flood in again like a river in spate. It is turning and seething and murmuring.

How can you stop this crowd choking the show? Here is 'actor-audience intimacy' with a vengeance—and it goes so far that we have also to recognize a possible impact of the *audience* on the *actor*! That must be controlled.

In point of fact I believe there is no possible way that it could be controlled with the elements which we have at present included in our picture. We have a blank in our reconstruction—a quite inevitable requirement and no functionary to fulfil it.

But we also have remarked some time ago one functionary in

the story to whom we could not then assign a job. May we now bring these two things together?

I refer, of course, to the styteler. Before we can take another step towards solving the audience problem which we have brought up, we must turn aside and ask what is to be discovered about the act of styteling.

A Definition of Styteler

The definitions of 'stytelerys' given in glossaries and notes appear to be a little conflicting at first. Thus the glossary in our edition of *The Castle* gives—'orderers, arrangers, managers'. While Sharp in *A Dissertation on the Coventry Mysteries* (1825) interprets the word as 'marshalmen', and is thus quoted by Pollard in *English Miracle Plays* (1890 and 1927). But both Thurston C. Peter in *The Old Cornish Drama* (1906, p. 12), and Chambers in *Literature*, p. 55, give the apparently very different meaning of 'sticklers'. Chambers, in fact, goes much farther than this; he not only employs the word but adds a very curious, and it may be misleading, phrase, for in his description of *The Castle* in *Literature*, p. 55, he says (and I italicize the phrase): 'There must not be too many sticklers *to prevent a good view.*' This remark follows directly on his mention of the circular place being kept free of spectators and ringed with a ditch, and thus he appears almost certainly to be quoting the legend round the plan (which we have studied on p. 18) and to be referring to the 'stytelerys' by his word 'sticklers'. Yet we have seen that, though the Plan warns us against over many stytelerys being within the Place, it does *not*, in fact, anywhere give as reason that they would 'prevent a good view'. It is, on the other hand, the sitting of people in the midst of the Place that is given as a cause of 'lettynge of syt'. Chambers here seems to be mixing up the information in two quite separate legends from the Plan, and the result is to give the impression—which is indeed held by some people—that certain *captious persons* might gather together in quantities in the Place and stand in such a way as to block the view, and that for this reason such captious persons in the audience must be kept few in number.

Clearly, now, one will begin to feel that there is something wrong at this point with the interpretation. The fault might be in Chambers's interpretation of the text or in our interpretation of Chambers's meaning of 'sticklers', but in any case we are heading for a false position if we assume a warning against something that could not in fact be guarded against. For how can you keep a stickler, in the sense of a captious person, out of the show anyway? Let us, however, suspend judgement on Chambers till we look at the definitions of the word.

We have at present: (*a*) 'orderers, arrangers, managers', (*b*) 'marshalmen', and (*c*) 'sticklers', all offered as meanings of 'stytelerys'. Let us try to get nearer the root meaning of the word.

We turn to *The Oxford English Dictionary* only to find, at first sight, no help; for 'stytelerys' is not given. But with early words the spelling is variable. When we ask if the term is included under another spelling we find ourselves at last on the track. Under the entry 'stightler' we learn that this word had, in the fifteenth century, the variant 'styteler', and that it is formed from the verb 'to stightle' plus the usual '-er' termination to form the noun—one who stightles.

Inquiring further we are told that 'to stightle' is a frequentative form of 'to stight'. 'To stight', we see, is defined as 'to set in order, arrange, place', and the example quoted is from about the year 1350, *The Romance of William of Palerne*, l. 4425: 'þan rauȝt sche forþ a ring a riche & a nobul, þe ston þat þeron was stiȝt was of so stif vertu, þat . . .' (etc.). So, we learn of a rich and noble ring, whereon a stone was *stight* (or placed) that was of so great a virtue . . . etc.

Turning now to 'to stightle' itself, we are given three groups of definitions and three examples—one of which is highly illuminating for our present inquiry. The three meanings of 'to stightle' are:

1. to dispose, arrange, to rule, govern, to set in order;
2. to strive;
3. to intervene as an umpire.

Here already we see the shades of meaning given in the *Castle* glossary. Of the three examples of these uses of 'stightle', the first is from the same source as that for 'stight' and reads: 'þat oþer was his stiward þat stiȝtled al his meyne', or 'that other was his steward who arranged, or governed, all his household'.

The second is from *Merlin*, just a hundred years later (1450): 'And so haue thei medled and styghtled till they haue founde the kynge Boors vpon foote.'—'And so have they mingled and striven till they have found the King Boors upon foot.'

The third and last reference illustrates the use of the word in

the sense of 'intervene' between parties, or as an umpire, and it is
this one which we believe is especially to our purpose. It is a quotation from a medieval play. We give it, because of its interest, in
a somewhat fuller context than the limited space allows the *Dictionary* to do. It is from No. xxxi of the *York Mystery Plays*, at
l. 75; this belongs to about 1440; and we quote from Lucy Toulmin
Smith's edition of 1885.

The situation is that Herod has just gone to bed when he is
aroused again at the call of some soldiers bringing a prisoner to
him. One says:

> . . . My lorde, yondir is a boy boune þat brought is in blame;
> Haste you in hye, þei houe at youre ӡates.

To which Herod (rather understandably) testily replies:

> What! and schall I rise nowe, in þe deuyllis name?
> To stighill amang straungeres in stales of a state.
> But haue here my hande, halde nowe!
> And se þat my sloppe be wele sittande.

> (My Lord, yonder is a boy ready, that brought is in blame;
> Haste you with speed, they stop at your gates.
> HEROD. What! and shall I rise now, in the devil's name,
> To *umpire* among strangers in conspiracies of state?
> But catch hold my hand. Steady now!
> —And see that I've pulled my gown down properly!)

The glossary of the edition gives: 'stighill—to decide, to establish, order, to part combatants.' (In which I cannot help thinking
the comma after 'establish' is a misprint, and unintended.)

All the above then seems (I think) fair and understandable, and
looks to be leading us towards a goal at which we shall be able to
determine the function of a styteler at a theatre performance. But
just as we seem on the point of full interpretation, we encounter a
show of resistance from our subject that tells us our analysis is not
yet quite complete.

I have referred to the *Dictionary* entry under 'stightler', but I
did not then continue and give also the definition which there follows. Instead I chose to look into the meaning of the verb 'to
stightle' before taking the noun 'a stightler' or 'styteler'. What now
is (at first sight) so surprising is that, after these definitions of the
verb which are at some length, and paint a picture into which one
can begin to read some intentions, the *Dictionary* should give the

definition of 'stightler' very curtly, without any informative alternatives as, simply, 'stickler'. And so we are brought back to the puzzle in Chambers and those other writers who accept this equivalent for the term.

What in fact is a 'stickler'?

We are conscious of I suppose only one common usage employing the word today in general speech—and that is in the phrase 'a stickler for etiquette', conveying the idea of someone who is particular in his manners—even a little fussy—and must have everything done 'by the book'. Perhaps we suppose it means one who is *sticky* about things. The last supposition itself would be misleading but the main impression before it is indeed not an incorrect one. Yet to turn up 'stickler' as we did 'stightler' in the *Dictionary* is to receive at first something of a surprise and then—suddenly— a shaft of illumination in which all the parts of this curious picture fall into place.

There are no less than six shades of meaning given for 'stickler':

1. an 'umpire at a tournament' . . . hence 'one who intervenes as a mediator between combatants';
2. 'an active partisan';
2b. ' meddler, busybody';
3. 'an opponent' or objector;
4. 'one who insists on' 'a form', etc.;
5. a second in a contest.

Thus a 'stickler' is in reality, not a 'sticky' person, but one who 'stightles'.

Let us now review all this.

We will begin with my last remark: 'A stickler is one who stightles.' It may also be written: 'a stickler is one who stickles.' That 'stickle' and 'stightle' are not only words of similar meaning but are in fact the very same word may not be immediately obvious, but this is true. In the mystery of the transmutation of consonants between versions of words in different languages, such things are well known and scientifically tabulated. It is similar with words in different dialects. In the case of this particular consonant change, we have a striking parallel example in a not dissimilar word that the reader may have noticed on an earlier page of this book (p. 31). That word is 'pightle' in the sense of 'an enclosure' or 'small field' or 'close'. Its transmuted form is shaped on just the same lines as 'stickler', though it is perhaps a little unexpected—'pightle' is the source of the transmutation 'Pickles' as a Yorkshire surname, and therefore: 'stickle' is to 'stightle' what 'Pickles' is to 'pightle'.

We are now able therefore to equate 'stickler' with 'styteler', provided always that it shall be understood to mean 'one who stightles'.

Now what have we got, up to this? We have a 'styteler'—a functionary obscure enough at the moment save that we know his function is 'to arrange' or 'to intervene', or some action of that nature relating to 'proper ordering'.

We have also the certainty that persons called 'stytelerys' were present in the Place.

We have further deduced that when the audience was present, sitting, standing, or moving, in the Place, it appears unescapable that for the unhindered progress of a show acted in the Place-technique, there must have been some means of *arranging* them, *controlling* them, or *intervening* between them and the actors in somewhat the sense that a cordon of policemen 'intervenes' between a crowd and a procession.

On top of all this we can very well see how such a cordon of policemen, if their rank becomes too closely packed, might act not as a help to keeping the proceedings clear so much as a hindrance. The first, obvious way in which they might become a hindrance if there were too many of them is that, coming as they would between show and spectators, they might block the view. But there is, I feel, another and still better reason to justify the warning that they should be kept as few as practicably possible—and that is that a bustling multitude of them would intrude on the *atmosphere* of the occasion, might swamp the show and quite possibly irritate the onlookers more than organize them. Some control there had to be, but it required to be kept tactfully unobtrusive so that it would not detract from the spectacle. We can easily realize how, though *some* policemen would need to be present on such an occasion, yet we should not wish to have over many of them in the place . . . .

Thus we have proved a need to control the audience; we have proved that the form of action implied in the word 'styteler' is on every count consistent with the actions involved in controlling such an audience; we have no hesitation in understanding that the persons who performed such a controlling action might become a nuisance; we have a specific warning in our text that 'over many stytelerys' were not to be present in the Place.

I therefore submit that we have made out a very fair case for our definition of the word 'stytelerys'.

What I believe is as follows: on some occasion before the day of the show, a kind of recruitment would be made among the worthies of the neighbourhood. Its object would be to collect a number of persons who would consent to act as controllers or marshals. One would be inclined to expect that they would be drawn from what I might call the semi-authoritative classes, and that they might be offered some inducement such as free entrance to the show, and perhaps the knowledge that they would see part of it at least from the 'front row'. To all which there might be added the pride of appearing on a public occasion in a privileged position.

It is worth noting that the pre-selection of a number of persons in this way exactly fits the implication in the words 'Let not over many stytelers be' permitted in the Place. For before each occasion of a performance it could be estimated what sized circle would best serve the density of the local population, and hence just how many stytelers were likely to be sufficient to control an audience of the expected size. So many and no more were to be recruited. The instruction in the legend can now be seen both to have point and to be capable of being observed.

These men, once collected, would be given their instructions. We would suppose these instructions included a requirement to be present in the Place before the arrival of the audience; to see that, when the audience came, those members of it who were privileged to sit on the Hill (if such a distinction were made) were admitted to their seats, and the rest kept in the Place proper; to see that the audience in the Place was concentrated in those areas in which (as we have shown) the view would be generally good and to prevent their gathering in other areas where they might obstruct vision or action—that is, they would be instructed to keep them out of the lanes and concentrated in the shaded sectors we have pointed out in our Fig. 13; and finally each styteler would be told to keep a sharp look-out for any signs that an actor on a scaffold near him was about to descend into the Place, and that on every such occasion it was his duty to ensure that a way was clear for the actor, and to *intervene* between actor and crowd whenever the need arose to preserve the smooth running of the performance.

I think their instructions would not be more detailed than this. I do not imagine, for instance, that the stytelers were told beforehand of every cross and descent in the play and of the point at which it occurred, because I do not see how they could have effectively remembered such instructions unless they had been present at one or more rehearsals. We have no evidence that such an opportunity was, or could be, offered them. And to suppose that specially trained members of the company travelled with the troupe solely to act as stytelers (which is otherwise the only way in which the styteler could have had such detailed knowledge of the script) seems very unlikely. Following upon this idea, it is of course not impossible that the company might travel one or two 'stytelers major'—if I may use the phrase—to guide the locals. Or that the whole business might not have been in the hands of the 'ordinary' or Prompter, whose function in the performances of those days was perhaps a very important one. Carew's oft-quoted comic story (see, for example, Nicoll, *The English Theatre*, p. 20) of a Prompter once having to deal with a non-regular actor who insisted on speaking aloud the directions whispered to him as well as his lines, is an example both of the oddities such performances sometimes encountered and of the importance of that rather nebulous figure the medieval prompter-stage-manager. Taking his functions all into account, a styteler might well be defined as a contemporary A.S.M.

I do not therefore suppose the local stytelers were fully rehearsed in every cue which preceded a descent or a cross. As we shall see when we come to examine the progress of the whole performance, these crossings of the Place are going to be pretty numerous and are going to follow many different paths—for instance an actor may be required to leave any one of the five scaffolds and go to the centre, or he may be required to go to any one of the other scaffolds, or he may be required to go to any intermediate spot in the area of the Place to meet some other actor or take part in some action at that spot; or he might be required merely to 'walk about' the Place to suggest a long journey or even to fill time during the performance by another actor of a quite separate action.

So it seems hardly likely that the stytelers could be expected to keep clear from the very beginning all paths which were eventually to be used by actors at any part of the play; I think they had to use their own discretion about this. When an actor showed signs of an intention to descend into the Place, one (or more) of the stytelers would move through the crowd, part it and clear a lane from the scaffold in the particular direction along which the actor began to go. This in some sense is not bad theatre technique. After a more or less lengthy harangue from a scaffold, the actor gathers his skirts about him, the stytelers see that action is about to follow; seated boys would be brought to their feet, a knot of listening citizens would be suddenly called to earth and hustled back a yard or two, a stir would spread through the audience, those far away would rise on tiptoe. Something would be about to happen.

The long speech ended, the player would begin to come down. A period of silence would ensue in which eyes would concentrate on the descending figure. Minds would ask, What is he going to do? At each step down, less of him would be seen. A sensation almost like the sensation at the descent of a deity would spread, a hush rule all spectators. Now his moving head-dress alone would be all that most of them could see, and he would be striding across the grass of the spectators' world, bringing the play into their midst.

The stytelers would guard his path, the crowd under their control would give way, and the player would walk on without interruption to the appointed spot where another phase of the action would begin and another section of the audience find itself privileged to have, for the time, the nearest and most intimate view. How well such a technique *spreads* a performance throughout all parts of a big audience! How well it is adapted to playing to crowds, in the streets or in the fields!

This, then, is our opinion of the meaning of 'stytelerys', and their relation to the performance.

And incidentally we have added yet another item to the evidence which demonstrates that the audience must have been *in* the Place, not outside it and leaving it clear. For stytelers 'within the Place', yet controlling an audience *outside* the Place are to my mind a contradiction in terms (and that appears to be the picture created by Chambers).

Here, our preliminary study of the Place, so far as evidence contained in *The Castle* goes, is complete save in one particular detail; we have been able to say very little about the nature of the scaffolds, and to these we must now turn our attention.

PART THREE

THE SCAFFOLDS
ROUND THE 'PLACE'

8

SCAFFOLDS OF THE FOUQUET
MINIATURE

The Theatre of the Miniature * *Scaffold No. 3* * *Scaffold
No. 1* * *Scaffold No. 2* * *Scaffolds Nos. 4 and 5* * *The Gap* *
Scaffold No. 6 * *Scaffold No. 0* * *The Spectators kneeling on
the Ground*

WHEN we begin the study of what, on the *Castle* Plan, are
called the *scaffolds*, we are very fortunate in that Time has
left us a document bearing much evidence. This document
is in France and seems at first sight perhaps to be worlds away
from the play we are studying. But many writers have pointed out
what a close connexion there was between France and Britain in
these matters. (Copies of French plays were made in England—
for instance, at Canterbury as early as *c.* 1275. It is said that all
classes in England understood French in 1350. The authorship of
Le Mystère d'Adam is possibly Anglo-Norman. One of the English
mystery-cycles is said to be based on a French original. The reader
is referred to Grace Frank, *The Medieval French Drama* (1954) and
Hardin Craig, *English Religious Drama* (1955).) The document of
which I am speaking has been much reproduced in books on
theatre history but it has been generally very inadequately examined in their texts. It was the juxtaposition of a photograph of
this document with one of the *Castle* Plan that first suggested to
me that it might be possible to reconstruct the form of the medieval
theatre in the round. The document is Jean Fouquet's miniature
of the martyrdom of St. Apollonia, painted probably between 1452
and 1460 for *Le Livre d'heures d'Etienne Chevalier*, which is now
in the Musée Condé, Chantilly, near Paris, see Pl. 2.

In this picture we see a shape of things which is strikingly like
the one we have reconstructed so far for the *Castle* circle; but this
likeness is not perhaps obvious at once, for the most interesting
detail of the Fouquet miniature is just that which is most obscure

in the *Castle* Plan—that is to say, the scaffolds; while the most notable detail of the *Castle* Plan is one of the least obvious in the miniature—that is the circular Place, and the relation of the audience and the play to that Place. Indeed (as we shall see) several commentators deny that a regular Place is shown in the picture at all.

But upon close study we find much that is related or complementary in the two documents:

Firstly, there is the circular Place.

Secondly, the whole thing is confined within the limits of the Place; that is to say, all the audience and all the action are in the Place itself or on the scaffolds immediately surrounding it.

Thirdly, though a number of actors are to be seen in the miniature on certain of the scaffolds, yet the immediate and sensational action that we see being performed is occurring in the centre of the Place itself.

Fourthly, the Place shown in Fouquet exemplifies the other kind of Place mentioned in the Plan, for it is a 'strongly-barred-about' Place, not one encircled with a ditch and hill.

As I have said, all these points do not necessarily strike a spectator at first glance, and we must give a word or two in development.

The Theatre of the Miniature

That the whole 'theatre', which Fouquet depicts, is circular has been disputed—it has been declared, for instance, to be semicircular—but after examination we see two facts; first, that the line of scaffolds at the back is most carefully and indeed skilfully drawn in perspective to show a concave curve; second, the hedge or fence in the foreground is still more obviously represented as a convex curve. Therefore, these two together must form some kind of circular shape. That the two curves meet outside the margin of the picture, and that the line of the fence would continue round and embrace the underparts of the scaffolds enclosing them in a ring, is admittedly not categorically stated in the miniature, but there are two considerations which suggest that this could be so—first, we have the circular theatre of the Terence miniature described above, not unduly distant in date and general conception from Fouquet. And second, we have the difficult task of offering an acceptable theory of what else—if Fouquet did not intend to represent a circle—he could possibly have meant by his drawing.

One attempt at an alternative is put forward, but not with any finality, by Nicole Decugis and Suzanne Reymond in their valuable book of pictures entitled *Le Décor de théâtre en France du Moyen Age à 1925* (1953). Here, at p. 18, they say of this miniature —'Ici la scène circulaire s'élève à un mètre au-dessus du sol, portée par des assemblages de fagots appelés "fascines". Le drame se passe sur la partie la plus avancée du plateau . . . au fond se trouvent les spectateurs . . .'.

For my own part I find this very difficult to translate fully and significantly. But I take it that what is implied is that before this 'elevated' *scène circulaire* and in front of the 'fence', there is to be understood some sort of a large auditorium at a lower level which Fouquet not only doesn't show, but which, with remarkable lack of ingenuity for a medieval artist, he does not even suggest. Such an auditorium, in fact, is something which the presence of his four figures in front of the fence actually tends to deny.

But this view of a sort of 'circular', raised stage banked up above the rest of the ground so that (although itself bearing some spectators at the back) it can be watched by more spectators again, disposed below in front—seems to see the medieval miniature too much through eyes accustomed to a twentieth-century picture-frame stage. Moreover, there is this consideration: we have already felt surprise at the physical task involved in digging a circular trench round a Place and banking the earth beside it. This new theory about the Fouquet involves a far greater task—the building up of a vast, flat platform of earth extensive enough to take the main action of the play *and* all the huge massed crowd of spectators we see behind *and* the considerable row of high scaffolds beyond. What an earthwork! Where did all this earth come from? Could it really have been dug and shifted merely to make a raised stage so that a further mass of spectators could have been disposed in front at a lower level? To what advantage could it be?

In their details, these authors perhaps follow Bapst who, in his *Essai sur l'histoire du théâtre*, 1893, p. 31, says of this picture— 'L'estrade, à peu près de la hauteur d'un homme, est établie sur des fascines; elle coupe diamétralement l'hémicycle formé par la ligne des loges.' That there is any 'platform' (*estrade*) which 'cuts diametrically the semicircle formed by the line of boxes' (or scaffolds) seems to me a suggestion incompatible with the facts in the miniature. But apart from this, the evidence in these arguments for a platform or *raised stage*, seems to receive most of its weight from the word *fascine*. Yet the one thing to be said on reference to the miniature is that what are shown in front are categorically *not* fascines—so far as I can understand the picture. If they were fascines it might be a different matter, because 'fascine' is a military term meaning (see *The Oxford English Dictionary*) 'A long cylindrical faggot of brushwood or the like, firmly bound together, used in filling up ditches, constructing batteries, etc.' (one was familiar with them in the *fascist* badge). But there is nothing in Fouquet's drawing to suggest long cylindrical bundles of sticks—nor, therefore, that he intended a raised earthwork, into the construction of which fascines entered. On the other hand he shows—surely quite clearly—a fence of stakes interwoven with strips, basket-fashion, and resembling a wattled hurdle. This is scarcely a reinforcement for an earthen embankment some 4 to 6 ft. high; but it is a perfectly acceptable method of enclosing a space, or a pen, or a 'croft'. Furthermore, the projection of unstripped, leafy twigs at the top of the stakes, over the wattling is—surely again—to obscure any vision over the fence, rather than to offer help to supporting any earth.

Thus I take the view that what is shown is part of a circular barrier-fence, designed to prevent outsiders getting into, or seeing, the show; and that the ground-levels inside and outside the fence are the same. This despite the fact that Fouquet has clearly shown the colour of the trampled earth inside the fence as grey, while outside is bright green grass.

On the basis of the above I believe, then, that the miniature shows a situation basically very like the situation in the *Castle* Plan; I believe it shows a circular Place with spectators in, and round, it and that Fouquet has elected faithfully to take a view of the action as from a spectator in the Place near the centre. This spectator sees the action happening in his immediate foreground (that is, in the 'midst' of the Place); beyond the action stretch the heads of other spectators similar to himself on the far side of the Place, and behind them again is part of a ring of scaffolds. I believe this was all Fouquet decided to show, and that he succeeded in showing it with very faithful effect and little distortion or overlapping of happenings. But he did *not* show the imaginary spectator

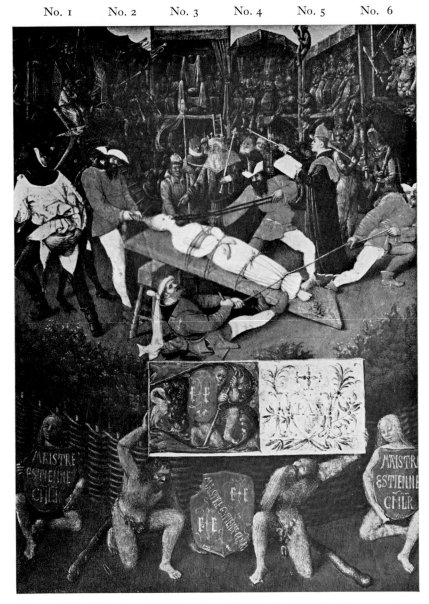

PLATE 2. The Miniature of the Martyrdom of St. Apollonia, by Jean Fouquet, about 1455. Showing half the interior of a Circular Theatre. *From* Le Livre d'heures d'Etienne Chevalier, *Musée Condé*, Chantilly

PLATE 3. Detail of the Fouquet miniature showing centre scaffolds Nos. 3 and 4; Decius' Seat and the Noble Spectators' Stand

from whose position he took the composition, nor did he show any of the nearer half of the audience or of the Place. What he did do—in order to finish off the foreground of his miniature and provide a suitable background for the lettering and the shields and their supporters at the bottom—was to cut his Place at that point and round off the front of his picture with a representation of part of the curved outer fence, that ultimately enclosed the whole theatre. This is the only distortion, or condensation, that he allowed himself and it seems to me a piece of characteristic conventionalism exactly in consonance with the kind of medieval pictorial composition that was also employed in the Terence miniature.

Perhaps the most remarkable divergence between Fouquet and *The Castle* is in the number and closeness of the scaffolds. In *The Castle* there are only five round the whole circle. But in Fouquet there is of course no hill to accommodate any audience. How near is this to the truth? Let us now consider these scaffolds in detail.

Scaffold No. 3

There are six scaffolds shown in the miniature and each will bear studying in turn. One of them is, however, outstanding in several ways and it offers us, so far as my experience goes, the best portrayal of a medieval theatre scaffold that history has left to us. With it therefore we will begin.

It is No. 3 in the row, counting from our left-hand side of the picture, and it faces us clearly, nearly in the centre, see Pl. 2, and for enlarged detail, Pl. 3, also Fig. 14.

Its floor is raised well above the heads of the audience. If this audience is standing, the floor must be some 8 ft. above the ground. This floor is supported on posts, or legs, and one is reminded momentarily of the tower on legs in the plan of *The Castle*. There are clearly indicated a pair of brackets (or braces), running in from these legs, either side, to help support the floor.

The front posts very clearly continue up past the floor and rise to support a roof over the scaffold; beyond this they rise again for 6 inches or so, in the manner of finials. Thus we have an upper story to the scaffold, itself apparently some 8 ft. in height. This upper part forms the stage. The overall width seems also to be about 8 ft.

We cannot tell whether the roof is flat or falls in a slope towards the back (the latter is perhaps more likely). But it seems to be formed of fabric of some kind supported on a frame, and it very clearly has a front extension falling like a short valance or pelmet, some 12 in. deep, across the top of the stage.

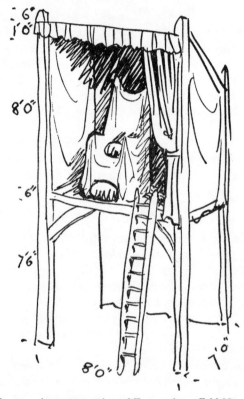

Fig. 14. A reconstruction of Fouquet's scaffold No. 3 showing estimated dimensions.

The colour, in the original miniature, of all the scaffolds appears to be the same—a kind of goldish-brown. One might have expected a display of brilliance here, but the whole of the background of the picture is treated in a sort of tinted monochrome, and may be intentionally subdued by the artist in order the better to show up the brightness of the costumes of the actors in the Place in front—and in these he has certainly achieved a brilliant effect.

The scaffold would presumably be built on a rectangular plan, and no doubt had at the back corners two posts similar to those at the front corners—though maybe not so high. There is every reason to suppose that the sides of this scaffold would be closed in with curtains on the upper story, as are the sides of other scaffolds in the picture; but this one is so placed that we cannot see the sides. It is worth noting that no appearance of daylight is shown between the heads of the audience below and the floor above them, therefore the back of the scaffold was presumably curtained-in down to the ground. Whether the curtains on the sides would be continued down to the ground also, so dividing the spectators, or whether they stopped at the floor of the scaffold, it is not possible to be sure—but one supposes the sides would not be curtained below. So much for general description.

Now we may go on to some of the particular details. Chief of these is the fairly pretentious draped seat or throne, with its back-cushion and foot-cushion. We can well appreciate now why one of the Latin names for such a scaffold was *sedes*, a seat. References to elevated 'seats', or 'chairs', in this particular sense are to be found in several English stage directions. When the occupant of such a seat was a robed king, then clearly the scaffold might stand as his palace—and the king, whose seat it was here, can be finely seen below, full in the centre of the Place.

But apart from this seat we have another piece of information of almost greater importance to our study—there is shown to us the means by which an actor descended into the Place from such a seat. And we find that it is no more than an ordinary, humble ladder! This ladder is, all the same, a vital element in medieval theatre technique, and in our understanding of any presentation in this technique.

So recognized a feature of technique was this ladder that on at least one occasion it was deliberately brought in by a playwright as part of one of his pieces of business in the performance. The instance is to be found in Sir David Lindsay's *Ane Satyre of the Thrie Estaits* (performed 1540) where three stage directions come close together, in the interlude in the middle of the play, which point to a remarkably similar system of staging. They are, first (after l. 1941), 'Heir sall the Carle clim up and sit in the Kings tchyre'; then (after l. 1949), 'Heir Diligence castis away the ledder'; and finally (after l. 1953), 'Heir sall the Carle loup aff the scaffald'.

So a feature was made, not only of climbing a ladder to ascend to a king's chair on the scaffold, but of the shift to which an actor was put if the ladder was 'cast away', namely, that there was nothing for it but to 'leap off the scaffold'!

Returning now to our consideration of the detail of scaffold No. 3 in the miniature, we have a further item of the most signal importance for our understanding of the scaffold technique— namely that the upper story of the scaffold could be concealed by drawing a curtain over it. Here we are shown an unmistakable draw-curtain, pulled aside and held back with a guard to the side upright of the scaffold. The curtain probably ran on a rod hidden behind the pelmet, and worked by pulling a line. That the function of such a curtain was in fact to cover the upper stage we have several proofs, for instance in 'The Trial before Pilate', one of the N-Town (*Ludus Coventriae*) cycle of plays, there is (see E.E.T.S. edition, p. 283) a stage direction—'Here þei take jhesus . . . to þe herowde. And þe herowdys scaffold xal unclose shewing herowde in astat . . .' (Here they take Jesus . . . to Herod. And Herod's scaffold shall unclose showing Herod in state . . .). Thus the scaffold had been closed by the curtain up to this point.

The method of working the curtain is indicated in the King's line from *The Pride of Life*, l. 303—

> Draw þe cord, Sire Streynth,
> Rest I wol now take . . .
> [*et tunc clauso tentorio dicet Regina*

—and so, on the closing of the scaffold-curtain the Queen takes up the dialogue.

Such an 'opening' and 'closing' of scaffolds is a piece of technique that we have not had indicated before in our study, and we shall put the discovery aside to be called upon later.

The last direct piece of evidence offered us by this scaffold in the miniature is the number of persons upon its floor, beside and behind the throne. But we cannot tell what they are. Are they players or spectators? It is greatly to be regretted that Fortune has not left to us a script of the play in which this scene took place; as it is (save that we suppose the king or emperor in question to be Decius) we are unable to say whether his palace needed to contain a group of courtiers for the action. We can see in the picture four seated figures and at least eight indications of standing figures, so that, with the king, this scaffold floor must have held thirteen persons at least.

Scaffold No. 1

I turn next to the scaffold on the left of the picture where God is enthroned with several angels about him, see Pl. 4. Without any doubt the most immediately striking feature here is the way of access up to the scaffold from the Place. Instead of a ladder we have a long inclined way with slats fixed across to prevent the feet slipping, recalling exactly the walk up to a raised fowl-house in a chicken run.

It had seemed, up to this, to be a problem how these actors negotiated their ascents and descents with any scrap of dignity . . . maybe the medieval mind saw no incongruity in the picture of a king swarming up a ladder like a fireman. But here we have some indication that they did not necessarily subject their angels also to such gymnastics. True the negotiation of so stiffly inclined a gangway is not particularly easy, but experience in going aboard ship indicates that it would be a little easier than by a ladder.

There is one further great advantage, of course, to a gangway of this sort, and that is that some kind of a processional passage could be made along it; a ladder is generally available only to one figure at a time, but up this sloping path it might have been just possible that a succession of figures could have proceeded—even two by two—without splitting up their procession (but one realizes in that case how strongly the gangway must have been stayed from under to prevent sagging).

We are unfortunately allowed very little sight of other details of this Heaven-scaffold since much of it is cut off from us, and we cannot tell how richly (if at all) it was decorated. We do see, however, something of God, and may note that he appears to be holding an orb in his left hand. He is seated on a throne.

The costume of two of the angels, with belted robes and cowl-necks, is very plain to see at the top of the ascent. We also notice how clearly their wings are shown, and that by their size the actors are probably children.

Again, the costume of the archangel on God's left hand is very clear, and we see him bare-headed, with (apparently) a wreath or fillet round his hair, a spear in his hand, large wings at his back and his body in full plate-armour. Potentially a splendid figure! This scaffold, again, seems to be fairly filled with figures—and some ten faces appear to be visible. Presumably all these must be actors; no audience would be up here.

The margin of the picture forbids our seeing what might have been the appearance of any roof over this scaffold. But some sort of curtaining to form a side wall is certainly indicated. No draw-curtain appears to be present at the front.

Scaffold No. 2

Scaffold No. 2 clearly holds the orchestra, see Pl. 4. There are three triple-curved trumpets, two straight horns, one set of bag-pipes and an organ.

(It is not uninteresting to note that Hardin Craig, in his *English Religious Drama* (1955, p. 252), states that the presence of a reference to an organ in a stage direction 'is an indication that the play was played in a church'. Here we learn that the indication is by no means a trustworthy one.)

The organ is being played by one figure and its bellows are being worked from behind by a second. At least one further figure is glimpsed in the background of the scaffold between the heads of the musicians.

The floor of this scaffold is level with those of Nos. 1 and 3, but its roof is a very different and curious thing. It appears to be a loose cloth hung over three or more rods projecting over the stage from the back wall of the scaffold. The construction is puzzling here. One wonders why no solid cross-member over the front is present, as it was in scaffold No. 3. The odd, undulating effect which results from the bellying of the fabric between the rods is suggestive of a very temporary structure.

Scaffolds Nos. 4 and 5

Scaffolds 4 and 5, see Pls. 3 and 5 respectively, can be taken together as having one puzzle in common. Since no way of access is shown to either, one is led to wonder whether the many figures sitting and standing here have any part in the play, or are simply spectators. If the latter, then we should learn that very similar

PLATE 4. Detail of the Fouquet miniature showing left-hand scaffolds Nos. 1 and 2;
Heaven and the Musicians

PLATE 5. Detail of the Fouquet miniature showing right-hand scaffolds Nos. 5 and 6 and the Gap; Citizen-spectators' Stand and Hell

scaffolds were provided for certain of the onlookers to those provided for the players.

Cohen writes quite confidently on this point—in his *Livre de conduite du régisseur et Compte des dépenses pour le Mystère de la Passion joué à Mons en 1501* (1925, p. xlviii), he speaks of the occupants of scaffold No. 4 as 'le groupe des nobles dames coiffées du hennin pointu dont le voile transparent retombe en mille plis et qui sont, non des actrices, mais des spectatrices', and refers in a footnote to chap. III, sec. iv of his *Mystères et Moralités du MS 617 de Chantilly*, 1920, which deals with 'Modes féminines et Chronologie'. Next, he says of scaffold No. 5: 'Plus loin sont des bourgeoises, reconnaissables à leur chaperon plat.' So he decides on the score of their head-dresses that those in the No. 4 scaffold are ladies of quality and those in No. 5 citizens' wives. If this is true, then we have interesting additional information that the spectators seated at the sides might be in at least two classes of seats. (In these, and in other French references, I owe much to my friend Monsieur René Thomas of Paris.)

Another argument that seems to me to point to the occupants of scaffolds 4 and 5 as being audience not actors is the presence of the flirting couples. It might, I know, be argued that if the script were to be discovered, and were to show that these scaffolds represented, say, the Palace of Pleasure then such business would be appropriate there, and thus the figures we see would be actors. But I am not sure in the first place that the physical embrace was much a part of acting technique in the Middle Ages. In the second place I would point out that if we have here an isolated instance of such business, then we have to account for the fact that it is being performed by actors at whom no one is looking at the moment.

Again it may be argued that this is the result of medieval pictorial condensation—that successive actions in the play are represented simultaneously. But I believe this picture is singularly free from such 'medieval condensation', and is a clear and straightforward representation of a specific moment.

Further, I would point out the climbing figures on these scaffolds. They surely must be spectators. Indeed, generally, the action of most of these figures, admirably expressed by the draughtsman, indicates watching (when it does not indicate incidental flirting). None of it seems to me to be representative of waiting actors.

Thus I am very much inclined to agree with Cohen that these two scaffolds hold audience not players. If this is true, then what we have here is, in terms of the *Castle* Plan, simply this—that if a performance were such that no ditch and hill had been built, still the range of spectators along the side between any two actors' scaffolds might yet be accommodated on an elevation simply by means of more, similarly-built, scaffolds and moreover these might be protected from the weather by roofs or awnings stretched over them, similar to the roofs or awnings over the actors' scaffolds. The whole spectacle, audience and actors, would thus be bound together in a unity of arrangement.

Since no access is shown to these spectators' scaffolds (if they are such) we are perhaps offered some confirmation for an idea that the scaffolds had an entrance of some sort at the back. One scarcely imagines the noble spectators, after the play was done, waiting for the arrival of a ladder to let them get down to the ground again. . . .

The roof of No. 4 appears—strangely enough—to be built in yet another sort of construction; or perhaps it is, in fact, constructed similarly to that over the musicians but has its fabric cover pulled somewhat farther forward so that a sort of valance hangs down over the front. The purpose of such a hanging strip over the opening may well have been to help to keep the sun out of the eyes of the people within. (Notice that the scaffold which is *not* provided with such a hanging valance—the scaffold No. 2— is on the shady side of the picture, while those *with* the valances, Nos. 3, 4 and 5 are all on the side opposite the light.) The line of supports beneath the fabric gives the impression of being arranged so as to give an arch-shape to the roof. The roof of No. 5 seems, on the other hand, to be built similarly to that of No. 3 and has a straight, hanging pelmet, appearing to show marks of some three folds down the front as if it had been packed away in store.

The Gap

Before we go on to consider the sixth and last scaffold, there is an intermediate matter. With all the other scaffolds, the side posts of adjacent scaffolds were butted close together. But, in this particular instance only, the nearer post of No. 5 is not butted close against the post of No. 6 (see Pl. 5). Is this because—as appears at first sight—No. 6 scaffold is set slightly back from the line of the others? The idea seems a little unlikely. There might be another reason; perhaps the post of No. 6 is in the same alignment as the others, but situated so that there is an empty gap between 5 and 6. Why should such a thing be? Obviously there might be the very good reason that here there is represented to us what we have earlier come to expect—namely, a passage through between the scaffolds from the outer world into the Place, by which spectators entered the theatre; if this is so then we are glad to have some corroboration apparently offered that such a thing was in fact arranged by the medieval theatre-makers.

Scaffold No. 6

Finally we look at the No. 6 scaffold itself—the Hell-scaffold directly facing Heaven, see Pl. 5. Our attention is drawn at once, of course, to the one piece of elaborate scenic decoration obvious in the picture—namely, the remarkably realistic Hell-mouth. It forms a kind of entrance to the lower story of this particular scaffold, and thus we may see how not every scaffold in this picture had spectators under it. Hell occupied its scaffold totally, both upper and lower stories.

There is another difference from all the rest. It is that the upper story is provided with a sort of loose drapery 'balustrade' skirting the bottom of the opening. Above this the devils on the floor look out, and they are hidden by it up to the hips.

At the top of the side of this last scaffold we have one final detail of construction—a cross-corner brace (similar to the brackets supporting the floors) between the post of the side and the timber that presumably framed-in the top of that side.

Scaffold No. 0

If we look to our left of the miniature we notice one of the biggest problems of the whole picture. For there are two men shown high up outside the first scaffold where God and the angels sit, see Pl. 4. If we numbered God's scaffold as No. 1, then we may number the position which these men occupy as scaffold No. 0. What can we make of this mysterious scaffold No. 0?

We see a man with folded arms leaning apparently on a handrail, in a negligent attitude and watching the scene below. The floor he is standing on is level with the floor of the other scaffolds. He has one leg crossed over the other. Behind his shoulder is just visible the head of the second man. The wedging of these two so close together in this tiny corner somehow suggests that they are part of a larger group of figures, which we should see if the edge of the picture did not cut them off. This is guesswork, but it does not seem likely that such a crowded scene as this would suddenly give way to an empty space exactly at the point where the margin of the picture comes.

Are these two men in fact on a scaffold similar to those we see in the rest of the row? Or are they standing on a quite different sort of construction? There is one detail which may (or may not) tend to suggest the latter; that is the rail across in front of the figure, on which he is leaning. No other scaffold in the picture has anything like this rail. What then might these men be, and what might they be standing on?

Cohen is, I believe, the only authority who has commented on this detail. In the Preface to his *Livre de conduite* he says (p. xlviii):

Une petite indication du miniaturiste, un bonhomme penché sur la balustrade, dans la loge voisine du Paradis, me semble attester que le théâtre a été ouvert par l'artiste, pour nous en montrer l'intérieur, mais qu'un autre hémicycle, composé probablement de galeries réservées aux spectateurs, peut-être d'*autres mansions* et, en dessous, d'un espace constituant parterre, achève l'amphithéâtre, lui conservant la forme romaine et traditionnelle du cirque, avec cependant une tendance à réserver plutôt l'une des deux moitiés aux acteurs et l'autre aux spectateurs, ce qui explique l'aspect de nos théâtres d'aujourd'hui.

(A small indication of the miniaturist's—a goodman leaning over the rail in the scaffold next to Paradise—seems to me to prove that the theatre has been opened by the artist in order to show us the interior; that another semicircle—composed probably of galleries reserved for spectators, perhaps of *further 'mansions'* [his italics], and, at the lower level, of a space constituting a sort of 'pit' or 'stalls'—would complete the amphitheatre, so preserving the traditional Roman form of circus, with however a tendency to reserve one of the two halves rather for the actors and the other for the spectators, in a way which is explained by the appearance of our theatres today.)

Again, in the 'Avant-propos' of the new edition of his *Histoire de la Mise en scène dans le Théâtre religieux français du Moyen-Age* (1926), he says:

La forme de l'amphithéâtre a été celle du théâtre au moyen-âge beaucoup plus souvent que nous le croyons généralement, induits en erreur par une généralisation hâtive du *hourdement* de Valenciennes. Pour moi, il n'est pas douteux que Fouquet dans sa miniature . . . n'ait eu en vue un cirque; je n'en veux pour preuve que le personnage, penché sur la balustrade, à la droite du paradis, et qui montre qu'un hémicycle de galeries réservées aux spectateurs doit compléter l'autre hémicycle, occupé surtout par les *mansions*. . . .'

(The amphitheatrical form was adopted by the theatre of the Middle Ages much more often than we generally believe, led astray as we are by a hasty generalization based on the 'platform' of Valenciennes. For me, there is no doubt that Fouquet in his miniature . . . had in mind a circus. I need no more proof of this than the individual leaning on the handrail to the right of Paradise, who shows that a semicircle of galleries reserved for spectators should complete the other semicircle occupied chiefly by the *mansions*. . . .)

He thus states his case with full conviction, but still I am inclined, on the whole, to feel there is as yet insufficient evidence to enable me to describe this scaffold No. o with any certainty.

There is perhaps one conclusion of Cohen's which seems a little unfounded; granted that the circular 'theatre' has been opened so as to allow us to look into one half of it, I do not see that we are justified in supposing that the half which has been removed must necessarily have been a 'semicircle of galleries *reserved for spectators*'. I think (at any rate speaking from our approach through *The Castle of Perseverance*) that it is more likely that Cohen's other view—expressed, though less confidently, in the first quotation—is the true one; that is, that the removed half was very like the half we see and contained not merely spectators but a further range of actors' scaffolds. He has, further, the strange inconsistency, noticeable also in other writers, of judging a medieval stage according to the standard of another period, for instance that of the present day or that of classical Greece (or Rome). How curiously writers can become obsessed by this inconsistency is specially exemplified here, because Cohen after saying (in his first passage) that Fouquet's theatre conserves the traditional *Roman* form then says it conserves that form in a way that reminds us of the appearance *of our theatres today*! How could such a thing be?

The Spectators Kneeling on the Ground

Despite the small space of this miniature, it is a remarkable fact that Fouquet has represented—in the crowd of spectators behind the central action, and occupying the ground before and beneath the scaffolds—no less than between ninety and a hundred persons! This quite apart from the number who must also be supposed there, but who are totally hidden by some part of the group of actors in front.

This achievement, especially considering the vigour and character which he has put into the individuals, is in itself no small one.

But we have especially to inquire how these people are disposed. One thing that is very certain is that all those along the front of the crowd are kneeling or sitting on the ground, and are quite near to the central action. Behind these the representations of the heads rise in a manner which Cohen describes as 'l'échelonnement des rangées de tête'. This effective phrase is difficult to translate; but from this 'massing upwards' of the heads Cohen deduces that the more distant crowd is 'debout sur les gradins', or standing on stepped stands. This may, perhaps, be so; but the general impression I receive is that the 'échelonnement' of the heads is no more than might be presented if the spectators were standing on the ground itself—with perhaps the qualification that the shortest had slipped to the front while the tallest had been content to stay behind. But on this point we cannot press the miniature too far. We must be satisfied with one certain piece of evidence; that (however the farther spectators are standing) the nearer spectators are indisputably on the ground, in the Place; and those at the very front are either sitting or kneeling on that ground.

This is entirely consistent with the picture we had begun to form of the disposition of the people in the Place in our reconstruction of the *Castle* Plan. We even look to see whether, from the foot of Decius's ladder before scaffold No. 3, there stretches any sign of the lane that we had deduced would be kept clear by the stytelers for such movements as Decius's descent. But, alas! the Emperor's figure and those of his attendants entirely block our view, and we remain unsatisfied.

But on the whole our study of Fouquet's intriguing miniature has been very rewarding. When we return to the development of our reconstruction of the *Castle* Place, we need to be able to add a visualization of the kind of basic anatomy of a scaffold that is, at least, not inconsistent with recorded contemporary procedure. Before, however, we enter into a more detailed anatomy of the scaffolds we must assemble all available evidence. Leaving Fouquet on one side for a moment, what evidence is there about scaffolds in *The Castle of Perseverance* itself? After reviewing this we will be in a better position to return and anatomize the constructions in Fouquet.

9

REFERENCES TO THE SCAFFOLDS IN THE DIALOGUE

*What the Characters tell us about the Scaffolds * On the Existence or Not of Scaffold Curtains*

WHEN we were studying the Place, we found that there were in the text of the play certain references, direct or implicit, which helped considerably to the development of our picture of it. We now ask if the text will help in a similar way to a fuller understanding of the scaffolds.

Upon examination we find a number of hints. They are generally slight, but their total contribution is not insignificant. They are as follows.

What the Characters tell us about the Scaffolds

Line 181. In his opening speech, World refers to his Treasurer, Sir Covetyse. World has, as we know from the Plan, a scaffold of his own on the West, and he is pretty certainly speaking from it in this speech. But Covetyse also has his own scaffold—that on the North-East. He has nothing to do in the play as yet, and though we presume he is on his own scaffold, he may still be hidden behind its curtain. What is sure, I think, is that he cannot be on World's scaffold. So, from this reference we learn that it is possible for a character on a scaffold to refer to another character without the second being on the same scaffold. He need not be present—or, at most, he may be across the Place on a scaffold on the opposite side. Already, then, the introductory lines are linking some at least of the separate scaffolds together.

Line 196. The Devil's opening line is 'Now I sit, Satan, in my sad sin'. His scaffold is on the North and we learn from his words that there is a seat upon it, but at l. 232 he says 'on bench will I bide'—thus we are to suppose the seat on the Hell-scaffold was not a throne but a bench. (Possibly a throne—with its back and arms—would not accommodate his devil's costume!) In the middle of his speech the Devil refers to his three servants, Pride, Wrath and Envy, much more particularly than World referred to Covetyse —indeed, Wrath is addressed as '*this* wretch'. Thus both the lines and the action of the play (as we shall see later) suggest that the three servants are present with the Devil on his scaffold at the beginning of the show, just as Decius's courtiers sat on his scaffold with him in the Fouquet miniature.

Next; in Flesh's opening speech from the South, he alludes twice to his scaffold as 'these towers' (ll. 235 and 239)—indeed in the second reference he says, 'With cloths of taffeta I decorate my towers' and this, of course, conjures up a somewhat more colourful picture than we have had so far. But it may, or may not, be simply verbal imagery. Though the scaffold is alluded to as 'towers' we have no certain evidence that it represented towers—all we are given is that it could be referred to as such. At l. 248 Flesh refers (as the Devil did) to three servants; this time, Gluttony, Lechery and Sloth, and in doing so he confirms what we inferred about the first three servants, for he distinctly speaks of Gluttony 'sitting seemly here by my side'. Thus the servitors sat beside their masters.

Later World (l. 458) cries 'Now I sit in my seemly salle' and in 'my true throne'. So he treats his scaffold as his 'hall' and it has a throne in it. At l. 483 he brings in a new name and speaks of 'my dees' (dais). At l. 471, however, he sets us a pretty problem; so far, according to the lines, he alone of all the three Evils, the World, the Flesh and the Devil, has made no allusion to three servitors beside him. Now, in a particular way, this is strange; for there is a remarkable sense of 'symmetry', if I may so name it, about the speeches and the characterization of this play. We find it throughout the script, woven indeed into an elaborate and intriguing pattern, and after coming to appreciate its presence we note the appearance of World unattended, while his corresponding Evils *were* attended, as a quite jarring fracture of this symmetry.

But at l. 471 we begin to see we were wrong, and that World also has his servitors, for he there addresses directly 'Lust-liking and Folly, comely knights of renown', and they are undoubtedly up beside him on his scaffold (though silent till now), for at l. 492 they leave him at his bidding and descend. But, it will be objected, here are only *two* servants (and this with all due deference to Furnivall's editing the names as if they were three persons—Lust, Liking and Folly). What now are we to do? We have made Lust-liking only one character, but thereby we seem to break our desired symmetry again just as soon as we thought to have found it. There is, however, the curious sequence to be noted in the list of characters included with the script. In this, as we saw on p. 7, we have 'World *and with him* Lust-liking, Folly *and Garcio*'. At l. 2895, World unmistakably addresses Garcio directly, as being beside him on the scaffold.

What follows from all the above is that at the opening of the play the three main scaffolds of the Evils at West, North and South, all bore (*a*) a seat, (*b*) their chief occupant and (*c*) sitting behind him *three* servitors—though in one case one particular one of these servitors appears to remain seated and inactive for nearly three thousand lines of the play! All these tiny items help to build up a useful conception of the effect of the scaffolds in use.

At l. 579 it is suggested that a character could in some way 'retire' into his scaffold—or at least withdraw his presence from the action—to the extent that another character in the Place, coming and wishing to speak to him, must cry 'How, Lord! *Look out!* For we have brought a servant . . .', etc. Whether a front curtain was in use here, or simply an action on the part of the player, we do not know. But he has to be summoned to listen.

At l. 650 we have the problem of the attiring of Mankind in the World's scaffold. He comes 'naked'; he is ordered to be clothed 'with rich array'; and after a space he is announced again—redressed—by Lust-liking with the words 'Here is Mankind full fair in fold'. Where was he dressed? There are two possibilities; either a front curtain is closed to hide the whole scaffold, or Mankind goes out at the back into some sort of concealment. (Dressing in sight on the stage *might* be possible but the lines, we shall find, somewhat point against it.) During the whole of the dressing, fifty-one lines of 'filling-in' speech are spoken by a fresh character, Backbiter, from the Place. In sizing up Mankind's new appearance after his return, World says 'You have brought Mankind to my hall, certes, in a noble array'—thus at the same time giving us an example of the word 'hall' used directly to describe a scaffold, and also indicating pretty certainly that Mankind did not dress in sight on the scaffold.

At l. 788 Backbiter refers to Covetyse as *sitting* and awaiting 'us on his *stage*', thus giving the scaffold with its raised floor exactly the name we would use for it today. It is not likely to be a different sort of scaffold from the other scaffolds since it too is called 'thine hall' (l. 820), and thus presumably they were all just as much 'stages'. A seat on this scaffold is again referred to in l. 836. In l. 886 this scaffold is called by a fresh name—a 'bower' (as it is again in l. 1087) and it is also a 'throne' in l. 1239.

At l. 1350 Mankind, on Covetyse's scaffold, refers to Sloth as sitting *herein*—just conceivably this might imply a concealed place at the back.

At l. 1555 the central scaffold in the Place itself is called 'yon Castle', and at ll. 1697–1700 Mankind is invited by Mercy from the Castle to 'come *in* here' (not 'come *up*'), and to 'stand *herein*'— thus he enters the lower story.

At l. 1749 the Devil is apostrophized with 'Hail, sat in thy *cell*' which may be a new name or simply a variant of *salle* (the spelling in the text is 'selle').

Returning to the central Castle, we learn with interest that one could leave its lower part and ascend, for at l. 1804 Mankind is reported as 'gone up high into yon castle', and at l. 1996 he speaks —thus presumably he could appear above the battlements. At l. 2043 the Castle is spoken of as 'of stone' (presumably painted so). At ll. 2056 and 2575 it is called 'this hall' just as the scaffolds round the sides are, and at l. 2468 as (oddly enough) a 'dais'—again like a scaffold.

When, at l. 2704, Covetyse offers to lead Mankind away to his scaffold he speaks of it as his 'castle cage', and again as his 'bower (2705).

At l. 3078 the Devil's scaffold is alluded to (with a phrase we have noticed before) as '*high* hell'.

Finally at l. 3218 God's scaffold is pointed out as 'yon high place'.

As I promised, the above are not all sensational items. Taken together they add, however, certain touches to this growing picture.

On the Existence or Not of Scaffold-Curtains in 'The Castle'

This finishes the review of the text references relating to the scaffolds. But out of the last reference there rises a very curious consideration which it is worth stating in some detail.

This last reference was to God's scaffold—an appeal to 'yon high place'. Now though all the other four scaffolds have been brought into the action early in the performance, this one alone has had no allusion of any sort made to it till now. What sort of appearance has it had all this time? Was it empty? Were there motionless figures upon it from the beginning waiting for this moment? When was God's person first apparent to the audience?

We must make clear what we mean by 'all this time'. To do this we have to answer another question—how long is this play, and how long did it take to perform?

Its length on paper is some 3,700 lines. How long this would take to act is a very uncertain quantity. How fast did the players speak? How much time was occupied by business—by processions, by the battle for the Castle, by crossings of the Place, and so forth? These are all matters which to be properly settled would need an actual performance of the play. But we can get some way to what we want; we can time the reading of a hundred lines. This in practice, at a slow, quiet, but continuous rate of speech, ignoring space for business, gives us the time of about six minutes for 100 lines—or an hour for 1,000 lines; three hours for 3,000 lines; and something over 3½ hours for the whole play.

The appeal to God's scaffold is made at l. 3118, that is to say (again making no allowances for time given to business) something over three hours after the performance had begun.

What we now have to ask is whether:

1. God sat motionless in his scaffold all this time?

2. Or whether his scaffold was empty until just before the cue, and then God walked from some place of concealment and took his seat on the throne in time to be ready for the Four Daughters?

3. Or whether his scaffold was closed by a curtain until the moment of the appeal? In this case God would take his throne in concealment at his leisure, and be ready for a dignified (and very dramatic) discovery on the drawing of the curtain.

(And how dramatic it must have been for a spectator to watch these three hours of wrangling for the soul of Man, with four open scaffolds belching forth the vaunts and ill wishes of the Evils throughout and yet, in the East, one silent and apparently unmoved scaffold, that all this time seemed to take no part in the Destiny, but by its silent existence held attention and raised expectation!)

So far as I can find, we have no evidence to help us to decide between these alternatives. We might reject the second one because, according to modern ideas of production, it seems clumsy and un-dramatic. But we cannot call this a conclusive argument.

We can say that the third alternative is the only one that seems at all acceptable, and thus that the use of a curtain to the scaffolds is thereby proved by inference—but we have no other evidence for it which is unimpeachable in the whole of this play.

With all this we have to remember one strange fact in favour of the apparently 'impossible' first alternative—that is, for God's sitting there throughout the three hours. That fact is that it is categorically stated in the legend on the Plan that the Soul of Mankind should 'lie under the bed [beneath the Castle] till he shall rise and play'! The Soul rises at l. 3009, so that it is incontestable that he (poor player!) is, according to the instruction, condemned to spend exactly three hours lying under a bed. What this in-volved we cannot guess. Maybe he had some more comfortable place of concealment, and crept to the bed inconspicuously at the last moment. Maybe he had nothing of the sort and was forced to stay in that cramped situation all that time. But we do, at least, feel that the latter would be unlikely.

But there it is! We appear to have evidence which says that players waited for three hours and more to take part in an action, and waited moreover in a specific place to which there seems to have been no access (on the evidence we have) save before the performance began.

The same kind of argument holds good about the appearance of Covetyse on his scaffold—though that is only at the comparatively early moment of l. 830 of the play; and of the appearance of the Seven Virtues in the Castle-tower at l. 1605.

One is very much inclined to the belief that some method of con-cealment, either of the place where a character appeared or of the access to it so that he could creep in unseen, must have been pos-sible in this play. But it seems impossible to offer a certain decision one way or the other on the internal evidence. On the whole the conclusion seems to be that there undoubtedly is a need in *The Castle* for scaffold curtains, and we do know that in other plays there was also this need, and that in these plays scaffold curtains were used (see p. 98 above). We dare say no more at present.

10

THE PROVISIONAL ANATOMY OF A SCAFFOLD

*The Frames and their Braces * The Roofs * The Problem of the Siting of the Scaffolds*

AFTER this study of the Fouquet miniature and the other material, is it now possible by putting together the evidence we have gathered to get a little farther into the nature of a scaffold by the means of limited conjecture? On the whole, pure conjecture is of little use in a reconstruction unless it is so supported that it begins to rise above conjecture; but the following may be taken or rejected by the reader according as it seems to him to be safe conjecture or unsafe conjecture, and in the end it will lead us to a problem in the progress of our reconstruction that will have to be settled for better or for worse anyway before we can complete that reconstruction. Let us then attempt an anatomy of the scaffold, in the clear understanding that we may be venturing into the realms of the untenable.

We can begin on firm ground by pointing out one very interesting feature of Fouquet's scaffolds that we have only hinted at till now; it is that in no case do any two adjacent scaffolds appear to share a common, intervening upright post, but every scaffold has its own posts either side, and these butt close against the uprights of the neighbour scaffolds (save where the Gap comes). What is interesting about this feature is that it suggests the scaffolds are each self-contained in construction, and could thus be connected in any number with others. Were they all made, then, as stock elements so that they could be got out of store, pieced together and grouped as any occasion required?

With this unit-construction in mind let us consider the details of a single scaffold. At first they are simple—four posts; a floor some half-way up; the roof, sides and back of the upper story curtained; probably the back only of the lower story curtained. A pelmet may hang across the top. Brackets help to support the floor. Sometimes (as in the Hell-scaffold) we have signs of a cross-corner brace, at the top, in the framework of the side (see above, Fig. 14).

The Frames and their Braces

So far so good. Let us now go on to consider these *brackets* and these *braces*, as I have called them. And to begin, let us take the 'bracket' under the front of the floor, and understand its purpose. What did the floor have to support? And what was its span? We have already seen that on the floor of Decius's scaffold (No. 3) there had to be supported the weight of at least thirteen people. And the clear span bridged we can estimate by inspection as some 7 ft. or so. But this is by no means the limit; the details of the miniature are not precisely clear in this matter, but it would appear that the two audience-scaffolds (Nos. 4 and 5) actually hold sixteen or seventeen (or more) persons each—to say nothing of the weight of such chairs or benches as they may be sitting on.

Clearly this is a considerable weight for such a span in this form of temporary timber construction. One well understands therefore the value of these brackets which distribute the floor-weight in some proportion into diagonal thrust against the legs, reducing the unsupported span of the centre floor to some 4 ft.

We notice the brackets shown regularly under every floor, at each front corner—possibly the backs were similarly reinforced.

But now comes an interesting point. We have already seen that in the Hell-scaffold an apparently similar cross-piece is visible at the top of the side of the scaffold, *where there is no weight to support* except that of the light fabric roof. What is this for?

I have, in speaking of this member, carefully avoided calling it a bracket like those under the floors, and have spoken of it as a *brace*. This is the name I should use of a similar piece of timber in the construction of an ordinary stage 'flat' in a set of scenery in the theatre today. For there I should see a diagonal piece at the top corner, joining the vertical stile and the top cross-rail, identically as we see it in the side of the Hell-scaffold. (See further my article on the construction of a modern flat in *The Oxford Companion to the Theatre*, 2nd edition, under the entry 'Flat'.)

But this cross-corner brace in a modern flat is not intended as a weight-bearing unit, it is intended as a means of keeping the framework of the flat square at the corners, and so strengthening it against any cross-pressure that would else tend to push the flat out of square into a diamond-shape.

I cannot help concluding that this brace in the Hell-scaffold was for the same purpose—to keep the side frame true; not to bracket the top rail against the dead weight of some vertical load.

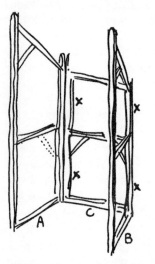

I may, or may not, be right in this (and Fouquet may have represented the scaffold correctly or incorrectly), but if such a piece were there, and were there for the bracing purpose that I have outlined, then we should be permitted to make a certain deduction; namely, that the side-frames of these scaffolds were all complete, independent frames, assembled beforehand, and carted, and joined with their neighbouring frames on the job.

Indeed, having pictured so much, the natural sequel is to suppose that two side-frames might be joined with a back-frame in a trio—either with hinges, or by lashings, or by some other means—after the fashion of a screen. The 'screen' unit would be of the

FIG. 15. Suggested scaffold 'screen' unit.

nature shown in Fig. 15—the two side-frames, A and B, have a sloping upper rail designed to accommodate the fall of the roof backwards. Each is shown here with its corner-brace at the top-front to keep it square. Whether there was a similar brace to the middle rail we do not know, but there might well have been. Again, we do not know whether there would be a bottom rail, as I have shown it, but, unless the vertical posts were to be sunk in the ground, such a rail along the base would be a great help to stability. These side-frames might, as I have said, be joined (at the points marked X perhaps) with the back-frame, C, if indeed the 'screen' technique were used. If it were not, the sides might be erected by digging a hole to take their bases, the joining members across between them being then built in on the spot. As soon as the front (and possibly back) floor-bearer is ready to go in position between the side-frames, the supporting brackets would be housed (perhaps in mortices) into posts and bearers.

Beyond this point we dare not go, for we should proceed without even such shreds of evidence as we have wrung out of the miniature so far. But I believe there is nothing inconsistent with the evidence in this construction as far as I have gone.

Before leaving the matter fully I would offer this consideration. Stage carpentry has been a long-traditioned and conservative craft; what we have just supposed is that these *scaffolds* (which, let us note, were sometimes called *houses*) were constructed by fitting pre-fabricated frames together on the job. Is there any other evidence that such a procedure was typical of the stage-carpenter's technique in these centuries?

There is such evidence. And it was because it was at the back of my mind that I had some confidence in venturing the theory I have outlined above. In my *Changeable Scenery* (1952), p. 29, I drew attention to the method of making the 'houses' for shows at the English court in the late sixteenth century, as evidenced by the Accounts of the Office of Revels. I remarked on p. 28 of that book that these shows were examples of 'the last phases of the medieval system of setting by means of "houses"'. Then, on the following page: 'we read of timber "frames for the houses" being made and transported to the place of performance, being joined together [when they arrived on the site] with "long vices" and covered with canvas for the painters.'

It seems to me that if this technique of setting shows was a last relic of the medieval 'houses' system (and I think it indisputable), then any apparent similarity in details of construction between *houses* and *scaffolds* may be a very real similarity, and the result of identical tradition. I think we may well be justified in seeing the ancestor of a 'house' at Elizabeth's court in the 'scaffold' of the medieval performance in the round.

The Roofs

Let me now leave the detail of the side-frames and floors, and turn to consider how the roof is affected by what I have said of scaffold-anatomy.

If I redraw the elemental 'screen' of a scaffold so as to look at it slightly from below (Fig. 16*a*), I show it in a similar aspect to that in which Fouquet showed the musicians' scaffold—No. 2. Let me now follow out the roof construction which I tentatively mentioned in describing this scaffold—that is, project three or so rods over the stage from the back wall of the scaffold.

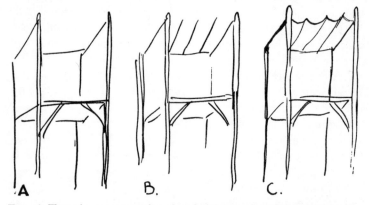

FIG. 16. Tentative reconstruction of roof of Fouquet's scaffold No. 2. (*a*) The bare scaffold, (*b*) the roof-rods added, (*c*) the rods covered with loose fabric.

The result is shown in Fig. 16*b*, which helps to show something else—namely, that if I projected such 'rods' it would be natural (given one reservation which we will consider in a moment) to project them so that they would *be parallel with the sloping top rail of the sides*, and thus accommodate the roof-fall which was the purpose of this slope in the rails. If, now, we throw a cloth over the lot to keep off the weather, it will clearly fall to a shape exactly like that shown in Fouquet's miniature—a sort of dragon's-wing effect—see Fig. 16*c*. And here we may (or may not) have the solution of his roof.

Again, take the other odd roof—that of scaffold No. 4. Could its curious, dome-like impression (or perambulator-hood impression!) be achieved in any way consistent with the above construction?

If instead of Fig. 16 we get our dome-like effect as in Fig. 17 with *curved* rods, clearly we should easily soon arrive at something which is not far from our model.

But we have not done with the roofs yet. I mentioned one reservation about the projected rods; what I had in mind was that the scheme was only workable provided the rods could be supported in their projected position—which as Fig. 16 suggests is a precarious one.

They *could* be so supported under one condition—that they were 'cantilevered' from the back; that is to say, if their ends projected some way beyond the back-frame and were there anchored down to something firm.

Fig. 18 attempts some impression of this. But something rather curious now follows. It is impossible (it seems) to work these rods as Fouquet shows them without projecting them *backwards* some distance and anchoring their ends down: this suggests a crossbar connecting their ends, which is itself anchored down. But immediately we think in such terms we are within sight of a covered back-way to the scaffold! Give it a floor by continuing

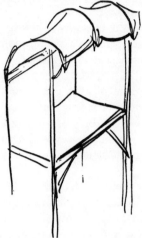

FIG. 17. Tentative reconstruction of roof of Fouquet's scaffold No. 4, employing curved rods.

FIG. 18. Further tentative reconstruction of roof of scaffold No. 2, indicating projection backwards of rods for support, and the suggestion so offered of a continuous, covered back-way behind the scaffolds.

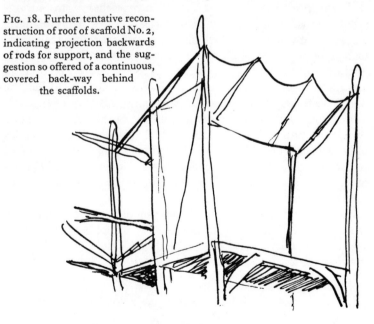

the scaffold floor back for a foot or two behind the back curtain—with a handrail to guard it—and you have our concealed place within the scaffold, to be approached from the stage through a gap in the curtains. Fit several of these scaffolds together in this way, and you have a continuous, outer, raised passage-way and a means of access to any stage. . . .

Again we have bounded beyond all our evidence and are in the realm of pure conjecture. It is pointless to continue. We may be right or wrong but there is nothing to prove, or even hint, which it might be.

Suffice to say a system of outer passages serving the scaffolds seems structurally quite possible.

Before I let the reader go away with the impression that I am making this picture too elaborate to believe in, and am beginning to imagine things which no medieval theatre could ever claim, I would recommend him to glance at p. 20 and onwards in Bapst's *Essai sur l'histoire du théâtre.* There Bapst quotes a performance at Metz in 1437 where, he says, the audience were accommodated in nine rows 'above and behind which were "great and long seats for lords and priests" '. Again at Vienna in 1510 there were 'magnificent scaffolds which were in two stories, besides the lower level for the general public, and which had ninety-six rooms (*chambres*) each equipped with a lock and key, and let at four crowns each'. Again at Autun in 1516 there were '240 rooms entirely separate so that the occupants of one could not go into the next. . . .' Here the *loges* (? scaffolds) were furnished with guard-rails ' "to keep people from falling; with a bar across for children;" they were reached by an outside stair.' Again in 1490, near Plessis-lez-Tours, Charles VIII (who caught cold easily) had a special box or room or scaffold at a show, wherein strips of paper were stuck along the cracks between the boards of the walls, and the whole hung with tapestry to keep out draughts. . . .

So it is not unreasonable to suppose some degree of complexity in a medieval 'theatre' building—and the scaffolds might signify much more than a few bare, raised platforms for indifferent, strolling rogues. . . .

The Problem of the Siting of the Scaffolds

Now we must take up a more immediate and teasing problem. Given that we were right about the anatomy of a scaffold, how was such a scaffold accommodated with regard to the Hill?

This is a new problem. Fouquet had no hill to complicate things; but before we can go on with our reconstruction of *The Castle* we have to settle this problem one way or another—even if only by guesswork. Otherwise we must abandon the reconstruction. Just what is the complication?

Let us suppose a performance of *The Castle* being prepared with the Ditch-and-Hill kind of circle, not the 'barred' or fenced kind shown in Fouquet. We then have to imagine a beginning to the work which would look exactly like what was shown in Fig. 9, p. 55. Now how are we going to set up our five scaffolds in regard to this? Are they to be on the open ground outside the Ditch? Or inside on the flat Place itself? Or between the two positions—that is to say, on the top of the Hill?

The first position, outside the Ditch, is what appears to be shown in the plan of *The Castle*; but we have seen it is quite impossible, for the Hill would hide the scaffolds, and the Ditch would isolate them. The Plan, then, only tells us at what point of the compass each was, and it must be ignored as evidence for the actual spot on which each was built.

The second position, inside the Hill and on the edge of the Place itself, is unsatisfactory since the back of the scaffolds would be presented to many of the audience on the Hill, and their bulk would intervene between spectators and action.

It seems we are inevitably reduced to the third alternative—which perhaps seemed at first the most unlikely—that the scaffolds were *on* the Hill. Or perhaps it would be better to say they were incorporated in the ring of the Hill.

If the Hill was 6 or 7 ft. high, did the scaffolds straddle it, with their back legs in the ditch and their front legs in the Place? This seems unworkmanlike. Could it have been that the back edge of the floor of the scaffold rested on the top of the hill and only the front legs reached down to the ground so that the scaffolds 'sat' as it were on the hill? Here we have no evidence so far to help us.

This point brings up another; if such a scaffold were so arranged on the Hill, what could those spectators see who were sitting on that part of the Hill directly beside the scaffold? Its curtained sides would mask any action upon it from them. Perhaps this was accepted. What suggests that it was accepted is that in Fouquet's picture it is clear that spectators standing directly under the floor of a scaffold could not have seen any action that went on on that floor. They may have heard the voices, but to see the speakers they had to wait till the action brought an occasion for them to descend and walk in the Place itself. Maybe spectators directly beside a scaffold were similarly unsighted.

We must gather our wits and go carefully here. And it seems better to take a new chapter for our construction.

11

RECONSTRUCTING THE THEATRE

Considerations on a Diagrammatic Section ∗ The Siting of the Scaffolds (resumed) ∗ The Rampart, and the Hill Used for Action ∗ Some final Points emerging from the Sections ∗ Scaffolds, Hill and Place assembled ∗ The Theatre in the Round

IN the present chapter I propose to sum up the evidence and fit it together into a reconstruction of the theatre which shall be as full as our knowledge can make it.

A certain disadvantage appears when one comes to write a report of the course of work which has led up to a reconstruction, as I am to do in this chapter. The disadvantage is that although one is tracing again one's exploratory steps for the benefit of a reader, one has now the unfair advantage over him of a perfectly clear picture of where it is all going to end up! He has not.

I hope to make the creation of such a picture one of the *results* of this chapter. But in case my reader feels something of this disadvantage, I have drawn that picture in detail and published it as Fig. 21. If he care to glance at it now, in anticipation, he will have as clear a view before him as I have of the ending to which the succession of steps to be described will lead.

I leave the matter to the reader's choice and set out to describe the steps of the study by asking: what is the best way to attempt a reconstruction on paper of so complicated a three-dimensional thing as a circular theatre, with a thousand freely moving spectators?

Perhaps the following considerations will open up the way.

Considerations on a Diagrammatic Section

It is extremely difficult to study three-dimensional things in one's head. There are three fields in which they can be studied— in actual fact (which is easiest and best); by visual examination with flat diagrams on paper (which has to be handled with care and as much experience as one can bring to it); and in the abstract—that is to say in one's head (which is wellnigh impossible).

In the realm of ideas, the difficulty of the fields of study is reversed. Practice often confuses us here or drives the ideas into the background. Paper-work is equally a help and a difficulty in both realms. While work in one's head gives ideas their widest scope.

The study of the theatre has been too often restricted to the examination of ideas in the head. To picture them on paper, or to analyse pictorial evidence about them, is a valuable corrective that too frequently is overlooked—and even sometimes pronounced bad scholarship. Practice, of course, is the ideal test. But to study the theatre in practice is a vast undertaking involving business organization and I know not what. Failing it, the study of diagrams and sketches can be, as I have shown in *Proscenium and Sight-lines*, a valuable substitute for, or even anticipation of, practice. It is not ideal, but it is an immense improvement on working in one's head.

One only needs to point out how one regrets that a vast study of the nature of Chambers's *The Mediaeval Stage* was put together almost wholly in words, and contains only two diagrams. No wonder that it is, in the event, confusing. Words alone (in theatre) do not explain what you mean. My own book here, even with its pictures, is already half a failure. An actual presentation of the play is the only real medium for study; but it is fleeting and cannot be looked up nor referred to—indeed can only be remembered fragmentarily or emotionally. Thus an analysis of a diagrammatic sort has got to be made.

I turn then for my next step in our study of the scaffolds and how they were sited to the drawing-board.

I propose to draw first a longitudinal section through a Place, and through the hill and ditch, and then try to set the scaffolds in their probable positions.

We begin by drawing a line to represent the level of the Place, and we add the sections of the Hill at either end (see Fig. 19). As to dimensions, those of St. Just are the most fully authenticated (because they still exist); moreover they offer us certain special features of the puzzle that it would be good to examine. So we will make the proportion such that the Place is 126 ft. across, and the

Hills 7 ft. high, 15 ft. thick at the base, and furnished on their inner face with seven steps, each 1 ft. high and 1 ft. 2 in. wide. Along the crest of each hill, let us suppose a flat walk 7 ft. wide. Outside all is the ditch. Now we have a disposition of parts according to the evidence of St. Just (see above, p. 65).

Let us then add to these beginnings as much as we can of the features of the *Castle* presentation, so far as our evidence of them goes, proceeding as if we were to put on a performance of *The Castle* in the Round of St. Just.

Let us at the same time construct a second diagram like the first but—since the dimensions of St. Just seemed to be extreme —to a different proportion; say such that the Place measures only 50 ft. across. Then we have represented possibly two extremes of size in these medieval theatres.

To these diagrams we add the scaffolds, the central castle-tower and the audience.

The results are in Figs. 19 and 20; and these two drawings and what they suggest to us we have now to consider at length.

The Siting of the Scaffolds (resumed)

One of the most difficult details in any reconstruction of this performance is the relation of the scaffolds to the people sitting on the Hill.

Several things complicate this. I may list them as follows:

1. The side walls of the scaffolds—as we have seen.
2. The question whether the stage floor of a scaffold ever projected in front of the front curtain, or whether it was always as is shown in Fouquet.
3. The question (at St. Just anyway) of the 'rampart'.
4. The problem of access to the 'stage-door' of a scaffold.
5. The possibility that the Hill was used for part of the action.

Our two sections through imagined theatres put most of these problems in a special light. Let us approach them by asking first how convincing our theory now appears that the scaffolds were situated on the Hill.

The Hill is shown slightly more developed in Fig. 19 than any we have shown so far, because it has added to it the steps for seating and the flat rampart along the top. The result is a pretty massive earthwork—possibly greater than can be supposed to have come out of the size of ditch that I have shown; but in this I have been influenced by the knowledge that the steps at St. Just were of stone and thus were (possibly) in addition to the quantity of earth that the ditch yielded. Whether dressed stone from a particular quarry

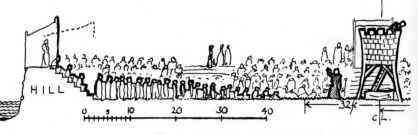

FIG. 19. Diagrammatic section through the centre of a showing 126-ft. diameter Place; set for a

was used we do not, at present, know, but we suppose the earth from the ditch—even on Cornish land—would not have yielded sufficient suitable stone of itself alone for the purpose. But, however that may be, it is definitely stated in Borlase that there were so many steps of such a size, with the rampart so wide at the top; such a Hill must then have had the bulk shown in my diagram.

FIG. 20. Diagrammatic section to the same scale through a small theatre with a 50-ft. diameter Place.

Upon this Hill now we set our first scaffold. At once it will appear how logically it takes its place *on* the Hill, as we had envisaged. Another matter vividly emerges; such an arrangement conveniently does away, not only with legs, but with all need for ladders to the scaffolds, for the steps of the Hill (though themselves not easy to walk up because of their size) are there to serve as access, either as they are, or with the addition of an intermediate six-inch step on each one to ease the climb.

In the diagram of the smaller theatre, Fig. 20, I have treated the Hill slightly—but only slightly—differently. I have supposed the whole to be less elaborate than the Round at St. Just, and have not here considered the Hill as provided with steps of stone.

circular theatre of the dimensions of the Round at St. Just,
performance of *The Castle* (see p. 125).

In fact I began by intending to make it altogether simpler—merely a pile of earth. When, however, the diagram developed and the spectators and scaffolds were added, it became clear that some at least of the elaboration would have to be included here too, after all. For instance, the inner face of the Hill would have to be stepped, even if the steps were only roughly cut in the earth, if we wished to accommodate seated spectators there at all. It then followed that we had to make the inner face of the Hill of a certain slope; it could not clearly be too steep or the spectators could get no seat-room or knee-room, whereas the outer face, towards the ditch, could be sheer—and the sheerer the better.

To support this inner slope, some thickish mass of earth would be needed between the sloping side and the sheer side—or the slope would not be stable. And in fact we find we have to imagine a body of earth which is, in section, remarkably like the mass of the hill in the other diagram of the larger and more elaborate theatre. Which is to say that some sort of 'rampart' on the top of the hill is apparently inevitable.

Whether, with this more roughly made hill, access to the scaffolds on its top could be by the rough steppings cut in the earth is less certain. Therefore, before one of the scaffolds in Fig. 20 I have shown a Fouquet ladder.

With the far-side scaffold—the one nearly hidden by the central tower—I have allowed two or three spectators to slip in front, to suggest the movement possible to the audience when no ascent or descent was being prepared for by the stytelers.

With such a form of Hill now, the siting of the scaffolds on the top becomes more likely still, and we will accept it provisionally.

We are beset at once, however, with a query. Should we put the back posts of a scaffold at the edge of the Hill—that is on the very brink of the drop into the ditch—or a little way in? And should we put the front posts at the inner edge of the rampart, that is on the top step or—again—leave a small space before we set them up?

If we set back the rear posts from the ditch, we might afford a narrow walk-round behind the scaffolds.

If we set back the front posts from the steps, we might leave a little space before the scaffold in the nature of a fore-stage.

I found myself a little tempted by this fore-stage. It would allow of much better vision by spectators, sitting close beside the scaffold, of a player upon it—who, otherwise, would be masked from them. It would also mean that the scaffolds as a whole approached the type-form which I have called elsewhere the Booth Stage (see my book *The Open Stage*, 1953, p. 15 *et alia*; also C. Walter Hodges, *The Globe Restored*, 1953, p. 40 *et alia*), which has an open acting-platform in front and a closed booth behind. One would like, perhaps, to see this fundamental, long-persisting stage type— so common in strolling-player pictures—echoed again in these scaffolds of the medieval rounds; but the fact must be accepted that Fouquet, at least, gives no sight whatever of any kind of advancing fore-stage. We therefore set the front posts forward at the top of the steps (but cf. Figs. 22 and 23).

The back posts are not so certainly decided, but the observation may be made that if a narrow section at the back of the scaffold were curtained off as a concealed place, then every available inch of space would be required, with nothing left for a walk-way. On the other hand, since outside access to such a concealed space could then only be from the rampart itself through a gap in the curtained side—then such a walk-way round the ring would be, in effect, provided although it involved passing *through* each scaffold as one went round, instead of behind it. But in practice, and supposing the concealed place existed, there would be merely a technical difference involved.

This is the basis, then, on which the scaffolds were settled in working out these diagrams.

The Rampart, and the Hill Used for Action

Two matters here will stand enlarging upon before we go on; they are the rampart and what I have alluded to, perhaps cryptically, as the possibility that the Hill was used for action in the play.

Borlase mentions, as we have seen (above, p. 65), that 'on the top of all' the steps, 'the Rampart is about seven feet wide'. What does he in fact mean to convey by this? It seems inevitable that he has in mind a flat top running along the circular hill, all the way round. In our reconstructions before this we had never felt the slightest need to incorporate such a thing. Why was it there?

Apart from its existence as the natural top of a big mass of earth, it seems at first sight meaningless as a part of the auditorium. It seems meaningless for a very good reason; and that is that although a *narrow* ledge along the summit of the hill might prove useful for one row of spectators standing and looking down beyond the heads of the others into the Place, yet for such a purpose this rampart seems quite unduly wide. In this elevated position even a second row of spectators would be badly unsighted, with regard to their view of the Place, by the first row. Several close-packed ranks, such as a rampart 7 ft. wide would allow, would clearly be very ill-adapted indeed in respect of seeing. Why then was the rampart so wide? Presumably there was a good reason for it, or the immense effort of massing all the earth that goes into a causeway 7 ft. wide and 7 ft. high would never have been expended on it.

The very name that Borlase gives suggests a reason. He calls it a 'rampart'; a rampart is a place for pacing, for circulation, as well as a vantage-place.

Is this a passage-way for circulation around the auditorium, much in the nature of the box-corridors in an opera-house today?

Is it not, perhaps, also a passage-way of connexion between scaffold and scaffold, should such be needed? Admittedly a costumed actor using such a path would be uncommonly close to the public, according to our present-day standards, yet, did he not in fact, during the action of the show, have to be in quite as close a contact when he walked through the crowd in the Place? Certainly, different standards might obtain at that period.

One is reminded, by this detail and that, of a circular theatre that followed this one at no impossibly distant interval of history. I mean the Swan Theatre of *c.* 1596 as shown in De Witt's sketch, some 171 years later. In this matter of the rampart, for example, how much one is reminded of the *porticus* at the top gallery of De Witt's theatre where, behind the row (or two rows) of seats, was a widish, unsighted promenade, where possibly one indulged in a 'quiet standing' or other social matters during the course of the play, but undistracted by its claim upon one's attention! (For details of this matter see my model-reconstruction of an Elizabethan playhouse for the British Council and the note upon it in their journal, *Britain Today*, April 1954, as well as the recorded talk made for the British Council to accompany this model on exhibition abroad.)

But I believe the flat space of this rampart had yet a further purpose.

It is a very remarkable thing that in no script we possess of any medieval play intended for circular presentation, and containing mention of the scaffolds necessary to it, is there a single example of a scaffold named 'a hill' for those scenes intended to take place on a hill. One is able to ascribe all other scenes—the palaces, the prisons and so forth—with some approximation to their scaffolds, but never is one able to approximate a scene on a hill to such a particular stage. And the scene on a hill is not rare.

We have Abraham cutting the mysterious rods on a hill in the Cornish *Origo Mundi* (ll. 1728 et seq.). We have the Devil taking Jesus up to the high place at the beginning of the Cornish *Passio*. We have the sacrifice of Isaac 'upon yon high hill' in the *N-Town Cycle* (E.E.T.S. ed., p. 46). We have the direction in *The Thrie Estaitis*—'Heir sall the boy cry aff the hill' (l. 2179). We have the references in *The Life of St. Meriasek*, at ll. 1145 and 1152 to a chapel and mount which do *not* seem to be scaffolds.

All these scenes demand hills and have hills deliberately referred to in the lines. Yet no hill is ever mentioned in such plans of scaffolds as survive. Apart from this, the plans provide for stages for every other needed subject of scene in the performance (save those scenes performed down in the Place—where clearly a *hill* scene could not properly be played!).

The conclusion therefore rises in a way not easy to be dismissed that when in a medieval circular presentation a scene had to take place on a hill, the existing Hill of earth itself might have been actually used for the purpose.

Let us turn to our diagram and see what exactly this would mean from the dramatic and visual point of view.

In Fig. 19 I have left a space in the ring of spectators just above the figures 20 and 30 on the scale. This I have done to remind us that it is not impossible that the stytelers might keep such a place free—the rampart at the top and the steps leading up to it. At the top I have shown three figures, as it might be actors, standing against the sky.

Let us now consider for a moment a scene that might have been played in this way, and see what effect it might have had. Suppose the scene to be Jesus on Mount Quarentana, just before his Temptation by the Devil, as in fact we find at the opening of the Second part of the *Ordinale* (The Passion), which begins with the direction (l. 1), *hic stat jhesus in monte quarentana versus jordanum et despicit intra jericho et jerusalem* ('Here stands Jesus in Mount Quarentana, near Jordan, and looks between Jericho and Jerusalem'). At the beginning Jesus and the Disciples probably moved across the Place towards this gap in the seated spectators on the Hill. Jesus ascends, followed perhaps by the leaders of the Disciples. He turns at the summit against the sky. The Disciples now are already, without calling on any producer's art, potentially spread over the steps at his feet in what might make as fine a picture as the theatre can show. Beside the Disciples are the spectators, some sitting also on the Hill and some standing, as perhaps the remaining Disciples did, on the plain below. Then Jesus speaks to the multitude. He delivers six stanzas of sermon to all before him. Then comes the direction (l. 26), *hic descendant omnes de monte* ('Here let all come down from the mountain'). The scene now continues for a space in the Place on a more intimate note, with Jesus conversing with Peter and Andrew. . . .

It cannot be denied, I think, that, with the technique we have been discussing, there would be no point in erecting a scaffold to stand for the mountain, when all that was needed was so easily and readily at hand. No finer setting for the scene could be conceived. The evidence suggests that in such a setting 'hill' scenes were played.

Some Further Points emerging from the Sectional Diagram

Some final points may be summarized to begin with as follows:

1. There is an area around the centre where (if the Castle is

raised on legs) an actor can be seen by anyone in the theatre, free of any obstruction. At St. Just, this would have been some 32 ft. in diameter. Presumably it is this that would have been kept clear, for 'here shall be the best of all' (see further, below).

2. If scaffolds were built on the rampart, this would forbid any entrances from *below* the scaffolds. (How then was Hell arranged?)

3. Were the Seven Virtues in a room, concealed in the tower, all through the play up to the assault?

(4. If so, these scaffolds might well be called *domus*, 'home'!)

5. Where did the actors dress? And eat?

One or two of these points will bear a little development.

In respect of Point 1, we see for the first time a really forcible reason why the Castle was on legs.

Perhaps this is not a fair way to put it; perhaps it would be fairer simply to think of the tower as complete skeletally, and standing on the ground, but deprived of its normal painted covering or skin up to a level some 7 ft. high. Thus the Castle-tower becomes, in its lower part, what Dr. Hotson has termed 'transpicuous' —in other words 'seethroughable'. (The reference is to the last page of the chapter called 'Shakespeare's Arena Stage' in *The First Night of Twelfth Night* by Leslie Hotson, 1954. But whether the present suggestion of a scaffold built in a tradition expressly intending it to be seen through is a support to Dr. Hotson's theory of Shakespeare's arena stage or not, we cannot alas discuss in this place.)

In Fig. 20 an interesting conclusion follows. I have there drawn a sight-line from the eye of a standing spectator on the highest point of the Hill through the point in the Castle-tower where it becomes clothed, or opaque. What is interestingly revealed is that an actor could be fully seen (right up to his head) from this position on the Hill, *even though he were 9 ft. on the far side of the Castle.*

Putting this another way, it means there was a circle 18 ft. in diameter at the centre of the Place, in any part of which an actor could be seen from any position in the theatre. If he went outside this circle, then the spectators standing on the opposite Hill would lose sight of the top of him because of the bulk of the upper part of the Castle in between.

Following out this line of reasoning in the diagram of the

larger round, we find that a circle of no less than 32 ft. in diameter (see Fig. 19) would be afforded—if *The Castle* were played at St. Just—wherein an actor would be totally visible at any part and from any viewpoint in the auditorium.

Concerning Point 5:

If there were no accessible actors' underparts to the scaffolds; and/or if there were no compartment above, which was concealed and large enough to serve as a dressing-room—then it follows that (*a*) certain entrances (for example, of characters who did not come down from scaffolds) would have to be made from outside the theatre altogether (unless the actors sat visible on benches in the Place; an idea I distrust as unlikely theatrically) and also (*b*) a dressing-tent or pavilion would have to be erected outside the theatre confines. The actors coming from without might then use this as a Green-Room, as well as a dressing-room, and enter the Place from it at their cue by the public entrance (or a similar gap in the ring elsewhere).

There are two facts which tend to confirm such an idea. First, the mysterious 'Palȝeoun' in ll. 1387 and 2315 of *Ane Satyre of the Thrie Estaits*. Second, the fact that the ship, in *Mary Magdalene* (where the stage directions are part Latin and part English), 'goth out of the place' at l. 1445; then it also '*venit In placeam*' at l. 1716; '*venit ad-circa placeam*' at l. 1879; and lastly, it again 'goth owȝt ofe the place' at l. 1923. It is very clear it must have come *from* somewhere to go into the Place and it must have gone *to* somewhere when it left the Place—a thing the size of a practical ship couldn't have ascended to a scaffold, or been popped behind a curtain. Again it could not, decently and theatrically, have been left naked for all to see in the open, outside the whole theatre. It must have had a concealment, or a shed, or a pavilion. Is such a thing provable?

Returning to the two *Thrie Estaits* directions; the first comes at the conclusion of a ribald piece of bawdry between the Sowtar's Wyfe and the Taylour's Wyfe. As it ends, the direction follows—'Heir sall thay depairt and pas to the Palȝeoun'. Neither appears again until after the Interlude, some 800 lines away.

Therefore, I believe we are fairly justified in supposing they leave altogether and go elsewhere for a time—and that, since their destination is stated to be the Palȝeoun (or Pavilion), therefore that pavilion is outside the theatre.

The other direction is somewhat different. At l. 2315, at the end of the comic Pauper-interlude, Diligence speaks and dismisses all this nonsense with a sharp appeal to pick up the thread of the main play again, announcing that the 'thrie estaits of this natioun' will now come to court with a 'strange gravitie'. And at the end of the speech the direction follows—'Heir sall the thrie estaits cum fra the pal3eoun gangand backwart led be thair vyces.'

This is a resumption of the plot and the beginning of what is in fact a new development of the play; it follows the interlude, during which 'The Kings, Bischops and principall players' were 'out of their seats', or scaffolds (hence the gag of the Pauper about climbing up to the King's empty chair), and it marks a return of the players after their interval. At such a point these players come *from the Pavilion* to pick up the show again. I have found all explanations of this 'Pavilion' unsatisfactory save this one—that it was outside the action altogether and functioned as a sort of dressing room and Green-Room. We have no proof of this, but the idea is worth retaining for testing eventually.

Taken by and large, there is much to suggest that there was some kind of private quarters outside the medieval arena. And thus that *some* entrances might be made from without, *via* the public entrance, into the Place.

One other detail in Fig. 19 ought to be explained. Above the Hill to the reader's left is a dotted line in the air somewhat like a fishing-rod, and more or less parallel to the roof of the scaffold.

This is the nearest I dared go to deciding the very uncertain question whether in the English circular theatre any sort of awning was erected over the seated spectators on the Hill to keep off the rain or the sun. If, on the basis of Fouquet, we were to presume such awnings, then perhaps they would have been in, or near, the position shown by this dotted line.

On a section of this nature it is not easy to show the lanes before the scaffolds, kept clear of spectators by the stytelers, but these have to be remembered to interpret the section rightly.

The most unfavourable positions in the whole theatre from which to get a view of the show—at least in the larger circle—must have been in those parts of the Place near the foot of the Hill. From this marginal area nearly all the action would have been masked by the standing spectators in front—that is between oneself and the centre. It would seem from the diagram that such areas would be the last to be occupied at the filling of the theatre.

Again, the first two or three steps on the Hill are bad, if their occupants were to sit, for then the people standing in the Place in front would mask all the action in the centre. It seems likely then that the lower steps of the Hill would not be occupied by spectators, and would serve only as a means of access to the less unsighted steps above, on which one might sit and still see the show over the heads of people standing in front.

Against all this we ought to set the idea that, in any but a very packed theatre, the standing audience must have been to some extent a moving thing, free to shift as the action shifted, and con-gregating thickly now in one part of the Place and now in another. (This must have been, from the comfort point of view, a great advantage—for to stand for over three hours and a half on the grass in rapt concentration, without intervals of welcome exercise, must have tried the stamina even of a medieval playgoer.)

Now at length, we may say that our picture of the medieval Place and scaffolds, with the encircling Hill, is beginning to take some character. As we proceed there grow a number of things about which we cannot be certain, but these losses in the clarity of the picture are, I think, outbalanced by the general scheme, of which sufficient features are of a reasonable likelihood to give us at least the confidence of retaining it for testing by future experience as more plays and more evidence come to our knowledge for analysis—e.g. the material set out in Appendix 2.

Scaffolds, Hill and Place Assembled

Our last step in these preliminaries is to attempt a still fuller picture, one that shall combine all those items which we have assembled in separate diagrams up to now, but drawn this time with the intention of conveying the visual impression of the whole scene as it appeared—or, one might say, with the intention this time not so much of studying it as of portraying it.

This impression which I earlier promised the reader is given in Fig. 21. (See folding diagram at end of book.)

With its help I want, in a few pages, to go on to study the performance from beginning to end. But before that final part of our study, we should add a few comments on what is portrayed in this picture.

At this stage in our work, and after the reader has possibly had the picture before him while reading the last few sections, there is little point in describing it in full detail. A great deal of what it shows will be very familiar by now. I add, however, the following brief list of things to be noted:

The drawing is not to any particular scale; it shows a theatre somewhat smaller than St. Just, but bigger than the circles described by Carew. It is between the two sections in size.

The drawing does not set out to represent any particular moment in the play; the procession of events in the performance we have yet to study. But there are shown certain salient acting-positions and production-details; for instance:

The Devil is seen rampaging and 'pomping' on his scaffold.

Covetyse has descended, and is inviting Mankind to come up and sit in his throne.

God's scaffold is silent and curtained.

A figure stands at the top of the Castle-tower, suggesting one of the Virtues.

Horses are being led inconspicuously through the public entrance and round the outside of the Place to be deposited at the scaffolds of the Evils in preparation for war.

The drawing shows how difficult it would be, with scaffolds having full side-curtains, to place them any nearer the centre than this—that is, forward of the Hill and its steps. So many adjacent spectators would be unsighted, both as regards what went on on the scaffold, and also because of its masking what went on on other scaffolds. Scaffolds *outside* the ditch are now clearly quite unacceptable. The position shown is a guess, but it seems to make the best sense.

The drawing shows the 'bad' rows of steps at the very foot of the Hill, where presumably people did not sit.

It shows the tendency to leave empty a rim round the outer edge of the Place—or at least to fill it with spectators only as a last resort—and how this might be used for horses and others coming from the Pavilion outside.

The flights of steps up to the top of the Hill either side the entrance bridge (and all details here) are entirely conjectural. But any use of the rampart as a means of circulation or as a way out from the back of the scaffolds would necessarily involve some such steps near the entrance.

We see the 'lanes' partly kept clear by the stytelers, but that leading from the entrance, and that leading from God's scaffold in the East, have been allowed to fill up slightly. They would have to be cleared by the stytelers before the lanes could be used.

Spectators entering before the show began would be fairly easily kept away from the lanes by the stytelers pacing up and down them. They might be less easily kept from the central area round the tower, for those who knew would choose to be as near this as possible. Constant surveillance would be needed to stop encroachment here.

It occurs to one to wonder: was there any barrier at the foot of the Hill, between it and the Place, as in a bullring?

The 'orchestra' is not shown because I do not know where it would be—presumably on a section of the Hill.

In the left foreground is the Pavilion.

This is a ditch-and-hill type of theatre. A similar theatre could, I believe, be built when the ground was unsuitable for ditch-making, by enclosing the Place with a strong fence, instead of a mound; by setting inside a considerable number of scaffolds so as to accommodate audience as well as actors and make up for the loss of the terraced hill (the theatre would then resemble that shown in Fouquet's miniature); by using scaffolds standing on their own legs, not sitting on the hill-rampart, and thus having an accessible under part (such as would serve for a Hell-mouth), and requiring a ladder for access to the upper part.

A theatre of this kind, without a hill, was what I first visualized when I began this study of *The Castle of Perseverance* after comparing the *Castle* Plan with the Fouquet miniature. At that early stage in my study I made a rough sketch of what I visualized. Sometimes these early sketches at the outset of a work of research have a freshness and atmosphere which it is not always easy to recapture when later one comes into possession of a mass of further facts. I think, therefore, that the sketch is worth reproducing and I add it as Fig. 22. In view of what I have just said, it will be understood that I do not offer it because of the correctness of its details but because of the general impression it conveys of the smaller type of fenced theatre. This general impression was confirmed by later work; the details are subject to modification in the light of that work as outlined in this book.

One thought, out of the many which rise up as one reflects on this attempt to portray a medieval theatre, concerns the Bed in the

FIG. 22. Tentative sketch of a small theatre of the 'barred' or fenced variety with self-standing scaffolds. This sketch was made at the outset of investigation and is included here for its value as a general impression rather than for its details.

centre. If one were trying to reconstruct a performance of *The Castle* from the text alone—supposing the suggestions on the Plan were lost—would it ever have occurred to one even for the very briefest moment to include a *bed* at all? I am sure it would not! The allusions to a bed in the lines, or the likelihood of its use in the action, seem so very slight and remote that one would never dream of introducing it, as I believe. Two things follow from this; first, might it not be possible that there was a very good reason for the bed in some piece of business of which we have no inkling? In other words, may there not be much in the production of the play that was added over and above the lines, and of which we can have not the slightest hint on the evidence available to us? Second, if this is true and such things as this bed were introduced for some separate purpose quite apart from the interpretation of the lines—then who knows what other, perhaps more elaborate, props and effects may not have got into the presentation of medieval morality plays?

The same thing, of course, applies to an object with even less apparent use than the bed, but which we know also existed—namely, that mysterious 'cepbord' of Covetyse's that was 'by the bed's feet'. This and the bed, then, we are prevented from omitting from our reconstruction purely because of their chance mention on a plan: How many other items that Fortune did not think to register are we missing altogether . . .?

The Theatre in the Round

The title of this book, *The Medieval Theatre in the Round*, may perhaps be held to have a somewhat 'opportunist' note about it. That is true; it knowingly uses a phrase—the theatre in the round —which today suggests certain contemporary experiments in production where the performance itself is in the centre of a room and the audience sit round it on all sides in a circle. Such a style has been particularly developed in America, though by no means exclusively so.

This form of presentation 'in the round' is one of the manifestations of a widespread movement belonging to the middle of this century, and designed to free the theatre from certain restrictions which are said to result from the orthodox style of presentation on the 'picture-frame' stage. (Another 'new' form of presentation which belongs to the same movement is what I have called the 'open stage' style.)

I have thus taken for my title a strictly modern term and applied it to a medieval form of theatre. I have done this partly with a purpose which, now that we have been able to complete the reconstructional diagram, can be explained.

So far as experiments with theatres in the round have gone today in France, Italy, the United States, Great Britain and elsewhere, it would seem that they have all had to be limited to small theatres seating comparatively small audiences. It seems that if the ring of seats reaches above five or six rows deep (say between 200 and 300 people), there will begin to be difficulties in hearing, because the actors must always speak with their backs to some of the audience.

Now there are certain economic factors always at work in the professional theatre, and one outstanding is that you must have a big enough audience to make your show pay, or you must close down—or be subsidized. For all ordinary purposes of professional-theatre work, a paying audience needs to be of the order of 600 or 800 people before even the prospect of covering costs from popularly priced seats becomes a fair one.

If the audience can be raised to 1,000, so much the better. M. Jean Vilar's Théâtre National Populaire, which has made such a name in France—particularly at Avignon—and in London and elsewhere, certainly owes some of its stability, not only to its being subsidized to the tune of some £54,000 a year, but to the fact that the *average* size of audience to which it plays is 1,680 per performance! (See the brochure put out by the T.N.P. on the occasion of their season at the Palace Theatre, London, in April and May 1956.)

This is a very remarkable figure in the circumstances.

M. Vilar, however, does *not* use a theatre-in-the-round. He uses a form of more or less 'open' staging; and this it is which makes possible the presentation of his shows before such large audiences. The normal theatre-in-the-round technique as used today would not allow him to serve anything like so many spectators.

What we have to ask now is: does the above mean that the form of staging in-the-round is doomed to grave financial limitations? Could a company using such a form ever hope to accommodate and satisfy an audience averaging as much as fifteen hundred per performance? Again: in a locality possessing no theatres, and where either open-air or roofed sports stadiums and such things are the chief available places for a show, is the form of presentation in-the-round totally ruled out because of the vast spaces?

It is to these questions that this diagrammatic reconstruction offers a qualified answer. It shows how formerly a kind of theatre in the round was developed to suit an audience of thousands. What it was like the diagram shows us, and what it shows us may now be described afresh from another angle, so as to lay special emphasis on the correspondence it bears with modern centre-staging. Putting it summarily, we should then describe the theatre in Fig. 21 as follows:

The 'stage' (if I may call it such) was a level area varying from some 18 ft. to some 30 ft. in diameter. It was not raised. In the centre of it might be set a piece of 'scenery', which could be elaborate provided it was designed with proper regard to 'see-throughableness'. On the ground all round this central acting-area, part of the audience were accommodated. They might sit or stand, but they were free to move as at a modern Promenade Concert. They were tactfully directed away from hindering the action of the play by officials.

In any roofed theatre today on circular lines—say perhaps the Royal Albert Hall, London—no doubt this portion of the audience would be provided with seats, which would add to their comfort but would make them lose their mobility. Possibly, also, some raking of the floor (so as to be saucer-shaped) would be contrived, to improve the vision of those sitting farthest out. These are matters in which a modern layout might be a little different from the one reconstructed in this diagram. But the remarkable point about the whole comparison so far is that they would be almost the only differences; we have not, in fact, come across anything yet in our present description which would not be quite relevant to any centre-stage theatre of today—always excepting the fact that I have been silent about the size of the audience in such a theatre.

Now, however, come the innovations which this medieval method brings to our notice, and which allow of presentation to a considerable audience.

There are to be added to the above, three major developments which are to be seen in no centre-stage theatre of which we have any record today (save perhaps that arranged by Okhlopkov at the Realistic Theatre, Moscow, in 1933 for his production of Gorki's *Mother*). That is to say, we have, coupled with the above: first, a number of subsidiary, highly raised, 'peripheral' stages, i.e. stages dotted round the outer edge of the audience; second, we have a system of linking those stages to the central area by means of steps and clear lanes preserved through the spectators; and third, we have, banked up all round the whole system, a high, circular 'Hill', or ring of multi-tiered boxes, whence a still further mass of the audience can see the show, and see it unobstructed by the mass of spectators in the Place below.

(Of course, we must very clearly recognize the presence also of a fourth factor, essential to the success of the whole, and that is a supply of plays especially composed with the technique of such a shape of theatre in mind!)

What is important is that we can make one major conclusion: whatever the qualifications, there is here a relatively elaborately worked-out system of presenting shows *in the round* which does admit of their being witnessed by an audience *reaching into the thousands*. This alone justifies a claim that the method deserves study by inquiring producers today. And it is partly to draw attention to that particular fact that I have called my present study by a title which links a modern movement with a medieval system.

One can see, I think, after such an approach, what a highly organized thing this Round Theatre of the Middle Ages was. It does not look like an odd occasional growth with no tradition. It must have been the product of some experience, and it begins more and more to have the look of a *professional* system. It is clearly not the crude, occasional, primitive work, hovering at the dawn of theatre history, that some writers have been inclined to suggest.

PART FOUR

THE PERFORMANCE

12

THE PRESENTATION ANALYSED

The Opening of the Play: 'This night I was of my mother born' ∗
The Investment of Mankind: 'To feed the fleshly flower' ∗ *The
Siege of the Castle: 'But forty winters old'* ∗ *The Fall of Mankind:
'A party well in age'.* ∗ *The Epilogue: 'Set him here by my knee'*

W E are now ready for the great performance.
Let us take the scene pictured in Fig. 21, possess ourselves of it as thoroughly as possible, and begin to alter it,
move it and make it work. We will first clear it by removing all the
figures of actors and closing the curtains of the scaffolds. The
audience can stay in their places.

A word about the sort of mind we have to use is prompted by
this 'closing' of the scaffold curtains. We have in what follows to
face up to the responsibilities of conjecture. In this, and many
other matters of detail, we have too little evidence to speak with
assurance. We do not *know* there were curtains to these scaffolds.
But we have now passed the stage where we can afford constantly
to be wrenching our picture with too candid comparisons of alternatives. We could do as much of this as we liked in our previous
study where we dealt with preparations. Now we have to leave
preparations and sail out, as little tremulously as we can, into the
event. And if we find our preparations prove too unsure to keep us
afloat, we must suffer drowning. We cannot cobble at the boat
when we have put to sea in it. For our reader, this present confession and our painfully acquired evidence up to this must be sufficient warning to bring his own judgement with him as he reads,
and must help him decide to what matters he needs most to
bring it.

Our shaping scene has to suffer two influences as it comes to
life; that of the day of the event, and that of the kind of mind
watching it. The influence of the day includes the weather and the

locality. That of the mind includes the profane element of expectant wonder, and the sacred element of religion.

As to the effect of the day, I do not wish to colour my picture by saying too much that must be purely conjectural about the sun and the blue sky (or the grey sky) and the grass. But I do wish not to deprive it of a certain legitimate richness which (for instance) Edwin Norris created when, in visualizing the presentation of a different performance in Cornwall, he gave us the following passage, refreshing us in our study:

The bare granite plain of St. Just, in view of Cape Cornwall, and of the transparent sea which beats against that magnificent headland, would be a fit theatre for the exhibition . . . of the great History of the Creation, the Fall, and the Redemption of Man. . . . The mighty gathering of people from many miles round, hardly showing like a crowd in that extended region, where nothing ever grows to limit the view on any side. . . .

And for the mental influences of expectation and religion I would very briefly point out that these waiting spectators to whom the show is presently to open are country people or from country towns, of an agricultural age, eager for any treat and now in crowd collected, among gay toys of costumes, Hills and banners, with a moat and barrier crossed that cut them off from all the workaday world. In addition, they are subjects of King Henry VI, with Agincourt fought say a decade ago, and in creed they are Roman Catholic. They are physically realists, and spiritually they are religious, conforming to the ritual and the teaching of the Church; constantly encountering theological issues and accustomed to the recognized symbols and arguments. Whether each was devout or not was probably dependent upon the individual, but the crowd as a whole belonged to an age with a dominant religious shape; and so, I think, they would be prepared to listen to the long argument on a theological strain that runs through this performance.

The Opening of the Play: 'This night I was of my mother born'

The crowd has gathered; the audience is in its place; the moment comes for the play to begin. How does it begin? This, unfortunately, is one of the things we do not know.

The people must have been talking; there was surely a babel of voices. It has to be stilled. Was there a trumpet call? Was there only the drawing of a curtain on the Western scaffold, whither all eyes turned, and at which the voices gradually dropped as the splendid World and his servants were disclosed? The script does not tell us. It simply opens at l. 157 (that is, after the twelve stanzas of the banns) with World's greeting and his opening announcement of himself.

This announcement is of some importance. It is a common convention in medieval plays at a player's opening. Sometimes a very interesting stage direction is used to introduce it. This kind of direction is not found in our play at all but in the Cornish cycles we frequently see such pageant-provoking words as *hic pompabit salamon*: 'Here Solomon shall "pomp"' (see *Origo Mundi*, l. 2376). This is a fine verb to describe the opening vaunt of a splendid figure—he shall 'pomp', he struts, proclaims his greatness on his high scaffold, and (all being well) ties his auditors' ears '(with golden chaines) to his Melody', to use the words of Dekker.

The regal, opening self-announcement reminds one of the vaunts in the ancient folk-plays of St. George, where each character on entering pronounces a speech announcing his name and celebrating his prowess.

So here also—whatever the means of silencing the audience—*The Castle of Perseverance* begins with a fine announcement from World's scaffold where he sits, or stands, with his three servitors, and while, as we suppose, the curtains of all the other scaffolds are yet closed. He 'pomps' and cries across the circular theatre these proud, resounding lines:

(l. 157) Worthy wyt*is*, in al þis werd wyde,
  Be wylde wode wonys, & eu*er*y weye-went,
Precyous i*n* prise, p*r*ekyd in p*r*ide,
 þorwe þis p*r*opyr pleyn place, i*n* pes be ȝe bent!
Buske ȝou, bolde bacheler*is*, vnd*er* my ban*er* to a-byde,
 Whe*r*e bryth basnet*is* be bateryd, & backys ar schent,
ȝe, syrys semly, all same syttyth on syde,
 For, bothe be see & be londe, my sond*is* I haue sent;
  al þe werld my*n* nam[e] is ment,
  al a-bowty*n* my bane is blowe,
  In eu*er*y cost I am knowe,
  I do men rawyn on ryche rowe
   tyl þei be dyth to dethys dent.

(Worthy wights, in all this world wide;
  By wild wood woning and every way-went;
Precious in price; prickëd in pride;
  Through this proper, plain place in peace be ye bent!
Buske you, bold bachelors, under my banner to abide,
  Where bright basinets be battered and backës are shent—
You, sirs seemly, all same sitteth on side.
  For both by sea and by land my scouts have I sent;
      All the world my name is ment [mentioned in];
    All about my bane is blow(n),
    In every coast I am known,
    I do men ravine in rich rows
      Till they be dight to deathë's dent.)

and he carries on in this strain for two further stanzas—39 lines,
probably a little over two minutes—'pomping' all the time, and
naming incidentally his 'tresorer, Syr Covetyse' across in the North-
East.

Readers will notice, in the above, several allusions whose great
significance we have already discussed—for example, the 'worthy
wights . . . through this proper, plain Place', that is, the people
standing on the grass; and then the swift turn to the side-audience:
'Bold bachelors . . . you, sirs seemly' that 'sitteth on side'. It is a
speech that—if ever there was one in English drama—contains
'attack'. Abruptness is the main feature of this opening; and it has
a power of dramatic effect. From beginning to end the speech is a
direct address to the audience.

At its close, what happens next? Perhaps World sits down in a
throne, and his scaffold is left uncovered. At any rate the sequel
is clear: from the West the whole audience is swung round to the
North by the announcement of what must have been in some ways
the most sensational figure of the show. We suppose the Hell-
scaffold suddenly opens and from it, with all eyes now switched in
his direction, Satan himself delivers his vaunt in turn, clad we may
be certain in all the panoply of a medieval devil. But it seems he
does not rise—at least, not at once—for he begins:

(l. 196) Now I sytte, Satanas, in my sad synne,
      As deuyl dowty, in draf as a drake;
    I champe & I chase, I chocke on my chynne,
      I am boystows & bold, as Belyal þe blake. . .

(Now I sit, Satan, in my sad sin,
 As devil doughty, in dregs as a dragon;
I champ and I chase, I chock on my chin,
 I am boist'rous and bold, as Belial the black . . .)

and so forth. At l. 209 he mentions (probably pointing to them by
his side as he does so) his three servitors:

Pryde is my prince, in perlys I-pyth;
 Wretthe, þis wrecche, with me schal wawe;
Enuye, in-to werre, with me schal walkyn wyth;
 With þese faytouris I am fedde; . . .

(Pride is my prince, in pearlës y-pight;
 Wrath, this wretch, with me shall go;
Envy into war with me shall walk brave;
 With these rascals I am fed. . . .)

He concludes, after a symmetrical speech of the same length as
World's:

gadyr ȝou to-gedyr, ȝe boyis, on þis grene!
In þis brode bugyl, a blast wanne I blowe,
 al þis werld schal be wood, I-wys, as I wene,
  & to my byddynge bende;
    wythly on syde,
    on benche wyl I byde,
    to tene, þis tyde,
     al holy, Mankende.

(Gather you together, you boys on this green!
On this broad bugle a blast when I blow,
 All this world shall be mad, I wis as I ween,
  And to my bidding bind.
    Swiftly on side,
    On bench will I bide,
    To plague, this tide,
     All wholly, Mankind.)

—a fair enough offer in all conscience! And one that we may well
now see could have had its effect when glowered down to the small
lads on the grass below. It ends amusingly briefly—almost with an
anticlimax—but with the threat of 'wait and see!' which well
sustains the growing drama.

Now perhaps there is a moment's pause. A sensation must have
sped through the audience as the Devil sat down again, and a

response to the awfulness of his threats. I have no hesitation in supposing that the medieval actor was just as capable of appreciating the value of a 'significant pause', when he felt he could hold it, as a modern actor, because such perception is not a result of sophisticated training but just of common theatre-experience—and I am supposing that if these were professionals, then they were in some degree experienced players.

At any rate, the moment is ripe for another surprise. And it surely comes. The audience is switched round from the North to the scaffold on the South. After the cold suavity of World, and the militant arrogance of the Devil, they have a fat and heavy grossness that can hardly be surpassed; the third scaffold opens to show Flesh and his three servitors, and with lip-licking satisfaction, he begins:

> (l. 235) I byde, as a brod brustun gutte, a-bouyn on þese touris.
> euery body is þe beter, þat to myn byddynge is bent.
> I am Mankyndis fayre flesch, florchyd in flowris;
> my lyfe is with lustys & lykynge I-lent. . . .
>
> (I bide as a broad, bursting gut, above on these towers.
> Every body is the better that to my bidding is bent.
> I am Mankind's fair flesh, flourished in flowers;
> My life is with lust and liking y-lent. . . .)

In his second stanza he says, in a way that removes all doubt:

> (l. 248) In glotony, gracyous now am I growe;
> þerfore he sytteth semly here be my side;
> In lechery & lykynge, lent am I lowe;
> & Slawth, my swete sone, is bent to a-byde:
>
> (In Gluttony gracious now am I grown—
> Therefore he sitteth seemly here by my side.
> In Lechery and liking sunk am I low;
> And Sloth, my sweet son, is bound to abide:)

And he ends (so as to make quite sure there is no mistake!):

> (l. 266) be-hold þe Werld, þe Deuyl, & Me!
> with all oure mythis, we kyngys thre,
> nyth & day, besy we be,
> for to distroy Mankende,
> if þat w[e may];
> þer-for, on hylle,
> syttyth all stylle,
> & seth wyth good wylle
> oure ryche a-ray.

(Behold the World, the Devil and Me!
With all our mights, we kingës three,
Night and day busy we be
For to destroy Mankind
If that we may!
Therefore on hill
Sit you all still
And see with good will
Our rich array!)

—and rich, I believe, it may have seemed!

However, here now is our beginning. Three scaffolds have opened, each containing a Major Evil and his three Servants. Each has given his vaunt in no uncertain terms. Each is probably now sitting in position with his court about him, and each curtain (as I believe) is still open. The play is well begun. The audience have already tasted of splendour and of high-boasting promise. The three symmetrical opening speeches have been 'pomped' through down to this culminating order that all those spectators sitting so comfortable on the hill are to look well to what follows.

And what now does follow?

I believe another spectacular moment, and something containing another dramatic surprise. Although here we cannot be sure and still we have no stage direction, yet I think we cannot avoid the impression that at this moment there would be achieved a complete contrast. For the most tender and pathetic little speech now begins, and we must pause to consider one or two details.

The former speakers have all been Great Fellows, vaunting to the full across the broad circle from their scaffolds high; and the eyes of the crowd have swung wide and large from one to another at command. Now comes something entirely new. No turning to yet another scaffold—swinging round on one's waist to left or to right and listening across the grass and sunshine to the voice above the crowd—but instead the whole atmosphere is suddenly concentrated inward. The outward scaffolds are all forgotten (are their curtains closed now? We have no hint either way, but in a little while we shall have to refer to this puzzle again), and each man is called to look directly and intently in front of him. Under the Castle something little moves and rises and comes out into the light from the very hub of the all-surrounding theatre. It is

Mankind—and in how touching a figure his lines will sufficiently paint! He quietly begins:

(l. 275) aftyr our*e* forme fader*is* kende
    þis nyth I was of my mod*er* born.
Fro my mod*er* I walke, I wende;
    Ful feynt & febyl, I far*e* ʒou be-forn;
I am nakyd of lym & lende,
    as mankynde is schapy*n* & schorn;
I not wedyr to gon ne to lende,
    to helpe my-self mydday ny*n* morn:
        for schame I stonde & schende.
      I was born þis nyth in blody ble,
      & nakyd I am, as ʒe may se.
      a! Lord God in t*r*inite!
        Whow Mankende is vnthende!

Where-to I was to þ*is* werld browth,
    I ne wot; but to woo & wepynge
I am born, & haue ryth nowth
    to helpe my self in no doynge.
I stonde & stodye, al ful of þowth;
    bar*e* and por*e* is my clothynge;
a sely crysme, my*n* hed hath cawth,
    þ*at* I tok at myn crysteny*n*ge: . . .

. . . ij au*n*gels bene a-synyd to me;
    þe ton techyth me to goode:
on my ryth syde ʒe may hy*m* se;
    he cam fro C*r*iste þat deyed on rode.
a-noþ*er* is ordeynyd her to be,
    þat is my foo, be fen & flode;
he is a-bout, in eu*er*y degre,
    to drawe me to þo dewylys wode,
        þat in helle ben thycke. . . .

(After our former father's kind,
    This night I was of my mother born.
From my mother I walk, I wend;
    Full faint and feeble I fare you beforne.
I am naked of limb and loin;
    As mankind is, shapen and shorn.
I [know] not whither to go or to lean—
    To help myself, midday nor morn;
        For shame I stand and shend.

I was born this night in bloody blee;
And naked I am as you may see.
Ah, Lord God in Trinity!
How Mankind is unthend! [miserable]

Whereto I was to this world brought
I not wot, but to woe and weeping
I am born, and have right nought
To help myself in no doing
I stand and study, all full of thought.
Bare and poor is my clothing.
A blessed chrism [anointing cloth] mine head hath caught
That I took at my christening . . .

. . . Two angels be assigned to me.
The one teacheth me to good—
On my right side you may him see;
He came from Christ that died on rood.
Another is órdained here to be
That is my foe, by fen and flood.
He is about in every degree
To draw me to those devils wood
That in hell be thick . . .)

There are 53 lines of this superb opening speech. There is much we wish we could know about its delivery. Mankind must have almost surely come from the place, where the bed is, under the Castle-tower. But how was he hidden up to the moment of his entrance? He points to the Two Angels that accompany him. Whence did they come? Probably also from this spot. But from what concealment? Since we have supposed Mankind to have 'entered' from the centre, where did he stand to speak? And to what direction did he deliver his lines? Some answer to this is hinted in his words 'I walk, I wend'—one sees that this might be a processional speech, spoken on a slow travel round the area of the central space, perhaps (since there are four stanzas to the speech) with four pauses before the four cardinal points of the massed audience, so that all should have a chance to hear part. If this is true we have a designed piece of technique in playwriting for a circular theatre.

Often one is inclined to see in speeches spoken in a similar way, a kind of somewhat repetitive, symmetrical construction that at first seems pointless and boring, but that would allow them to be delivered, as it were in series, to successive sections of the audience.

At any rate, over the green grass of the fens and under the Lincolnshire sky, this figure of baby Mankind slowly wends, his Good and Bad Angels pacing at his heels, with their great wings overshadowing him. He passes round the inner ring of audience, and there is sufficient impression, I believe, to justify our saying the great play is well begun.

The next passage is between the two Angels. In alternate stanzas they exchange barbed contempts, speaking from either side Mankind in the Place. Says the Good:

(l. 331)   . . . neuyr-þe-lesse, turne þee fro tene,
                & seruë Jhesu . . .

                (. . . nevertheless, turn thee from teen
                And serve Jesu . . .)

and the Bad retorts:

(l. 340)   Pes, aungel! þi wordis are not wyse!
                þou counselyst hym not a-ryth; . . .
(to Man:)   . . . Cum on with me, stylle as ston!
                þou & I, to þe werd schul goon. . . .

                (Peace, Angel! Thy words are not wise;
                Thou counselest him not a-right . . .
                . . . Come on with me, still as stone!
                Thou and I to the World shall go. . . .)

Mankind is baffled:

(l. 378)   I wolde be ryche in gret a-ray,
                & fayn I wolde my sowlë saue:
                        as wynde in watyr I wave.

                (I would be rich in great array,
                And fain I would my soulë save—
                        As wind in water I wave.)

At the Bad Angel's urging, he resolves:

(l. 397)   but with þe Werld I wyl go play,
                certis, a lytyl þrowe.
                In þis World is al my trust,
                to lyuyn in lykyng & in lust;
                haue he & I onys cust,
                        we schal not part, I trowe.

(But with the World I will go play,
Certes, a little throw.
In this World is all my trust,
To live in liking and in lust;
Have he and I once kisst,
We shall not part, I trow!)

But the Good Angel cries:

(l. 408)   man! þynke on þyn endynge day
Whanne þou schalt be closyd vnder clay!

(Man, think on thine ending day,
When thou shalt be closed under clay!)

to which, the Bad replies:

(l. 413)   ʒa, on þi sowle þou schalt þynke al be tyme.
Cum forth, man, & take non hede!
Cum on, & þou schalt holdyn hym Inne;
þi flesch þou schalt foster & fede
with lofly lyuys fode. . . .
wanne þi nosë waxit cold,
þanne mayst þou drawe to goode.

(Yah! On thy soul thou shalt think *in good time*
Come forth, Man, and take no heed!
Come on! And thou shalt hold him in;
Thy flesch thou shalt foster and feed
With lovely life's food . . .
When thy nosë waxeth cold
Then may'st thou dräw to good!)

Mankind is won (so pathetically he pleads!):

(l. 425)   I am but ʒongë, as I trowe,
for to do þat I schulde . . .

(I am but young, as I trow,
For to do what I should . . .)

and so the Bad Angel, very strikingly, says:

(l. 436)   Now go we forth, swythe a-non!
to þe Werld us must gon;

(Now go we forth, quick anon;
To the World we must be gone;)

—thus indicating a movement impending, and possibly giving a warning to the stytelers that the passage between the centre and World's scaffold (where he sits waiting) must be cleared ready. Man agrees to go. The Good Angel would seem to stop in his tracks and give up the struggle:

(l. 451)   I syë sore, & grysly grone . . .
               I not weder to gone.
               Mankynde.hath forsakyn me!

               (I sighë sore and grisly groan . . .
                 I [know] not whither to go.
               Mankind hath forsaken me!)

and so, clearly, he leaves him behind and the conflict falls to silence as Man and the Bad Angel pass along the grass to the Western scaffold, and the Good Angel retires—perhaps to a little, insignificant stool by one of the Castle's legs.

And then, like a moment in melodrama, underlining a great sentiment, music suddenly breaks in. We have a direction, in what is said to be a different, but nearly contemporary, hand, to 'pipe up, music'. The whole air is lifted up again to lead into a tremendous new vaunt from World's scaffold. It is worth noting the nature of this transition. The scene between Man and the Two Angels lasted 172 lines—possibly ten minutes. There is now to come a passage of 72 lines *before* the meeting between Mankind and World's messengers takes place. We shall see shortly what happens to World in that time; but the question that is not answered is: What, during these five minutes, are Man and the Bad Angel doing?

One is tempted to suppose that they make use of a well-worn technique, and stroll unobtrusively round the Place, not going directly to the scaffold but symbolizing a long journey before at length the encounter comes. Perhaps the piped-up music accompanies part of this walk, and marks the transition in the drama. At any rate, the picture we are to have in a moment is of World's scaffold wide open and of World speaking from it, of the Good Angel slipping out of the action, of Mankind and the Bad Angel strolling, suspended, in the Place, and of World's three servants visible behind him on his scaffold. What now of the other scaffolds?

The question is relevant because no character speaks from any of these between l. 274 (when Flesh finished his vaunt) and l. 829

when Covetyse is to appear on his scaffold—and apart from this, not till l. 909, when Pride answers Covetyse's call, with Wrath and Envy, from the Devil's scaffold.

This offers us a problem such as we have met before; were these scaffolds in fact closed again after the opening vaunts, and did they remain closed all this time? Or did the characters remain silent on them for some good half-hour? There does not appear to be a conclusive answer, but hints in the text suggest, as I hope to show, that the closed curtain seems more likely. We thus conclude our picture by supposing the other four scaffolds are closed, and return to that pipe-music and World's cry.

World's cry suggests that the intention is to distract the audience for the time from Man and the Angel in the Place, for a sort of short sub-plot now intervenes, and until the two threads join we hear no more from the couple on the grass. What World cries is:

(l. 458)   Now I sytte in my semly sale;
         I trotte & tremle in my trew trone;
         as a hawke, I hoppe in my hende hale; . . .

     (Now I sit in my seemly salle.
         I trot and I tremble in my true throne.
         As a hawk I hop in my lovely hall; . . .)

(then, summoning two servitors):

(l. 471)   Lust Lykyng & Foly,
         comly knytis of renoun,
     be-lyue þorwe þis londe do crye
         al a-bowtyn in toure & toun.
     If any man be fer or nye,
         þat to my seruyse wyl buske hym boun

     (Lust-liking and Folly,
         Comely knights of renown!
     Betimes through this land go cry
         All about in tower and town,
     If any man be far or nigh
         That to my service will busk him boun [ready].)

Lust-liking and Folly spring to this command from their seats on World's scaffold and, standing up there beside him, Lust-Liking says:

(l. 484)   lo, me, here! redy, lord, to faryn & to fle,
         to sekyn þee a seruaunt dynge & dere. . . .

þis werldys wysdom ȝeuyth no[t] a louse
of God, nyn of hye heuene
[tunc descendunt in placeam pariter.

(Lo, me, here! Ready, Lord, to farë and to flee,
To seek for thee a servant, worthy and dear . . .
This world's wisdom giveth not a louse
For God nor for high heaven!
[*Then they descend into the Place together*.)

It is of course at this point that the great moment, which we studied in such detail in an earlier chapter, occurs—namely, the descent of Lust-liking and Folly from the scaffold of World down into the Place of the ordinary people. It is, as we have seen, the first occasion in the play on which such a highly dramatic action as the intrusion of a splendid figure from an elevated stage into the crowd below has happened, and it must have had a great effect.

Coupled with the effect itself as the two begin to descend the steps is the dramatic preparation for such a move, first in respect of the World's sending messengers among ordinary humans to find a man, and second in respect of there being in the very Place itself a Man in particular, whose Bad Angel has just succeeded in convincing him of the desirability of enlisting in the World's service.

Upon such a leading-up we can well savour the significance of the continuance of Lust-liking's speech when, after descending, he turns to the nearest audience at the foot of the steps and, after apologizing for disturbing them, plunges straight into his message:

(l. 493)　　　Pes, pepyl! of pes we ȝou pray.
　　　　　　syth & sethe wel to my sawe!
　　　　　Who-so wyl be ryche & in gret aray,
　　　　　　to-ward þe werld he schal drawe. . . .
　　　　　　　Who-so wyl with þe werld haue his dwellynge,
　　　　　　　& ben a lord of his clothynge,
　　　　　　　he muste nedys, ouyr al þynge,
　　　　　　　　euere-more be couetowse:

(Peace, People! Of peace we you pray!
　　Sit and list well to my sawe.
Who-so will be rich and in great array,
　　Toward the world he shall draw . . .
　　　Who-so will with the World have his dwelling
　　　And be a lord of his clothing,
　　　He must needs, over all thing,
　　　　Evermore be covetous.)

Folly echoes this call to service, and both urge the people around them to accept.

And then, just at that particular moment, they encounter the Bad Angel in the Place, among the people they are cozening! He cries:

(l. 530)   How, Lust Lykyng & Folye! . . .
               I haue browth, be downys drye,
                   to þe Werld a gret present;
               I haue gylyd hym ful qweyntly . . .

               (How! Lust-liking and Folly! . . .
               I have brought, by downës dry,
                   To the World a great present!
               I have guiled him full quaintly . . .)

These three gossips continue in high feather, and Lust-liking replies with glee—the poor figure of Man without doubt standing beside all the while and dumbly uncomprehending their drift:

(l. 555)   Lechery schal ben hys fode;
                   Metis & drynkis he schal haue trye.
               With a lykynge lady of lofte,
               he schal syttyn in sendel softe,
               to cachen hym to helle crofte
                   þat day þat he schal deye.

               (Lechery shall be his food;
                   Meats and drinks he shall have rich.
               With a liking lady of loft [position]
               He shall sit him in sendal soft,
               To drag him to hell-croft
                   The day that he shall die!)

And at last poor, bedazed Man speaks:

(l. 575)   Syn þat þou wylt makë me
               boþë ryche of gold & fee,
               goo forthe! for I wyl folow þee
               be dale & euery towne

               (Since that thou wilt makë me
               Bothë rich of gold and fee,
               Go forth! For I will follow thee
               By dale and every town.)

And then, of course, there is a blast of trumpets! ('Of course'

because there is no doubt that these men had a sense of theatre!)
The four figures—rich Lust-liking, gay Folly, the sombre Bad
Angel and little, growing, but still 'naked' Man turn on the green
among the people and begin to make their way through the fanfare
towards the cleared lane that leads to the scaffold of the World.

Whereupon we may for a moment (having traversed a sixth of
the play) draw breath and pause.

We have at this point our third stage direction of the play. It
runs '*Trumpe up. Then* Lust-liking *and* Folly, *the* Bad Angel *and*
Mankind *go to* World, *and* (Lust-liking) *shall say*;'—we break off
before the speech to remark how clearly our picture is confirmed
by the direction. These four strangely assorted figures are shown
incontestably crossing the grass to the Western scaffold where the
World waits and where, hidden or revealed, there skulks behind
him that malignant Boy who signifies nothing yet, but who in the
end shall bring the last heart-stab to fallen Mankind.

At this pause we should perhaps notice some of the other stage
directions beyond these three that are to be found up to this point
in the edited version. They are all modern interpolations and they
do much, I believe, to hinder our understanding of the presentation. For instance, the word *exit* is used (ll. 195, 274, 457, etc.).
This is a misnomer as well as, in some respect, an anachronism.

It is a misnomer because, as we begin to see, there is very little
'going-out' or 'coming-in' in this circular method of presentation.
There are pauses; there are 'suspensions' of action; there are 'fill-
ups' where something takes place while certain people are doing
something else; there are 'ascents' and 'descents'; and of course
there may (or may not) be the opening of curtains. But goings-out
—as of a player leaving a stage by going through a door or curtain—
are very rare. Similarly with entrances.

We find *Exit* inserted by the editor at the end of World's opening
speech, and at the end of Flesh's opening speech but (rather
shrewdly) *not* at the end of the Devil's opening speech—because,
presumably, the editor noticed that that speech ended: 'on bench
will I bide', so the Devil could not have gone out or 'had an exit'.
But this of course begs the whole question; if the phrase is shown
by the text to be inapposite in one case, then it must be inapposite
in the other two parallel cases—it cannot be apposite in one instance and inapposite in another similar instance: it must be
unsuitable in all.

Again, '*exeunt* MAL. ANG. *and* HUM. GEN.' at l. 448 (after Mankind agrees to follow his Bad Angel to the World) is very misleading. It looks most authentic with its abbreviations, but it is not justified at all. It would raise the question: Where do the Bad Angel and Mankind exeunt *to*? Further, what justification is there for interpolating '*Re-enter* MANKIND' after l. 565, in the middle of Folly's speech at the meeting with the Bad Angel? None at all. Neither of the figures, I believe, left the scene, and there is no need for such a modernization. And in any case, a theatre-man has a hatred of any instruction to *exit*, when there is no shadow of a hint at all where and whither the *exit* means him to go.

After l. 457 we get a plethora of these inserted directions. At the end of the Good Angel's speech an *exit* is marked, but with no indication whither. Immediately following on the early direction '*pipe up, music*', there comes the anomalous insertion—[SCENE V. *Before* World's *Scaffold, on the West.*], and finally—a triumph of tinkering!—there is added to all the above: '(*On the Scaffold*, World, Pleasure, Liking, Vain-Glory.)', that is to say, Lust-liking has been split into two characters and Folly has been given a new name which is not the one he is usually called by in the script. No wonder the action of the play is not easy to follow!

But with the shape of theatre and disposition of details that we have studied, the picture is reasonably consistent: Mankind's entrance, the present place of the Good Angel, and the problem of the use or not of scaffold curtains, are all that have worried us.

The Investment of Mankind: 'To feed the fleshly flower'

To resume. We left Lust-liking, Folly and the Bad Angel leading Mankind to the World's scaffold, with Lust-liking about to speak as they arrive at the foot of the steps. What he says in his opening line offers a suggestion concerning the scaffold-curtain problem, for he stops below the Western scaffold and calls 'How, Lord! Look out!' Surely such a call would scarcely have come if World had been sitting, openly watching all that has happened! It suggests much more that World took no part after the departure of his servants, and that the curtain was drawn again over his scaffold until their return. Then there would be logic in the call, and we would suppose the curtain responded by flying back and disclosing a complacent World, scarcely concealing his satisfaction, as he sat and looked down at the conquest brought to his feet.

Lust-liking's full speech runs:

(l. 579)   How, lord! loke owt! for we haue browth
        a serwant of nobyl fame;
    of worldly good is al h*is* þouth;
        of lust & folye he hath no schame;
           he wolde be grat of name,
          he wolde be at gret hono*ur*,
          for to rewlë town & tour*e*;
        he wolde haue to h*is* p*a*ramour*e*
           Sum louely dyngë dame.

    (How, Lord! Look out! For we have brought
      A servant of noble fame.
    Of worldly goods is all his thought;
      Of lust and folly he hath no shame.
          He would be great of name;
         He would be at great honour
         For to rulë town and tower;
         He would have to his paramour
           Some lovely, well-born dame.)

(In respect of the last line, one is almost tempted to adopt the reading of an Australian visitor: 'Some sweet, humdinger dame'!)

World condescendingly replies with a stanza of welcome to the group below, and Mankind then offers his hand in seal of service with an answering stanza. World then clinches the whole bargain with a speech containing the very significant line: 'Come up! My servant, true as steel . . .' (l. 618) which is immediately followed by the fourth stage direction of the play—'*Then* Mankind *shall ascend to* World'. Thus, as World finishes his speech we have a clear picture of what is happening—the little, naked figure of Mankind is joyfully ascending the steps to the Western scaffold, with these lines ringing in his ears:

(l. 623)   lust & lykynge schal be þin ese;
    louely ladys þ*ee* schal plese:
    who-so do þ*ee* any disesse,
        he schal ben hangy*n* hye.

    (Lust and liking shall be thine ease;
    Lovely ladies thee shall please.

Who-so doth thee any dis-ease
He shall be hangëd high.)

Now the sequel is interesting—the whole tempo of the play
changes; the metre alters and quickens; a new, sharp atmosphere
comes over us. The little poor-clad Man goes up, but what do the
others do? There is no stage direction, yet the lines tell us sufficiently; for World issues quick orders to them immediately:

(l. 627)   Lykynge! be-lyue
late clothe hym swythe
In robys ryve
    With ryche a-ray. . . .

(Liking! alive!
Let clothe him swythe [quick]
In robës ryve [fine]
    With rich array. . . .)

Lust-liking leaps to it, and thus must have ascended the scaffold
with the others to respond so quickly. He answers:

(l. 635)   trostyly,
lord, redy,
Je vous pry,
    Syr, I say.
in lyckynge & lust
he schal rust,
tyl dethys dust
    do hym to day.

(Trustily,
Lord, ready,
Je vous prie,
    Sir, I say.
In liking and lust
He shall rust,
Till deathë's dust
    Do him to die!)

Folly responds in eight equally short lines, and then a direction
to sound trumpets comes again!

Thus World has invited Mankind up from the Place to the
scaffold; he is followed up by his three seducers; once aloft, World
orders them to take Mankind away and dress him fittingly.

And so we encounter another problem.

This question of the dressing of Mankind we have discussed in a previous chapter. We suppose, now, that all that is involved is that they simply pass through the curtain into a concealed place at the back of the scaffold, or even merely draw the front curtain over as before. However it be, the play now suddenly changes. A practical necessity is of course involved; Mankind must be given time to change. How is the show to be kept going?

As the trumpet notes die away, we see the form this interlude is to take—we find ourselves distracted from World's scaffold by the introduction of a new character.

He is not heralded by any direction, so we do not know exactly whence he comes; but there are two observations to be made— that he speaks as a *travelling* character or as one having no fixed home, and that he speaks unmistakably as from the Place, not from a raised scaffold.

The inclination, under such conditions, is to suppose the entrance to be from the Pavilion, by way of the bridge and gap. If this is true here, then what happens is as follows; when the curtain closes over the Western scaffold and hides the growing Man and his investment in the rich garments of the World, and as the trumpet flourish fades, so a voice is heard from the grass at the South-West, and there comes across the bridge over the ditch, and through the Gap in the hill, a motley figure, not unlike Autolycus trolling his wandering entrance in *A Winter's Tale*. The audience turns to take in this new-comer strolling forward along the path by which they themselves entered from their own streets and homes. And they hear him call:

(l. 651) all þyng*is* I crye a-gayn þe pes
    to knyt & knaue; þis is my kende. . . .
    of talys vn-trewe is al my mende;
      Man*n*ys bane a-bowty*n* I ber*e*. . . .
    I am þe werldys messengere;
      my name is Bacbytere.

    (All things I cry against the peace
     To Knight and Knave; this is my kind. . . .
    Of tales untrue is all my mind;
      Man's bane about I bear. . . .
    I am the World's messenger;
     My name is Backbiter.)

It is a rich speech of 52 lines. Like Mankind's first, 'wandering'
speech, it is divided into four equal stanzas, and it is, in an exactly
similar way, studded with references to 'walking' and 'wending'—
therefore again, perhaps, we have here an instance of a 'processional' speech addressed to successive groups of audience in turn.
There are some memorable passages. Backbiter says his pro-
fession is:

(l. 668)   to speke fayre be-forn, & fowle be-hynde,

(l. 672)   . . . I am feller þanne a fox.
        fleterynge & flaterynge is my lessun;
        with lesyngis I tene boþe tour & town,
        with letterys of defamacyoun
        I bere here in my box. . . .

(l. 679)   to may not to-gedyr stonde,
        but I, Bakbyter, be þe thyrde. . . .

    (To speak fair before and foul behind.

        . . . I am feller than a fox.
    Flettering and flattering is my lesson;
    With lyings I injure both tower and town,
    With letters of defamation
    I bear here in my box . . .

    Two may not together stand
    But I, Backbiter, be the third . . .)

So he goes strutting and boasting—an ill-famed pilgrim, with a
pouch on his back; and as he draws to the end of his parade, his
lines show the reason for his introduction; they conclude:

(l. 696)   For whanne Mankynde is cloþyd clere,
        þanne schal I techyn hym þe wey
        to þe dedly synnys seuene.
        Here I schal a-bydyn with my pese,
        þe wronge to do hym for to chese,
        for I þynke þat he schal lese
        þe lyth of hey heuene.

    (For when Mankind is clothëd clear,
    Then shall I teachë him the way
    To the deadly sinnës seven.

Here I shall abide and hold my peace,
The wrong to do him for to choose,
For I think that he shall lose
The light of high heaven.)

And his purpose of filling in the interval of the investment of Man now over, he presumably squats on the grass in the crowd and complacently awaits events, and plots. . . .

These events follow at once. World's curtain opens again and discovers the familiar group on the scaffold—but now with a striking difference, as is shown in Lust-liking's opening lines:

(l. 703) Worthy World, in welthys wonde,
    here is Mankynde ful fare in folde!

(Worthy World, in all wealth dwelling,
 Here is Mankind, full fair in fold!)

Man is invested! The vaunting description goes on. Folly echoes it as usual, and then World, oozing with satisfaction once more, thanks them:

(l. 729) now, Folye, fayre þee be-fall!
    & Lustë, blyssyd be þou ay!
   3e han browth Mankynde to myn hall
    Sertis in a nobyl a-ray. . .
   welcum Mankynde! . . .
    loke þou holde myn hendë feste,
     & euere þou schalt be ryche.

(Now, Folly, fair thee befall!
 And Liking blessed be thou aye!
Ye have brought Mankind to mine hall,
 Certes, in a noble array. . .
Welcome, Mankind! . . .
 Look thou hold my handë fast
 And ever thou shalt be rich!)

Man's compliant answer is:

(l. 742) Whou schul I, but I þi hestis helde?
    þou werkyst with me holy my wyll . . .

(How should I but in thy hestës hold?
 Thou workest with me wholly my will! . . .)

And World makes many promises to him.

But the time is now ready to begin a further development in the drama—to move Man away from this scaffold and on into other spheres of action. World prepares for this with a command to him:

(l. 768)   go to my tresorer, Syr Couetouse!
          loke þou tell hym as I seye!
        bydde hym make þee mayster in his house,
          with penys & powndis for to pleye.
        loke þou ȝeuë not a lous
          of þe day þat þou schalt deye.
        messenger, do now þyne vse!
          Bakbytere, teche hym þe weye!

        (Go to my Treasurer, Sir Covetyse;
          Look thou tell him as I say.
        Bid him make thee master in his house,
          With pennies and pounds for to play.
        Look that thou give not a louse
          For the day that thou shalt die!
        Messenger, do now thine use!
          Backbiter, show him the way!)

The transition is engineered neatly. The scandalmongering wanderer below on the grass sits up at his Lord's call to him, and trots to the foot of the scaffold, eagerly lifting his face up to its splendid occupants, and he cries:

(l. 783)   haue don, Mankynde, & cum doun!
          I am þyne owyn page.

        (Have done, Mankind, and come down—
          I am thine own page!)

Then—swinging his arm round to the North-East, and pointing right across the circle:

(l. 787)   lo, where syr Coueytyse sytt,
          & bydith us in his stage.

        (Lo, where Sir Covetyse sits
          And bideth us on his stage.)

So Covetyse's scaffold is now open, with a solitary figure waiting there.

Mankind and World exchange farewells and Man is ready to descend to Backbiter, leave the World's scaffold and all those upon

it, and take the longish journey through the people in the Place to
Covetyse. No stage direction shows this, but the lines are quite
clear. How, now, is this journey to be filled up? For the crossing
will take some minute or two.

It is interesting to see that another 'fill-up' scene is now inserted.
Two stanzas—that is, 26 lines, perhaps taking a little over a minute
—follow, with an interesting indication in them, for they are divided between the Good and Bad Angels; therefore we must understand that the Bad Angel has descended with Mankind. The Good
Angel we left forlorn, not quite certain where to place him, but
supposing him on a stool, inconspicuous against one of the legs of
the Castle. As Mankind and Backbiter, with the Bad Angel, begin
their cross, the Good Angel is stirred by this significant descent
into action once more. From his place he cries:

(l. 791) alas, Jhesu, jentyl justyce!
 wheder may mans Good Aungyl wende?
now schal careful Coueytyse,
 Mankende trewly al [to-]schende . . .

(Alas! Jesu, gentle justice!
 Whither may Man's Good Angel wend!
Now shall Careful Covetyse
 Mankind truly all to-shend [tear] . . .)

and so forth. . . . The Bad Angel hears the plaint and lifts his head
at his old enemy's voice, retorting in fine contempt:

(l. 804) ȝa! whanne þe fox prechyth, kepe wel ȝore gees!
 he spekyth as it were a holy pope.
goo, felaw, & pyke of þe lys
 þat crepe þer up-on þi cope! . . .
  tyl man be dyth in dethys dow,
  he seyth neuere he hath I-now;
  þer-fore, goode boy, cum blow
   at my neþer ende!

(Yah! When the fox preacheth, keep well your geese!
 He speaketh as it were a holy pope.
Go, fellow, and pick off the lice
 That creep there upon thy cope! . . .
  Till Man be dight in deathë's do
  He sayeth never he hath enough;
  Therefore, good boy, come blow
   At my nether end!)

And with such angelic bawdry, the passage across the plain is over
and the Good Angel left in contempt, and Man and his leaders are
arrived at Covetyse's scaffold. Or perhaps the party splits and only
Man and Backbiter go to the scaffold, leaving the Bad Angel to
turn his back on the Good and stay glowering in the centre on his
stool. This is the more likely because the Angels take no more part
in the action nor have anything to say until l. 1263, which is some
half an hour away. Covetyse watches the new-comers and waits to
learn the nature of the visitation. Backbiter enlightens him:

(l. 819)   I, Bakbytere, þyn owyn knaue,
        haue browt Mankynde vn-to þine hall.
    þe Worlde bad þou schuldyst hym haue. . . .

(I, Backbiter, thine own knave,
    Have brought Mankind unto thine hall.
The World bade thou shouldst him have. . . .)

Covetyse—perhaps rising—here takes full hold of the plot. Now
we are well engaged with the particular conception of the playwright's that is going to be the kernel of his drama. With infinite
courtesy this figure on the North-Eastern scaffold receives Mankind, and gives us in his lines both the gist of the dramatic argument and a perfect example of the technique of medieval, circular
staging. Addressing the pair below he says:

(l. 830)   Ow, Mankynde! blyssyd mote þou be!
        I haue louyd þee derworthly many a day,
    & so I wot wel þat þou dost me;
        cum up & se my ryche a-ray!
    it were a gret poynte of pyte
        but Coueytyse were to þi pay.
    Sit up ryth here in þis se;
        I schal þee lere of werldlys lay,
        þat fadyth as a flode.
    with good I-now I schal þee store;
    & ȝyt oure gamë is but lore,
    but þou coueyth mekyl more,
        þanne euere schal do þee goode.

(Ow, Mankind! Blessed may thou be!
    I have loved thee dearworthily many a day,
And so I wot well that thou dost me.
    Come up! And see my rich array!

It were a great point for pity
  But Covetyse were to thy pay!
Sit up right here in this seat;
  I shall thee learn of worldë's lay,
    That fadeth as a flood.
  With goods enough I shall thee store;
  And yet our gamë is but lost
  Unless thou covet'st mickle more
    Than ever shall do thee good!)

And he explains in detail how Man must give himself to simony, extortion and false assay, help no one without repay, avoid giving his servants their due, destroy his neighbours, fail in his tithes, turn the deaf ear to beggars, be subtle of sleights in business-dealings, buy and sell by false weights. And Mankind falls for it all. He mounts the North-Eastern scaffold as he is bid, and sinks in smug satisfaction into the throne that Covetyse has vacated.

What happens now to Backbiter?

This question is typical of several that arise in this play, when we find that a character, after finishing his speeches and his immediate business, has no direction marked for him to go off. In point of fact, Backbiter now has nothing to do from the moment when he hands over Mankind to Covetyse at l. 829 until l. 1734, when he is to come crying into the ring at the Bad Angel's shout, after Mankind has slipped into the protection of the Castle. Thus he is suspended for something like a thousand lines, or a quarter of the play.

One feels he could not well have stayed in the Place for getting on for an hour. He might have followed Man up to Covetyse's scaffold and then left them both by slipping out at the back. But he is a terrestrial creature; on no occasion in the play do we meet with a clear indication that he ever ascends any scaffold. He might, perhaps, have turned on his heel and quietly walked back over the grass across the whole theatre to leave by the Gap, and so take refuge in the Pavilion again. Yet this long cross would distract from the scene which is to come.

I am inclined to one of the following alternatives: either that he ascended Covetyse's scaffold, went out the back of it and made his way to the Pavilion round the crest of the Hill, behind the spectators; or simply that he did not ascend, but turned and circled the Place along that 'dead' rim, between spectators and Hill-foot, where few people stood—and where I have shown the horses being led in in Fig. 21. So, he would also get back unobtrusively to the Pavilion. And there, for the time we leave him.

Returning to the show; we are soon to see one of the most colourful passages of pageantry, of poetry and of moralizing that the play contains. Before we begin it, let us take the opportunity to pause and make sure that we are clear about the disposition of all the players so far.

Only one scaffold is open at this moment—the one in the North-East where Covetyse is chatting to Mankind. World, the Devil and Flesh are withdrawn and probably hidden. Pride, Wrath and Envy are still with the Devil on his scaffold, also hidden; and Sloth, Lechery and Gluttony are with Flesh. Lust-liking and Folly we last saw on World's scaffold, after the investiture of Man. They too are now hidden, and in fact have probably slipped out the back of the scaffold and round the Hill to the Pavilion, and are (perhaps) now changing—for they have no further appearance to make in the play. The next new-comers are to be Shrift and Penance; these two new characters could well be played by the same two actors. Back-biter has slipped away as we have seen. The Good Angel is unaccounted for, and possibly still sits on his stool by the Castle, while the Bad Angel (similarly unaccounted for) may be hunched waiting on another stool by the opposite leg of the Castle—still chewing the cud of their recent argument.

Now we may begin to listen to what Covetyse is saying to Man and hear how he stirs up the play at this point to one of its high passages. He is concluding:

(l. 892)   here I feffe þee in myn heuene
             with gold & syluer, lyth as leuene;
             þe dedly synnys, allë seuene,
                I schal do comyn in hy.

             (Here I feoff thee in mine heaven
             With gold and silver, light as leaven;
             The deadly sins, all seven,
                I shall have coming in haste.)

And thereat he comes to the front of the scaffold and cries aloud over the arena:

(l. 896)   Prydë, Wrathë, & Envye,
             Com forthe, þe deuelys chyldryn þre!

Lechery, Slawth, & Glotonye,
  to mans flesch ȝe are fend*is* Fre;
  . . . com to Mankynde & to me,
    fro ȝour*e* dowty de*n*nys!
  as dukys dowty, ȝe ȝou dresse!
  wha*n*ne ȝe sex be comme, I gesse,
  þa*n*ne be we seuene, & no lesse,
    of þe dedly sy*n*nys.

(Pride, Wrath and Envy!
  Come forth ye Devil's children three!
Lechery, Sloth and Gluttony!
  To Man's Flesh ye are fiendës free.
  . . . come to Mankind and to me
    from your doughty deans.
  As dukes doughty, ye you dress.
  When ye six be come, I guess,
  Then we be seven (and no less!)
    Of the deadly sinnës.)

Now the pageantry begins. First, the Devil's scaffold opens, with its occupants in full panoply. The Servants hear the summons and in turn take leave of their Master before preparing to descend. Pride speaks first, saying:

(l. 909)   Wond*er* hyȝe howt*is*, on hyll, herd I houte:
      Koueytyse kryeth; . . .
      . . . Syr Belyal, bryth of ble!
      to ȝou I recomau*n*de me:
      haue good day, my fad*er* fre,
        For I goo to Coveytyse.

      (Wonder-high shouts on hill heard I hailed;
      Covetyse crieth . . .
      . . . Sir Belial, bright of blee,
      To you I recommendë me.
      Have Good Day, my father free;
        For I go to Covetyse.)

Then Wrath speaks, answers the call and bids farewell also:

(l. 931)   Syr Belyal blak & blo,
      haue good day! now I goo
      for to fell þi foo
        W*ith* wyckyd wage.

> (Sir Belial, black and blue!
> Have Good Day; now I go
> For to fell thy foe
>   With wicked wage.)

Lastly Envy:

(l. 944)
> Belsabubbe! now haue good day!
> for we wyl wendyn in good a-ray,
> al þre in fere, as I þe say,
>   Pride, Wrath, & Envye.

> (Beelzebub, now have Good Day!
> For we will wend in good array,
> All three in fere [brotherhood], as I thee say—
>   Pride, Wrath and Envy.)

And the Devil wishes them well and tells them to catch Mankind. Immediately the curtain of Flesh's scaffold opens and similarly there the three Servants take leave of their Master and receive his blessing:

(l. 1000)
> Glotony & slawth, Fare-wel, . . .
> & Lecherye, my Dowter so dere . . .

> (Gluttony and Sloth, farewell . . .
> And Lechery, my daughter so dear . . .)

(thus we are clearly informed that Lechery is played as a woman; the rest are men). The sixth stage direction now follows: '*Then* Pride, Wrath, Envy, Gluttony, Lechery *and* Sloth *shall go to* Covetyse. . . .'

Therefore we are clear of guesses here. We are informed that the six decked Sins go down from the scaffolds, one trio on the North and one on the South, and begin to promenade across the Place. Possibly they take a direction such that the two parties can meet; then, having joined, they bend their way all together to the feet of Mankind, where he sits waiting them with Covetyse on the North-East scaffold.

As they form up in the lane before the scaffold, Pride announces their arrival in response to the summons. There now follow some 240 lines of magnificent boast and answer as each Sin dedicates himself to Mankind, is accepted and, in his turn, climbs the scaffold and seats himself in court about Mankind's throne. This is the longest, single, sustained 'scene' so far, and it is carried off with fine, large poetry and a good deal of shrewd moral advice. The Seven Sins speak with cynical frankness among themselves, and the whole effect is heightened because, through it all, Mankind sits beaming from his throne, hearing every word they say, yet missing the drift from the first to the last. For instance, Covetyse can say (as he explains to the others standing below why he called them) the following, without Mankind appreciating an inkling of it:

(l. 1041)   late Iche of vs take at othyr,
        & set Mankynde on a stomlynge stol.
          whyl he is here on lyve,
          lete vs lullyn hym in oure lust,
          tyl he be dreuyn to dampnynge dust;
          Colde care schal ben hys crust,
              to deth whanne he schal dryve.

(Let each of us take at other
  And set Mankind on a stumbling-stool.
      While he is here alive,
      Let us lull him in our lust
      Till he be driven to dampening dust.
      Cold care shall be his crust,
          To death when he shall drive.)

Now follow six symmetrical groups of speeches; in each of them one of the Sins gives a stanza describing the quality he bestows on Man, then Man replies with a stanza of his own in acknowledgement and appreciation, and finally follow two couplets —one from the Sin and one from Man—neatly bringing the Sin up from the Place to sit with Man on the scaffold. Says Pride:

(l. 1055)   bete boyes tyl þey blede . . .
        Frende, fadyr, & moder dere,
        bowe hem not in non manere . . .
    . . . blowë mekyl bost,
        with longe Crakows on þi schos;
        Jagge þi Clothis in euery cost . . .

(Beat boys till they bleed! . . .
  Friend, father and mother dear,
  Bow [to] them not in no manner . . .
. . . blow mickle boast,
  With long Cracows [toes] on thy shoes;
Dag thy clothes on every side . . .)

And—'Pride, be Jesu! thou sayest well!' answers Man. Pride ends:

(l. 1087)   I þi bowre to a-byde,
             I com to dwellë be þi syde.

             (In thy bower to abide,
             I come to dwell by thy side.)

This is intended literally (as we shall see from the other speeches)
and Pride now climbs up the steps, and appears in all his glory on
the stage with Man.

Wrath speaks next, and he so intoxicates little Man with his
incitements that Man cries in reply, drunken with power:

(l. 1104)   Wrethë! for þi councel hende,
                haue þou Goddis blyssynge & myn!
             what caytyf of al my kende
                wyl not bowe, he schal a-byn;
             with myn veniaunce I schal hym schende,
                & wrekyn me, be Goddis yne.
             raþer or I schulde bowe or bende,
                I schuld be stekyd as a swyne
                     with a lothly launce.
                be it erly or late,
                who-so make with me debate,
                I schal hym hyttyn on þe pate,
                     & takyn a-non veniaunce.

             (Wrath, for thy counsel kind
                Have thou God's blessing and mine!
             What caitiff of all my kind
                Will not bow, he shall abyne [suffer]!
             With my vengeance I shall him shend
                And wreak me, by Goddë's eyes!
             Rather than I should bow or bend,
                I would be stuck through like a swine
                     With a loathly lance.
                Be it early or late,
                Whoso make with me debate
                I shall him hit upon the pate!
                     And take anon my vengeance!)

Envy advises Man:

(l. 1123)   whanne any of þy neyboris wyl þryve,
             loke þou haue Envye þer-to . . .
             bakbyte hym . . .
             Kyll hym a-non, with-owtyn knyve. . . .

(When any of thy neighbours will thrive,
  Look thou have envy thereto . . .
  Backbite him . . .
  Kill him withouten knife. . . .)

Yes, yes, calls Man eagerly—'for ilke man calleth other "whore"
and "thief"! . . . Come up to me above . . .'. And Envy quietly
responds, as he mounts, with the interesting line which we noted
earlier:

(l. 1147)   I clymbe fro þis crofte,
             with Mankynde, o, to syttyn on lofte.

             (I climb from this croft
             With Mankind, ho, to sit up aloft.)

Gluttony ends with gay grossness:

(l. 1159)   . . . chyde þese fastyng cherlys!
             loke þou haue spycys of goode odoure,
             to Feffe & fede þy fleschly floure;
             & panne mayst þou bultyn in þi boure,
                 & serdyn gay gerlys.

                 (. . . chide those fasting churls!
             Look thou have spices of good odour,
             To feoff and feed thy fleshly flower—
             And then may'st thou bolt thee in thy bower
                 And get into gay girls!)

Man ruefully agrees that:

(l. 1166)   I am no day wel, be sty nor strete,
                 tyl I haue wel fyllyd my mawe . . .

             (I am no day well, by sty nor street,
                 Till I have well filled my mawe . . .)

Lechery sweetly takes up:

(l. 1181)   ȝa! whanne þi flesche is fayrë fed,
                 panne schal I, louely Lecherye,
             be bobbyd with þee in [þi] bed;
                 here-of serue mete & drynkis trye.
             In louë, þi lyf schal be led;
                 be a lechour tyl þou dye;

þi nedys schal be þe better sped,
  If [þou] ȝyf þee to fleschly folye
    tyl deth þee down drepe.
  lechery, syn þe werld be-gan,
  hath a-vauncyd many a man.
þerfore, Mankynde, my leue lemman
    I my cunte þou schalt crepe.

(Yes! When thy flesh is fairly fed,
  Then shall I, lovely Lechery,
Be bobbëd with you in your bed!
  Thereto, serve meat and drinkës rich.
In loving thy life shall be led;
  Be a lecher till you die—
Your needs shall be the better sped
  If you give you to fleshly folly
    Till death you down drip!
  Lechery, since the world began,
  Has advancëd many a man.
  And so Mankind, my dear leman,
    In my cunt thou shalt creep.)

Mankind:

(l. 1194)   a, lechery, wel þee be!
    mans sed in þee is sowe;
  fewe men wyl forsakë þee,
    In any cuntre þat I knowe
  spouse-breche is a frend ryth fre;
    men vse þat mo þanne I-nowe; . . .
      þerfore, cum vp, my berd bryth,
        & reste þee with Mankynde!

(Ah, Lechery! well thee be!
  Man's seed in thee is sown.
Few men will forsakë thee
  In any country that I know.
Spouse-breach is a friend right free—
  Men use it more than enough . . .
    Therefore, come up, my birdë bright
      And rest thee with Mankind.)

She counters, as she climbs up:

      I may soth synge:
      'Mankynde is kawt in my slinge.'

> (I may sooth sing—
> Mankind is caught in my sling!)

and he caps with:

> For ony erthyly þynge,
> to bedde þou muste me brynge.

> ('Fore any earthly thing,
> To bed thou must me bring!)

Sloth follows hard upon, with:

(l. 1211) Ʒa! whanne Ʒe be in bedde browth boþe,
> wappyd wel in worthy wede . . .
> whanne þe messë-bellë goth,
> lye stylle, man, & take non hede!
> lappe þyne hed þanne in a cloth
> & take a swet. . . .

> (Yah! When ye be in bed brought both
> Wrappëd well in worthy weed . . .
> When the mass-bell go'th,
> Lie still, man, and take no heed;
> Lap thine head then in a cloth
> And take a sweat. . . .)

After the last ascent is done, Man rises to give his new, grouped companions a final speech of welcome which includes the lines:

(l. 1252) I se no man but þey vse somme
> of þese vij dedly synnys . . .
> . . . with on or oþer he schal be take. . . .

> (I see no men but they use *some*
> Of these seven deadly sins! . . .
> . . . with one or other he shall be taken. . . .)

So ends a splendid, mounting scene, as sustained as any in the play, with Mankind growing in power and desire (and age) through it all and finally triumphing in the peak of perfect manhood. But there is now an interruption. A somewhat bitter comment comes out of the blue, from the centre by the Castle where the Good Angel was, whom we have forgotten:

(l. 1263) So mekyl þe werse, (wele a woo!)

> (So mickle the worse—well-a-way!)

and he bewails the case: What am I to do? Mankind 'doeth me bleykin, bloody blee . . .'.

(l. 1273)   I am a-bowte boþe day & nyth,
              to brynge hys sowle in-to blis bryth;
                  & hym-self wyl it brynge to pyne.

              (I am about it both day and night
              To bring his soul into bliss bright—
                  And himself will bring it to pain!)

This stirs the Bad Angel to scurrilous retort. Then the Good lifts his voice again, trying to pierce the atmosphere of this riotous feast of promises that has just gone on and to bring balance and reason to things again, but 'Alas, Mankind is soiled and sagged in sin!'—when suddenly there pace into the arena, from the opposite side, two sombre figures, one carrying a high lance.

The Good Angel pauses, struck by the sight. The murmuring on Covetyse's scaffold is stilled. The Bad Angel gives one sharp glance and looks away, and sits eyes dropped. The two stride on with even step, the lance's pennon steadily flickering aloft. Every eye in the ring will be turned to them as they pass from the entrance at the Gap and begin to make their way straight along the lane towards the Good Angel in the centre. So grave and sternly do they come that there might be no need for stytelers—the greatest enjoyer of the previous scene might well fall back. . . .

The leading figure reaches the Good Angel and speaks:

(l. 1301)   What! mans aungel, good & trewe!
                  why syest þou, & sobbyst sore?
              sertis, sore it schal me rewe,
                  If I se þee make mornynge more. . . .
              For all felechepys olde & newe,
                  why makyst þou grochynge vnder gore,
                      with pynynge poyntis pale?
                  why was al þis gretynge gunne
                  with sore syinge vndyr sunne?
                  tell me, & I schal, if I cunne,
                      brewe þee bote of bale.

              (What, Man's Angel, good and true!
                  Why sighest thou and sobbest sore?
              Certes, sore it shall me rue
                  If I see thee make mourning more. . . .

> For all fellowships, old and new!
>> Why makest thou grouching under gore—
>>> With pining pointës pale?
>> Why was all this greet begun,
>> With sore sighing under sun?
>> Tell me, and I shall, if I can,
>>> Brew thee boot of bale.)

The Good Angel recognizes him—'Sweet Shrift', he says to him, 'Mankind is set in seven sinne's seat.'

(l. 1323)   þerfore, Schryfte, so God me spede,
            but if þou helpë at þis nede,
            Mankynde gety[t]h neuere oþer mede,
              but peyen with-owtyn ende.

            (Therefore, Shrift, so God me speed,
            Save that thou help him at this need,
            Mankind gets never other mede
              But pain withouten end!)

This does not worry the upright figure or his lance-bearer; Shrift and Penance (they say) will put all that right. And they stride across, pennon flickering again, to Covetyse's crowded scaffold, with Man in the midst of it. The direction is perfectly clear in this; '*Then they shall go to* Mankind, *and* Shrift *shall say*':

(l. 1340)   what, Mankynde! whou goth þis? . . .
            þese lotly lordeynys, awey þou lyfte,
            & cum doun & speke with Schryfte,
            & drawe þee ȝernë to sum thryfte!
              trewly it is þe best.

            (What, Mankind! How goeth this? . . .
            These loathly lordings away thou lift,
            And come down and speak with Shrift
            And draw thee quickly to some thrift—
              Truly, it's the best!)

Man answers: 'Please—Sloth says "Thou might'st ha' come . . . on Palm-Sunday": Thou art come too soon. Therefore, Shrift, go forth till on Good Friday. 'Tend to thee, then, well I may; I have now else to do.' Which, as might be expected, brings the retort from Shrift:

(l. 1358)   ow! þat harlot is now bold!

            (Ow! That harlot is now bold!)

How very fast and vigorously this scene might go with hearty playing, and the audience well worked-up!

In passing, it is interesting to note a small point in the above. Mankind's full opening lines in answer to Shrift are:

(l. 1349)   a, Schryfte! þou art wel be note
here to Slawthe, þat syttyth here-Inne . . .

(Ah, Shrift! Thou art well beknown
Here to Sloth, that sitteth herein . . .)

Is the phrase 'that sitteth *herein*', used of Sloth, some indication of the enclosing scaffold-walls and -top that hooded the group? Or is it a suggestion that in fact Sloth (and the other Sins) have gone *in*, at this point, to sit behind the curtain at the back of the scaffold? The answer is not certain. Either way might prove equally effective for the coming scene.

But to resume Shrift's forthright attack: He goes on: 'Sey, Slawthe, I preyd hy*m* þat . . .' (etc.). If this means, as it seems to do, 'Tell Sloth I asked him that . . .', then it certainly suggests that Sloth is not now present, and that the other Sins have disappeared with him. This we may never be able to decide; but however it be, the gist of the speech is:

(l. 1360)   Sey, Slawthe, I preyd hy*m* þat he wold
Fynd a charter of þi lyue.
Man! þou mayst ben vndyr mold
    longe or þat tyme, . . .
    be-hold þy*n*ne hert, . . .
    & þy*n*ne owyn consyense,
        or, sert*is*, þou dost a-mys.

(Tell Sloth I prayed him that he would
Find a charter of thy life.
Man! Thou may'st be under mould
    Long ere that time! . . .
    Behold thine heart . . .
    And thine own conscience,
        Or, certes, thou dost amiss!)

Man answers, naughtily:

(l. 1371)   3a, Petyr! so do mo!
we haue etyn garlek eu*er*ychone . . .
I dyd neu*er*e so ewyl trewly,
þ*at* oþer han don as ewyl as I . .

(Yeah? By Peter, so do more!
  We have eaten garlic every one. **. . .**
  I did never so evil, truly,
  But others have done as evil as I.)

But—and here the struggle between the two forces takes a very strong note and the gayness dies away—the silent lance-bearer lifts his head to face Man on the scaffold.

Whether it is Man alone who takes the look, or whether all the roisterous Sins are there beside him, we do not know. What is to come might be profoundly effective if Man had to face it alone and deserted; but it might be profoundly effective also if Man spoke through a hypnotized matrix of the Sins, each of them powerless to deflect the point that is being levelled steadily home at Man's heart.

In any event, Penance, the lance-bearer, speaks. This is his only speech in the play, and it is a still and dignified one, after the 'bobbaunce' of all the garrulous Sins, and it well fits into this longish scene of some 300 lines that forms the present period of the play.

(l. 1380)   wi*th* poynt of penau*n*ce I schal hy*m* preue,
      mans pride for to Felle.
    wi*th* þis launce I schal hy*m* leue,
      I-wys, a drope of me*r*cy welle.
    Sorwe of hert, is þat I mene:
      trewly, þe*r* may no tungë telle,
    what waschyth sowlys morë clene
      ffro þe foul[ë] fend of helle,
          þa*n*ne swete sorwe of hert. . . .
    wi*th* my spud of sorwe swote,
    I rechë to þyne hert[ë] rote;
    al þi bale schal torne þee to bote:
      Mankynde, go schryue þee ȝerne!

(With point of penance I shall him preve,
  Man's pride for to fell.
With this lance I shall him leve,
  I wis, a drop of mercy's well.
Sorrow of heart is what I mean—
  Truly there is no tongue can tell
What washeth souls more clean
  From the foul fiend of hell

> Than sweet sorrow of heart! ...
> With my spud of sorrow sweet
> I reach to thine heart's root;
> All thy bale shall turn to boot.
> Mankind, go shrive you soon!)

The last line but three is spoken, I believe, as the accompaniment of the actual action. Thus we see the meaning of this long lance which, without the actor leaving the Place or mixing with the crowd of the Sins, can reach up to the high scaffold, thread through the throng, and pierce to the bared heart of Man with its easing touch.

Mankind answers in a tempest of remorse, and from his stage he even turns to the people watching: 'Lordings! Ye see well all this . . .'. Shrift gently takes over from him:

(l. 1432)   Schryfftë may no man for-sake . . .
        Whanne sorwe of hert[ë] þee hathe take . . .
        . . . torne not a-geyn to þi Folye,
            ffor þat makith dystaunce.
         & if it happe þee turne a-geyn to synne,
         For Goddis loue, lye not longe þer-Inne!
         he þat dothe alway ewyl, & wyl not blynne,
            þat askyth gret venjaunce.

(Shrift may forsake no man . . .
When sorrow of heart thee hath taken, . . .
. . . Turn not again to thy folly,
    For that maketh distance.
And if it hap thou turn again to sin,
For God's love, lie not long therein!
He that doeth always evil and will not blench—
    That asks for great vengeance.)

Man replies:

(l. 1448)   I wyl now al a-mendë me:
                    [tunc descendit ad Confessionem
        I com to þee, Schryfte, al holy, lo!

(I will now all amendë me:
                    [*Then he descends to* Shrift
I come to thee, Shrift, all wholly, lo!)

So we get a further movement in the action, and Man goes down from Covetyse's scaffold to come to Shrift's feet in the Place, and there:

(l. 1493)   but to þe erthe I knele a-down,
        boþe *with* bede & orisou*n*,
        & aske myn absolucio*un*:
          syr Schryfte, I ȝou pray.

        (But to the earth I kneel adown,
        Both with bead and orison;
        And ask mine absolution,
          Sir Shrift, I you pray!)

Shrift assoils him in three quiet and deliberate stanzas. Afterwards Man rises and asks where he may now dwell in safety. Shrift replies, pointing to the tower in the centre of the Place:

(l. 1555) goo ȝone Castel, & kepe þee þe*r*-Inne,
      For [it] is strenger þa*n*ne any in Frau*n*ce: . . .
      Who-so leuyth þere, h*is* lyuys space,
        no sy*n*ne schal hy*m* schende.

     (Go to yon Castle and keep thee therein,
       For it is stronger than any in France . . .
       Whoso liveth there his lifë's space,
        No sin shall him shend.)

And Man:

(l. 1562) a, Schryfte! blessyd mote þou be!
      þis castel is here but at honde;

      (Ah, Shrift! Blessed mayst thou be!
      This castle is here just at hand.)

and he moves on over the grass and comes very close to the Castle.

The Siege of the Castle: 'But forty winters old'

Let us here recapitulate the state of the scene. The Three Evils are closed in their scaffolds. The Seven Sins are still possibly watching from the one open scaffold at the North-East (or, as we showed, they may have slipped out and left it empty). Backbiter is out of it. Mankind, Shrift and Penance are moving to the centre. That accounts for all the characters save two—the Bad Angel and the Good. We left them at opposite corners of the Castle's feet.

Now, therefore, Mankind is coming very near to them. And, sure enough, his approach arouses them; the Bad Angel leaps up and cries out, barring the way:

(l. 1575)   Ey, what deuyl, man! wedyr schat?
        woldyst drawe now to holynesse?
        goo, felaw, þi goodë gate!
          þou art forty wynter olde, as I gesse; . . .
          late men þat arn on þe pyttis brynke
          ffor-beryn boþe mete & drynke,
          & do penaunce as hem good þynke,
          & cum & pley þee a whyle!

        (Hey! What the devil, Man! Whither set?
        Wouldst draw now to holiness?
        Go on, good man, thy present pace—
          You're but forty winters old, as I guess! . . .
          —Let men that are on the pit's brink
          Forbear both meats and drink
          And do penance, as them good think—
          And come *thou* and play awhile!)

(The reference to Mankind's age as now being forty years, is most significant in suggesting how this comprehensive role turns over the whole cycle of man's life in its few hours; we see him growing in strength and power all the time up to this, and it might very well be grimly implicit in his playing that we were also to see him grow on into age and decline.) Next the Good Angel takes up the cudgels in his ancient battle, and begs Mankind 'forth wend thy way, and do nothing after his rede'. Mankind here gently responds to him, his first age of wholesale sinning done:

(l. 1601)   goode aungyl, I wyl do as þou wylt,
        In londe whyl my lyfe may leste;
        ffor I fynde wel in holy wryt,
          þou counseylyste euere for þe beste.

        (Good Angel, I will do as thou wilt
        In land, while my life may last,
        For I find well in holy Writ
          Thou counsel'st ever for the best.)

And at that point we very unfortunately have a break in the manuscript.

       *   *   *   *   *

This matter of the break is not without complication. Pollard offers a study of the facts in his 'Introduction', p. xxxi. What in effect seems to have happened is that the scribe of this manuscript has copied an earlier manuscript from which there were two leaves missing—one at this particular place in the section, and one at the corresponding place on the opposite side of the sewing-together of the section, that is to say at l. 3030, later on.

As, however, the make-up of the section in the present manuscript seems complete (it is folded up into the same number of leaves as the section bound beside it), we may say nothing is missing from this particular version; but it is a version copied from one that *had* these two leaves missing. The hiatus, therefore, is indicated here by no evidence except the sense, the rhyme and the break in the stanzas. In other words, though no leaf is missing in the binding, the *contents* of a leaf are missing in the sense of the play.

How far can we build up the missing passage?

We may go some way. To begin; a page of this manuscript contains on an average some fifty lines, therefore we lack at this point about a hundred lines, fifty on either side of the leaf.

But it is very likely indeed that the first nine of these formed the completion of Mankind's stanza, of which four lines occur before the break—the stanzas at this point in the play being of thirteen lines.

We can also reconstruct a little at the end of the break in a similar way. The following page begins a series of speeches, each in one stanza of thirteen lines, from Charity, Soberness, Chastity, Busyness and Largity. They speak in turn welcoming Mankind to the Castle. These are the last five of the Cardinal Virtues in the order given in the List of Characters. For the first two of the Seven on the list, Meekness and Patience, we have no speeches. Thus, it is almost certain that the last twenty-six lines of the missing passage consisted of two thirteen-line stanzas, one from Meekness and one from Patience.

This would leave us with some 65 lines unaccounted for (50+ 50)—(9+26). If the stanzas were of regular length at this point, we should thus have five stanzas unaccounted for. On pure guesswork alone we might allow ourselves to expect that the missing two pages were made up as follows:

ll. 1604/1–1604/9, part stanza finishing Man's speech.
       10–22, possibly a final protest from the Bad Angel.

23–35, possibly a counterspeech from the Good Angel.
36–48, possibly a reaffirmation from Man.
49–61, possibly his introduction by Shrift to the Virtues.
62–74, possibly Man's first speech to the Virtues.
75–87, most likely Meekness's welcome to Man.
88–100, most likely Patience's welcome to Man.

The welcomes of the other Virtues we have.

What, however, is more hazardous to guess is: what stage direction came here? Was there any instruction to Shrift and Penance to leave the scene? Possibly not; yet we hear no more from them, and they must be supposed to have gone away as they came. Was there any instruction to Mankind to go towards the Castle—something like 'Then Mankind shall go to the Seven Virtues'? This seems more likely. At any rate, it appears that that is what happened.

But whence did the Seven Virtues appear? This is one of the great problems of the presentation, and we have spoken of it before. Unless they came in procession from the Pavilion through the main entrance at some point in the missing pages, there is only one thing to suppose, that is that they have been hidden in the upper part of the Castle-tower all this time, and here come down by a ladder to the space beneath the tower and stand round Mankind's Bed, ready to greet him.

As I have said, the manuscript picks up again with Charity's speech. This we have in full. She begs Man to have an eye to charity in all things.

Maybe here the Seven Virtues are in circle, round the tower, facing outward, and Mankind goes to each in turn. At any rate, by each he is greeted in the same kind of speech and advised to observe that virtue represented by each speaker. Soberness says:

(l. 1618)   In abstinens lede þi lyf!
                take but skylful refeccyon;
             for gloton kyllyth w*ith*-owty*n* knyf,
                & dystroyeth þi co*m*plexion. . . .

             (In abstinence lead thy life;
                Take but rational refection.
             For gluttony killeth withouten knife,
                And destroyeth thy complexion. . . .)

187

And Busyness:

(l. 1650)   . . . Do sum-what al-wey for loue of me,
þou þou schuldyst but thwyte a stycke;
with bedys, sum tyme þee blys!
Sum tyme rede, & sum tyme wryte,
& sum tyme pleye at þi delyte:
þe deuyl þee waytyth with dyspyte
whanne þou art in Idylnesse.

(Do somewhat always for love of me,
Though thou should'st but thwyte a stick;
With beads sometime thee bliss,
Sometime read, and sometime write,
And sometime play at thy delight.
The devil thee waiteth with despite
When thou art in idleness.)

Mankind answers these Ladies, lovely and light, in two stanzas. Then Meekness, as leader, makes a concluding speech which contains a matter of significance for the action. Man asks for mercy; she replies:

(l. 1696)   Mercy may mende all þi mone:
Cum in here at þynne owyn wylle!
we schul þee fendë fro þi fon
if þou kepe þee in þis castel stylle;
stonde here-Inne, as stylle as ston;
þanne schal no dedly synne þee spylle: . . .

(Mercy may mendë all thy moan.
Come in here, at thine own will;
We shall thee fendë from thy foes
If thou keep thee in this Castle still.
Stand herein, as still as stone,
Then shall no deadly sin thee spill. . . .)

But now we have to record a curious aberration of editing. Some way ahead, at l. 1909, in the E.E.T.S. edition is printed the short stage direction 'tunc mutabit'. It occurs in a raging, ramping speech of the Devil's, as he rouses his forces to war against the Castle. But it has no bearing whatever on that speech.

On turning to the facsimile of the manuscript we are surprised to find that this stage direction is not present. But there is some reason for this; at this point (just to add still another complication) two leaves have become misplaced. Because of this, the stage direction in question was itself misplaced in the transcription, when the position of the leaves was corrected, but not the stage direction. In fact, the stage direction actually appears at the point we have reached—or rather after the words 'in this Castle still' in the above speech.

But, having restored its position we are, for the moment, just as puzzled by it. We have recorded it as No. 9 on pp. 36 and 38. There it will be seen that we have differed on the transcription of the abbreviated original, and believe it to be 'tūc intᵃbit' not 'tūc mtᵃbit'.

This reading was decided before the full study of the course of the performance was undertaken, and its significance was put aside to be examined later. Now it comes to our attention; and now the significance of the position and of the interpretation of the word seem amply vindicated. For, in fact, what we now have is the speech, with its direction included—'Come in here . . . keep thee in this Castle still. (*Then he shall enter*) Stand herein as still as stone. . . .' This would seem a proper reading.

Furthermore, I think there is now brought out a suggestion of significance—that after circling round outside the ring of Virtues, Mankind is invited to penetrate it and thus to come not only into the circle, but into the area under the tower: he is invited ('Come in')—he does so ('*Then he shall enter*')—and then he stands inside ('Stand herein . . .'). The action seems indisputable.

If our reading is just, Mankind is now securely encircled by the guardian Virtues in the shadow of the Castle. This done, there follows the tenth stage direction, after l. 1708—'*Then they shall sing "Eterne rex altissime," etc.*' And this was quite probably a fine chorus, accompanied by organ and other instruments, and sung in the church tradition.

During all this the Bad Angel is silent. We have no indication of his position, as usual. Perhaps he is sitting disgruntled at the edge of the central area, watching. (Or it might even be that the Two Angels have a pair of pulpits of their own at some unspecified places, and speak from them as the angels are seen to do in some of the alabaster tables.) As soon as the song is over, however, Meekness sums up with a stanza of blessing, and at this the Bad Angel can no longer keep silent, and brings in discord with all his might. Perhaps the Virtues' circle contracts here, leaving the central 'stage' clearer. At any rate the Bad Angel 'takes the stage' in all conscience. He cries:

(l. 1718)   Nay! be Belyals bryth bonys,
        þer schal he no whyle dwelle . . .
        þe synnys seuene, þe kyngis thre, . . .
        scharpely þei schul helpyn me,
        þis Castel for to breke.

        (No! By Belial's bright bones!
        There shall he no while dwell . . .
        The Sins seven, the Kings three . . .
        Sharply they shall helpen me
        This Castle for to break.)

And he calls out at the very top of his lungs:

(l. 1727)   Howe! Flypyrgebet! Bakbytere!
        ȝerne, oure message, loke þou make!
        blythe a-bowt loke þou bere!
        sey, Mankynde his synnys hath for-sake;
        with ȝene wenchys he wyl hym were.
        al to holynesse he hath hym take;
        In myn hert it doth me dere;
        þe bost þat þo moderis crake,
        My galle gynnyth to grynde.
        Flepyrgebet! ronne up-on a rasche!
        byd þe Werld, þe Fend, & þe Flesche,
        þat þey com to fytyn fresche,
        to wynne a-ȝeyn Mankynde.

        (Hey! Flippergibet! Backbiter!
        Quick; our message look thou take;
        Blythe about, look thou bear.
        Say Mankind his sinnës hath forsake;
        With yon wenches he will him wear;
        All to holiness he hath him take.
        In my heart it doth me dear,
        The boast that those 'mothers' crack;
        My gall 'ginneth to grind!
        Flippergibet! Run upon a rush!
        Bid the World—the Fiend—the Flesh—
        That they come to fight afresh
        To win again Mankind!)

Backbiter comes darting in with great, long beggar's strides from the Pavilion during this stanza, and runs to the Bad Angel in the centre, pausing to receive his orders in the last lines. Then he is off running again:

(l. 1740)   I go, I go, on groundë glad,
        swyfter þannë schyp with rodyr! . . .

        (I go! I go! On groundë glad—
        Swifter than a ship with rudder . . .)

and in nine lines he has rushed across, and up the lane to the Devil's scaffold in the North. Direction No. 11 leaves us in no doubt—'*Then he shall go to* Belial'.

The whole pace of the show has been lifted now. The slow and mazy motions that may have been suggested by the circling Virtues give way as dramatically as can be to alarums and excursions. At the Devil's feet, Backbiter's lines come tumbling out:

(l. 1749)   heyl, set in þyn selle!
        heyl, dynge deuyl in þi delle!
        heyl, lowe in helle!
        I cum to þee, talys to telle.

        (Hail, set in thy cell!
        Hail, dingë devil in thy dell!
        Hail, low in hell!
        I come to thee tales to tell.)

(Surely here is a piece of false alliteration! If ever a line called for '*high* in hell', the third one here does! Can it be that some careful improver could not easily brook the adjective, and ruined the sound with his logical 'low'? At any rate he overlooked 'In high hell shall be thyne house;' at l. 3078.)

Now, down to l. 2427, there is scarcely any break in a tearing scene of anger and excitement. Not till Covetyse turns the tide of battle after 675 lines of rising onslaught do the tempo and tension fall to the working-day pace. Our description will scarcely keep up with it. But we must, while there is yet time, make an attempt here to paint the picture in full as we see it at present.

The play has been going some hour and three-quarters perhaps. It is very nearly at its half-way point. The picture before us is the thronged circular theatre, with the Seven Ladies enclosing Mankind in the protection of the central tower; an outraged Bad Angel has sent a message hot-foot to summon all the evil powers to attack them. The Virtues possibly withdraw and mount into the body of the tower to await the outcome. Meanwhile the messenger has reached the Northern scaffold and hailed the Devil.

What follows is perhaps a slight confirmation of the use of scaffold curtains, since, if the Devil had been evident on his scaffold all this time, and watching the refuge of Man, then one presumes he would not have needed to be advised of it by the messenger, Backbiter. But advised he is, and thus we are led to suppose that the Devil did not see the passage to the Castle, and that either he had retired into the booth behind his scaffold, or that the curtain upon it had been drawn to conceal him and his seat. On the whole I tend to favour the latter idea.

The Devil's curtain, then, flashes open and we look to hear the Messenger explain the situation to him. This Backbiter does in a normal stanza, saying that Mankind has gone under the protection of Meekness into the refuge of the Castle. At the end of his speech we are faced with something of a puzzle. The Devil does not immediately reply, but instead we have a stage direction; and it is one that is not easy to read. It is No. 12 in our list. Furnivall records it as 'tunc vertunt Superbia, Invidia, & Ira'. We are unable to interpret his verb *vertunt*. The manuscript seems rather to offer 'vtanᵗ' but the handwriting is not clear. We have proposed 'intanᵗ' expanding it to *intrant*, 'they enter'. But there is only one other possible example of the use of this word in the whole of these stage directions, and that is in No. 8—itself difficult to read, but seeming to relate to a movement when Mankind did in fact *enter* the Castle.

Here, however, it is difficult to see just what it is that Pride, Envy and Wrath can be said to *enter* or to go *into*. If they be supposed to enter the theatre, then this is the only example in the play of the use of this word in such a connexion. If they be supposed to enter upon the Devil's scaffold, then their action is rather one of *coming out* (from concealment behind), than of *going in*. We must beware of investing the term, familiar as it is today on the stage, with a modern flavour. In short, here is a stage direction of which I find it very difficult to make a convincing interpretation.

But whatever it means in detail, the general effect is clear, for Pride, Envy and Wrath do appear and begin to speak at once. Whence they come we do not know.

Pride, as spokesman, evidently having heard the news, immediately states that he and his companions are all ready 'throats to cut', in two quick lines.

But the Devil turns on them in a great rage, loads them with abuse for letting Mankind slip through their fingers, and we straightway come upon another puzzling stage direction (No. 13), which appears to read '& verberab^t eos sī terrā'. This we can translate 'and he shall beat them over (?) the ground'—that is to say, expanding the last part into 'super terram'.

But the significance of 'super terram' is very uncertain. The general impression is straightforward enough, but the phrase is puzzling so far as conveying exactly what was done. Undoubtedly the Devil sets upon the Three Sins—but where were they standing? If they were on his scaffold when he began on them, then does 'he beats them *over the ground*' mean that he beats them to the ladder, and down it, and so into the Place? Perhaps it does. But what does the Devil himself do? Does he remain triumphant at the top of the ladder when they have gone, or follow them down and continue beating? The puzzle is that the preposition 'super' (if we have read 'sī' aright) certainly suggests the latter; and yet the action appears clumsy and undignified. What happens next? Do the Sins and the Devil become motionless at the foot of the scaffold while Backbiter, as he is next to do, goes on to the other Evils? Or has the Devil remained above, waiting for the next action? Or do some or all climb the ladder again and sit aloft?

(At moments, I am almost tempted to allow myself to wonder if a Gallicism has not crept into the Latin here, and whether the stage direction should not read 'et verberabit eos *sur* terram'—'and he shall (come down and) beat them on the ground'; that is, he shall come and beat them where they are, in the Place.)

It is clear that we are now entering a passage of some difficulty. Let us, however, go on.

The Devil having beaten his three Sins, Backbiter withdraws a little, laughing at the sport he has caused. He has a whole stanza to himself in which he proposes to play the same trick again upon Flesh's henchmen. Perhaps this stanza is spoken while he moves away from the Northern scaffold, for at its last line is the stage direction (No. 14)—'To Flesh', and he immediately thereafter hails Flesh. Thus he is now before the Southern scaffold, having run across the Place.

The above scene is now repeated with Flesh and Lechery,

Gluttony and Sloth. But there are some curious minor differences, which in so 'symmetrical' a playwright cause us to wonder.

The first is that after Backbiter's stanza of announcement we have a clear direction this time, instead of the obscure 'intrant', and one using quite a different verb; it is 'tunc Caro clamabit ad Gulam, Accidiam, & Luxuriam' (*Then* Flesh *shall call to* Gluttony, Sloth *and* Lechery).

Yet it is odd to see in a verse play, where metre is presumably very important, that no words are provided for Flesh to use in his call. Does he just shout 'Hi!'? Does he call their names? If so he must surely upset the measure of the verse?

Further, there is again the problem—where did he call them *from*? Why did not the Devil also call *his* servants in this way? Is some distinction implied in the mode of entrance of the trios in the two cases? Again we cannot tell.

But Flesh is instructed to call; and Lechery answers swiftly with a couplet, speaking for all three. Flesh rounds on her, just as the Devil did on his, and calls her a 'scallyd mare' and abuses the others. And then comes stage direction No. 16, but again with a difference. The difficulties here in interpretation we have noted on p. 38; but, putting these aside, the point that strikes us now is that we have 'tunc verberabit (?) eos in placeam' ('*Then he shall beat them into the Place*') instead of '. . . super terram'; certainly, now, this suggests that these beatings began on the scaffolds and consisted of driving the three servitors (who must thus have entered on the scaffold) down into the Place—the Master Evil, in each case, remaining aloft.

We go on to see what happens in the third symmetrical case.

Again Backbiter has a stanza of glee at seeing the trouble he is bringing, and runs 'ad Mundum' ("To World'). World greets him just as did the two others before. When, however, Backbiter tells him the bad news, World's action is different from his predecessors'. True, he has to call, not three Vices, but only one—Covetyse. And it seems clear whence he has to call him, for Covetyse has a scaffold of his own, as we know, and we might suppose he would be waiting there. At any rate, World calls him, but calls him (apparently) with a *trumpet*. That is to say, stage direction No. 18 is 'tunc buccinabit cornio (?) ad Avariciam' ('*Then he shall blow on a trumpet* (?) *to* Covetyse'—the difficulty in the interpretation of *cornio* we have stated on p. 38).

Covetyse immediately answers with a couplet. World gives him nine lines of abuse, during which time Covetyse must have come up to him, for direction No. 19 immediately follows—'tunc ver-berabit (?) eum' ('*Then he shall beat him*'), and thus we have a third variant of this culminating direction, but are still no more certain whether any significance lies in the variations.

At all events, this piece of beating ends the particular triple sequence, and we are now to see the play go into the next phase of its action.

Covetyse takes his beating much more practically than the other six, and pleads that, if the beating stops, he will win Mankind back again.

In World's reply the new phase in the action is initiated. World is more businesslike than the Devil and Flesh, and seizes the sug-gestion at once. He cries to Covetyse:

(l. 1880)   by-lyue, my baner up þou bere,
              & be-sege we þe castel ȝerne . . .

              (Be quick! My banner up thou bear,
              And besiege we the Castle sharp! . . .)

and swears of Meekness that 'she shall die upon this green', and snorts terrible vengeance all round. Upon which follows direction No. 20; and here, I think, a reader may see we were not wrong when we warned him of difficulties ahead. This is possibly the most corrupt stage direction of the lot, and we must pause to try and sort it out.

Already, on p. 39, we have noted an error in the version given in the edited text. This version reads:

tunc Mundus, Cupiditas, & Stulticia ibunt ad castellum cum vexillo & domino Demon.

We believed the original should be expanded as 'et *dicet* Demon' not 'et *domino* Demon'.

But we now have to face another, and completely different, puzzle about the direction—namely, that it mentions one name that is not generally used of any character in the play, and another name which is that of a character that has already left the action for good! That is to say, after World, it mentions *Cupidity* and *Folly*! There is, I believe, no explanation but that the scribe has blundered. Presumably he means Covetyse by *Cupiditas*, and Backbiter by *Stulticia*; but Covetyse is called *Avaricia* in Latin, not *Cupiditas*, and *Cupiditas* does not occur in the List of Characters at all. The name *Stulticia*, the Latin name of Folly, refers to Lust-liking's companion in the earlier scenes of the play, when naked Mankind was first led to the feet of the World. We have no reference to this couple after l. 790.

With these things in mind, I feel inclined to amend the direction to '*Then* World, Covetyse *and* Backbiter *go to the Castle with a banner, and the* Devil *(then) says*—'.

Hereafter we go a little more smoothly. The Devil's speech which follows is of two stanzas (in which, after l. 1909, is wrongly inserted direction No. 9 as we have remarked on p. 188) and is spoken amid the hideous hooting of trumpets and war-cries from the hills.

It is interesting to note, in passing, the number of references in this play, and especially in this present passage, to hills and to plains. Clearly, some feature was made of the striking difference in level between the flat, central Place, and the high circular Hill which enclosed it, with the scaffolds on top.

These references have some bearing on our reconstruction for, beside such allusions as we have noticed to the Hill as a place for the spectators to sit, we have also the word 'hill' (or 'height' or some such) brought often into the lines of a speech in which a character is describing something happening *on a scaffold*. The implication is clear; that both provided eminences, and eminences such that the same term could be used about both. This is some confirmation of the theory we adopted in Figs. 19, 20 and 21, that the scaffolds were actually situated on the 'rampart' crowning the Hill.

For examples, we may cite l. 1898, where the World closes his speech with the announcement that his fellow traitors 'howteth high upon yon hill' with their trumpets. Backbiter alludes twice to the Place in what follows; first, as 'yon green grass' (l. 1908), and then as 'yon field' (l. 1915). Flesh speaks of the din as 'an hideous hooting on height' (l. 1939).

But the action is fast proceeding. After stage direction No. 20, the Devil speaks of the World's trumpets as he 'walketh to war, for to cleaven yon Castle clean', and orders his own pennon to be spread, and his banner to be borne forth. Pride responds 'Now,

now! Now, go now! On high hills let us shout' and bears Belial's banner 'before his breast, with comely countenance'.

Flesh takes up and astonishes us with an allusion to his sitting 'in his saddle' (l. 1941)—whence our query whether war-horses were brought in here. (For a similar use of horses see Appendix p. 226.) He proposes to attack 'both with shot and with sling' (l. 1945).

Gluttony answers him with a promise to take a faggot in his hand 'for to setten on fire' (l. 1962) and a 'long lance'.

The passage ends at l. 1969 with stage direction No. 21. We have already noted some of the problems in rendering it (on p. 39); it is either '*Then he* (or *they*) *descend* (or *shall descend*) *into the Place*'. One is inclined to read it now as intending a plural, for clearly more characters than Gluttony descend into the Place to make the attack. We would rather suppose it is the signal for a concerted descent of all characters who are not at present on the ground, so that the complete force rings the arena ready to go to war.

The Bad Angel is transported with delight. He cries 'As armys' —(Aux armes!) and urges them on. Direction No. 22, at l. 1971, suggests he hurries as he speaks first to the Devil and shouts the attack in his face, then in a following stanza to Flesh (l. 1982), and to World (l. 1991). To all he calls for bloodshed.

Now, quietly, above all this warlike preparation, Mankind speaks. How does he dominate it? At first there is no hint, but at l. 2144 it is clear that the defenders of the Castle are 'aloft'. Thus Man must now be speaking from the battlements at the top of the tower, having climbed by a staircase inside. He addresses the audience directly (see l. 2009) in two stanzas and tells them of the lot of Man once he deserts his sins—namely, to be subject to their most vigorous attack.

The Good Angel follows, putting his hope in the Virtues, and comparing them to red roses (the emblems of Christ's passion).

Meekness, as the leader, replies, saying Mankind is safe so long as he stays in the Castle. She and the other Virtues are most likely aloft now, with Man. The Good Angel, as usual, offers no sign whence he speaks.

The Devil breaks in from the Place with a war-speech. Then Pride takes up and challenges Meekness, and a long symmetrical passage now follows, where each of the Devil's three Sins calls one challenging stanza in turn to his corresponding Virtue, and each Virtue has two stanzas of contemptuous return from the battlements.

It is during Patience's answer to Anger that she uses the line (l. 2144)—'If thou art fond enough to come aloft . . .' so demonstrating the Virtues' position. She also adds a point that makes us comment on the edited transcription of the text. Generally, so far as the normal, dialogue lines of the play are concerned (apart, that is, from the stage directions), the transcription seems careful. But when Patience is made to threaten her enemy 'with þese rolys swete & softe', we are sure that the word should be 'rosys' (roses), as indeed the later lines show—for it is with this emblem of the Passion that the Virtues repel the attackers.

Envy, at l. 2157, calls for Man to 'come to us down', thus proving again that Mankind is above on the Castle-tower; and he refers also to a bow he bears (l. 2160).

After these nine stanzas of exchange, the Devil loses patience and urges have done with the chiding! (Perhaps he here begins to blow off his fireworks!) Get to battle! 'Work these wenches woe and wrack! Clarions, cry up at a crack; and blow your broad bags!' (Were these bagpipes among the music, like those in Fouquet's miniature?)

Now follows direction No. 25: '*Then they shall fight for a long time*' (see p. 39).

What the fight consists of we can only guess. The Sins are armed with slings, lances, shot and bows (*not* with pitch-forks, as Chambers for some reason supposes—see *Literature*, p. 59), and the Virtues, it seems, pelt them with the symbolic roses. But did the Sins make any pretence at a real attack? Presumably these three Sins encircle the tower and attack from three sides.

Whether the three attacks are simultaneous from three directions, so that all the audience see some of the fight at the same time or whether each Sin attacks in succession and the audience awaits its turn to see, we do not know. We are pretty sure that Pride engages with Meekness, Anger with Patience and Envy with Charity. But do they put us on thorns about the result by using scaling-ladders? Or do they stay on the ground and merely brandish their weapons and hurl insults? That would seem a little unconvincing, I feel, after all their boasting! But, alas, the manner of the fighting must remain a mystery—or at most an idea!—upon our present knowledge.

After they have 'fought for a long time', the three Sins fall back and each bellows a stanza of outraged defeat; the roses (and the strength of Virtue) have been too much for them. Anger has the picturesque lines about Patience—'her roses fell on me so sharp, that my head hangeth as an harp . . .' (l. 2223).

So the first wave is repulsed.

Now the Bad Angel howls execrations upon 'all four' (that is, Pride, Anger, Envy and the Devil), and urges Sir Flesh ('with thine eyen sour') to try a second wave.

Then an exactly similarly patterned attack follows; with Flesh's battle-cry to Gluttony, Sloth and Lechery in concert—with Gluttony's vaunt to Soberness in one stanza and her two stanzas of reply—and the like with Lechery and Chastity—and then with Sloth and Busyness—with Flesh's final stanza of attack—and then with direction No. 26, '*Then they shall fight for a long time*' exactly as before.

(N.B. For those readers following this description with the printed text of the play, it should be noted that it is at this point in the 1924 reprint of the E.E.T.S. edition that the lines are incorrectly numbered from l. 2334 to l. 2742. See above, p. 40.)

Again the attack is repulsed, and the three beaten Sins cry off in a whining stanza of cowardice each. At this the Bad Angel is beside himself. He turns in last desperation 'to World' (direction No. 27).

World has of course only one knight, Sir Covetyse, to fight his cause, but he urges him—'Banner avaunt!' and promises him 'the gallows of Canwick' as a 'mede'—thus affording us our clearest suggestion of the neighbourhood of the performance; for Canwick Hill is not far to the south of the town of Lincoln, and in earlier days it bore its gallows.

Now comes what must have been one of the great dramatic moments of the play. With the triumphant Ladies, flushed with victory, aloft round Mankind on the tower; with the six Sins spread in a circle of misery round the Castle-foot, licking their wounds; with Flesh and the Devil fuming, sullen and despondent; and with the green of the Place littered with the battery of roses—Covetyse walks slowly out on his own and calls Mankind very softly and reasonably. If there were bees in the air to buzz over the flowers, or a skylark rising from the meadow outside, or a distant church bell sounding, you probably heard them now in the stillness after the boasts and the bawling, the trumpets and the shouts of pain had died away.

Covetyse says:

(l. 2428)   how, Mankynde! I am a-tenyde
        for þou art þere so in þat holde.
        Cum & speke with þi best frende,
          Syr Coueytyse! þou knowyst me of olde.
        what, deuyl, schalt þou þer lenger lende
          with grete penaunce in þat castel colde?

        (How, Mankind! I am a-tened
          For thou art there, so, in that hold!
        Come and speak with thy best friend,
          Sir Covetyse. Thou knowest me of old!
        What-the-devil! Shalt thou there longer lend
          With great penance in that castle cold?)

—and so forth. Largity is up in arms at once, but very 'dismayed'. She calls her two stanzas of opposition as her sisters did. But the result is different. Still gently, Covetyse inquires:

(l. 2467)   what eylyth þee, lady Largyte,
        Damysel dynge up-on þi des?

(and then, hardening viciously)

        & I spak ryth not to þee
        þerfore I prey þee holde þi pes.
        how, Mankynde! cum speke with me!
          Cum ley þi loue here in my les! . . .

        (What aileth thee, Lady Largity?
          Damsel dingë upon thy dais!
         As I spake right *not* to thee,
          Therefore I pray thee hold thy peace!
        How, Mankind! Come speak with me—
          Come, lay thy love here in my leash. . . .)

Man replies:

(l. 2480)   Coueytyse! whedyr schuld I wende?
        what wey woldyst þat I sulde holde?
        to what place woldyst þou me sende?
        I gynne to waxyn hory & colde . . .

>   as a ȝonge man, I may not hoppe;
>   my nose is colde, & gynnyth to droppe;
>   myn her waxit al hore.

>   (Covetyse, whither should I wend?
>   What way would'st that I should hold?
>   To what place wouldest thou me send?
>   I 'gin to waxen hoary and cold . . .
>   As a young man I may not hop;
>   My nose is cold and 'ginneth to drop;
>   My hair waxeth all hoar.)

Covetyse:

(l. 2492)
>   Petyr! þou hast þe morë nede
>   To hauë sum good in þyn age:
>   markys, poundys, londys & lede,
>   howsys & homys, castell & cage; . . .

>   (Peter! Thou hast the more need
>   To have some goods in thine age!
>   Markës, poundës, lands and lede [subjects],
>   Houses and homes, castle and cage. . . .)

Mankind pathetically still protests. Then Covetyse gives his fourth stanza.

(It is interesting to notice here the 'circular' technique again. Each trio of Sins surrounded the Castle in turn, speaking up to the circular battlements from different sides, so that each section of audience had at least one speech given in their own sector. Now Covetyse is alone; how can he 'surround' the Castle and deliver his supremely important speech so that no section of the surrounding audience misses the drift, any more than with the multiple Sins? The answer is clear. He speaks in movement. He is provided with four stanzas, and thus he can walk reflectively round the tower, pausing from time to time, so that each is delivered in a different quarter—in this way all may hear at least one passage of his pleading.) He concludes:

(l. 2521)
>   . . . þou schalt fyndë, soth to sey,
>   þi purs schal be þi best[ë] frende.
>   þou þou syt al day, & prey,
>   no man schal com to þee, nor sende;
>   but if þou hauë a peny to pey,

men schul to þee þanne lystyn & lende. . . .
if þou be pore, & nedy & elde,
þou schalt oftyn euyl fare.

(Thou shalt findë, sooth to say,
Thy purse shall be thy bestë friend.
Though thou sit all day and pray,
No man shall come to thee, or send;
But if thou have a penny to pay,
Men shall to thee then listen and lend . . .
If thou be poor and needy and old,
Thou shalt often evil fare.)

How few could withstand this prudent counsel! Mankind cannot. He will 'forsake the Castle of Perseverance'. The Good Angel, from wherever he is, cries out a stanza of protest, but ends:

(l. 2556)   a, swete ladys, helpe! he goth
a-wey with Couetyse.
[tunc descendit ad Auariciam

(Ah, sweet Ladies! Help! He goth
Away with Covetyse.
[*then he descends to* Covetyse.)

Each Virtue calls out a stanza of resignation. 'God hath given him a free will!' (l. 2561) says Meekness; 'He held the axe by the helve' says Patience; 'World's weal is like a three-footed stool, it faileth a man at his most need' says Soberness. And Largity ends with an appeal to all the audience present—'Now good men all that here be, hold my sisters excused, and me; though Mankind from this Castle flee, blame you Covetyse.'

The Bad Angel chortles in rapture:

(l. 2649)   Ʒa! go forthe, & lete þe qwenys cakle!
þer wymmen arn, are many wordys:
lete hem gone hoppyn with here hakle!
þer ges syttyn, are many tordys.

(Yah! Go forth! And let the queanies cackle!
Where women are, are many words.
Let 'em go hopping with their hackle!
Where geese sit, there are many turds. . . .)

Man, a little dazed, walks on: 'Penny-man is mickle in my mind. . . .' The Good Angel wails.

'Ah! Ah!' cries World suddenly (perhaps having retired to his scaffold), 'This game goeth as I would!'—and then (superbly reversing the famous lines of Knowledge in *Everyman*, 'Everyman, I will go with thee, and be thy guide; in thy most need to go by thy side') he ends:

(l. 2698)   For I, þe Werld, am of þis entayle,
        In hys moste nede I schal hym fayle,
          & al for Coveytyse.

        (For I, the World, am of this entail—
        In his most need I shall him fail;
          And all for Covetyse!)

The Fall of Mankind: 'A party well in age'

This gives us pause for a moment to ask a question that, I admit, is a stiff one to answer; where, now, are the other six Sins, and the three Kings of Evil? Save for the World, we hear nothing of any of them again in the whole play. Somehow they must have crept away at the end of the battle—possibly up to their scaffolds and out the back and round the Hill and home to the Pavilion. We do not know. But if the North and South scaffold curtains are now closed, at least the West is open; for one Evil remains still regnant over Man, and dominates his closing scenes—the World.

Man is growing very old. He is walking now with Covetyse, who gently warns him:

(l. 2700)   Now, Mankynde, be war of þis:
        þou art a party wele in age;
        I woldë not þou ferdyst a-mys;
          go we now knowe my castel cage!

        (Now, Mankind, beware of this:
        Thou art a party well in age;
        I would not that thou fared'st amiss—
          Go we now to (?) my castle-cage.)

There Man shall have full store, but must promise one thing—'And alway, alway say "More" and "More"; and that shall be thy song.'

Says Mankind, hanging on his lips as they walk, '"More and more!" In many a place, certes, that song is often sung!' (l. 2716).

The scene which here follows is not easy to visualize; we are offered very few hints, yet such as there are point to a dramatic passage of some importance. One factor which we should bear in mind as we read is that the play is approaching its climax, and is soon to take a changed and tragic note. We have now roughly only a quarter of the script left to run.

So far as we can tell, the arena is now empty save for: Mankind and Covetyse somewhere in the Place; for World watching from his Western scaffold; and for the ever-present, but consistently puzzling, Good and Bad Angels. The Virtues have no more to do, and are presumably hidden in the body of the Castle; the six Sins, Flesh and the Devil do not speak again and we suppose them to have left the scene.

Mankind and Covetyse, therefore, hold all our attention. But we have to consider their action with some care. It would have seemed, at Covetyse's line 'Go we now to my castle-cage', that the pair are moving to the North-Eastern scaffold. But two matters make us hesitate. The first is that a careful study of the succeeding script fails to show any sign whatever that they reach this scaffold. The second is that Covetyse's line in the original is a very strange one, and I may have interpreted it wrongly. The line in the original is (as we saw at l. 2704) 'Go we now knowe my castel cage'.

After Mankind's stanza of reply, Covetyse's next speech opens with a new idea that we must weigh carefully. He says: 'Have here, Mankind, a thousand marks. I, Covetyse, have thee this got . . .' and Mankind accepts this gift of money with: 'I vow to God it is great husbandry; of thee I take these nobles round.' There thus appears to be transfer of a considerable sum. Where does it come from? How does Covetyse get it? And what does Mankind do with it?

These may seem unimportant matters, but one's attention is called to that very puzzling legend on the Plan, to which we have already referred. The legend is in two lines, but the lines are divided in the middle by the drawing of the Castle-tower (see Fig. 1). The words appear to be as follows:

> Coveytyse cepbord⎞ ⎛schal be at þe ende⎤
> be þe beddys feet ⎠ ⎝of þe castel⎯⎯⎯⎯⎯⎦

Here is one of those puzzles that one suspects will be perfectly obvious to someone else, but which remain annoyingly obscure to oneself. I do not find myself able to decide in what order the parts of this legend should be read. The words themselves seem to be fairly clearly written, and I have only one variant to suggest of the reading of the letters that is commonly offered—that is that what seems to me to be *cepbord* is rendered by Furnivall as *copbord*. Unfortunately this seems to be the operative word in the group, and neither version makes much sense. The interpretation *cupboard* seems unavoidable—but what can Covetyse's cupboard be? And why, if it is Covetyse's, should it be under the Castle of all places, and not on his scaffold? Again, if this is true, why specify its relation to the bed, and why must the 'cupboard' be especially at the bed's *foot*?

One takes it for granted that a statement which it has been thought worth while to include in a plan of this sort must be a significant statement, having importance for the conduct of the play. But at the moment there seems to be no particular significance emerging.

Yet some impression of meaning is conveyed by the words: what is it? They strike one as saying: 'Covetyse's cupboard (?), (which is required) at the end of *The Castle* (that is, near the end of the play), shall be by the foot of the bed (under the tower)'. But the words can scarcely be twisted into that order without undue violence. Had they, then, such a meaning?

If, by any chance, we should be right in this reading, it is just possible that we have the answer here to our question: Where did Covetyse find the thousand marks? That answer is that he and Mankind were on the green, and Covetyse simply opened a small chest (?) at the nearest convenient place, that is by the bed under the tower.

But still one would like to be able to know why he did not go 'home' to his own scaffold, and get it from there. For some good reason, it seems, he could not do this. I do not know the reason.

To continue now with the play. Mankind's immediate reaction to the gift is: 'I shall me hurry, and that in haste, to hide this gold under the ground. There it shall lie till that I die .... Yet I am not well at ease. Now would I have some castle walls . . .' (l. 2742).

Does he now actually bury the gold or conceal it in a hole in the ground made for this purpose? We shall see later that World sends to have the gold taken away again.

At any rate, this greatly ageing figure is now in sad uncertainty. To comfort his unease, Covetyse proffers one of his most cynical, and most cryptic, stanzas, and—we write this with a pang of regret—it is his last in the play. We record it in full, and venture a very tentative, modern reading:

(l. 2753) al schalt þou haue al redy, lo,
     at þyn owyn dysposcyon.
    al þis good, take þee to,
     clyffe & cost, toure & toun:
    þus hast þou gotyn, in synful slo,
     of þyne neygboris, be extorcyon.
    'more & more' sey ȝyt, haue do;
     tyl þou be ded & drepyn doun,
       werke on with werldys wrenchys.
     'more & more' say ȝyt, I rede;
     to more þanne I-now þou hast nede;
     al þis werld, bothe lenthe & brede,
      þi coveytyse may not qwenche.

    (All shalt thou have; all ready, lo,
     At thine own disposition.
    All these goods, take thee to—
     Cliff and coast, tower and town—
    These hast thou gotten, in sinful slough,
     Of thy neighbours by extortion.
    'More and more' say yet, have do,
     Till thou be dead and dropping down.
       Work on with worldë's wrench.
     'More and more' say yet, I rede,
     Till more than enough thou hastë need.
     All this world, both length and breadth
      Thy covetyse may not quench!)

Though this is his last speech, it lacks any final stage direction or any finality. It leaves him silent in the field and we do not know what to do with him. May he perhaps turn inexorably away, and trail his robe across the grass to the main entrance, and go out in silence? Does he mount his scaffold, refusing Man its refuge, and vanish for ever behind its closing curtain? Or does he for a space remain and then have another and truly final speech *which is lost*, because of the corresponding text-break that we have yet to reach? There is, in fact, still one more reference to him by Mankind;

and it seems in the nature of a direct address (as we shall see at l. 2884); for this reason, we believe that Covetyse did not leave the theatre, but retired to a scaffold—either his own or his master's—and sat watching for a space.

As he goes, Mankind's next speech comes, to close this section of the play. It is the speech of a broken man. It is spoken in extreme old age. Perhaps Man sinks to his knees and buries his head in his arms. Here is a period, a punctuation-mark ending a passage:

(l. 2767)   me þynkyth, neuere I haue I-now . . .
    'more & more' ȝit I say,
      & schal euere, whyl I may blow; . . .
        'more & more,' þis is my steuene.
    if I myth al-wey dwellyn in prosperyte,
    Lord God, þane wel were me!
    I wolde, þe medys, forsake þee,
      & neuere to comyn in heuene.

    (Methinketh never I have enough . . .
    'More and more' yet I say,
    And shall ever while I may blow. . . .
      'More and more'; this is my steven.
    If I might always dwellen in prosperity,
    Lord God! then well were me!
    I would for that forsakë Thee,
      And never to come in Heaven!)

Then—if those Ages gave themselves to such play of emotion—he might have sunk his ancient, maddened head like Lear, and hidden his face from the world in solitude—a cipher-spot now, not far (I believe) from World's scaffold.

He thus would offer a perfect dramatic preparation for what now comes.

I am well aware of the dangers of dramatizing a description of the events in a drama (though some of my readers might, I fear, be justified in believing I am not), so let me leave what happens next with no description except the poet's words—save that I venture to suggest that the Figure who now speaks comes in at the main entrance, slowly walks down the lane in front of it, and will then circle anti-clockwise round the Castle. (Mankind is crouched in the lane before World.) The Figure says:

(l. 2779)   ow, now it is tyme hye
        to castyn Mankynde to dethys dynt.

In all hys werk*is* he is vnslye;
  mekyl of hys lyf he hath myspent.
To Mankynd*e* I ney ny;
  w*ith* rewly rappys he schal be rent. . . .
    ʒe schul me drede, eu*er*y-chone;
    wha*n*ne I come, ʒe schul grone;
    My name in londe is lefte a-lone:
      I hatte 'drery Dethe.'

(Ow! Now is it time high
  To cast Mankind to deathë's dint.
In all his works he is unsly.
  Mickle of his life he hath misspent.
To Mankind I now nigh;
  With ruly rappës he shall be rent. . . .
    Ye shall me dread, every one,
    When I come ye shall groan.
    My name in land is left alone.
      I'm callëd dreary Death.)

(The last line in the original—'I hatte drery Dethe'—is curiously reminiscent of the Swedish construction—'Jag heter', 'I am named . . .'.)

There are five stanzas in this speech. Thus, we are inclined to see a 'circulating' speech, with one introductory stanza and the other four spoken to the four quarters round the circle, the last bringing him up to Mankind. He bears a lance (l. 2808). His last stanza begins—'To Mankind now will I reach . . . with this point I shall him broach . . .'. Then suddenly the closing lines become a direct address to Man—'Now I kill thee with mine knap; I reach to thee, Mankind, a rap, to thine hear) root.'

Man cries (with immortal poetry):

(l. 2844)   A, Deth, Deth! drye is þi dryfte.
          ded is my desteny!

          (Ah, Death! Death! Dry is thy drift!
          Dead is my destiny! . . .)

He raises his arms in one last cry to World (and for this reason we planted him opposite World's scaffold): 'World, World! Have me in mind. Good Sir World! Help now Mankind . . . for old acquaintance, help me. . . .' And World very gently and silkily asks:

(l. 2870) owe, Mankynd*e*! hathe Dethe *with* þee spoke?
a-geyns hym helpyth no wage. . . .
our*e* bonde of loue schal sone be broke;
In coldë clay schal be þy cage . . .
þus haue I seruyd here be-forn,
a hundryd thousand moo.

(Ow, Mankind! Hath Death with thee spoke?
Against him helpeth no wage. . . .
Our bond of love shall soon be broke—
In cold clay shall be thy cage . . .
Thus have I servëd here before
A hundred thousand mo'.)

The writhing, yearning figure below gasps: 'Oh, World, World!
Ever worth woe!—And thou, sinful Covetyse . . .' (l. 2883), but
all to no purpose. A bitter change comes; all the foregoing was
probably slow and agonizing. How will the poet give a fillip to the
pace to stimulate contrast and attention? World calls, suddenly:
'How boy, arise! Now thou must wend on mine earth . . .' (l. 2896).
Since we have very good reason to suppose that Garcio, the Boy,
last of World's three servants, makes his appearance on the scaffold
behind his master, this speech, then, looks like an order to descend.
The response seems to bear this out, for the Boy says—presumably
as he slips down the ladder—'I thank thee for this great gift; I go
glad upon this ground . . .' (l. 2909). He threatens to 'lift' Man
'into a lake' (does this mean he will throw his body into the Ditch?),
and at the end of his stanza is the stage direction (No. 29) '*Then he
shall go to* Mankind'.

There he seems actually to lift him, for he says: 'He is heavier
than any lead'. Man rouses sufficiently to ask him 'What art thou?'
The Boy says 'I am come to have all that thou hast. . . . The World
hath for thee decided who shall have thine heritage.'

Man cries: 'What, devil! Thou art not of my kin! I had liefer . . .
some man had it of my blood.'

The Boy replies: 'Die on! for I am master here . . . the World
bade me this gold arrest. . . .' (Does he then pick up, or dig up,
Covetyse's thousand marks?) Man begs to know his name, and
hears: 'Look that thou it not forget; my name is "I-wot-never-
who"!' (l. 2968).

There is nothing now for Mankind. He speaks three stanzas of
despair and ends:

(l. 3001)   . . . as a flo*ur*, fadyth my face.
to helle I schal bothe far*e* & fle,
    but God me grau*n*të of his *gr*ace.
        I deyë certeynly:
      now my lyfe I hauë lore;
     myn hert brekyth; I syhë sor*e*;
    a word may I speke no mor*e*;
        I putte me in Godys m*er*cy.

    (. . . as a flower fadeth my face.
To hell I shall both fare and flee;
    Save God me grant of His grace,
        I dië certainly.
    Now my life I have lost.
    My heart breaketh. I sigh sore.
    No word may I speak no more.
       I put me in God's mercy.)

And he speaks no more to us.

Perhaps all curtains now are closed.

The next stanza opens with a curious aberration of the scribe's; he writes the name of its speaker as '*Domina*'. But the speaker addresses Mankind as 'Body' and thus seems to be Mankind's Soul, who was instructed to 'lie under the bed (in the Castle) till he shall rise and play' in the legend on the Plan (see above p. 27). Thus it is to be supposed that the scribe should have written *Anima* for *Domina*.

The Soul speaks a normal stanza of thirteen lines, and then nine lines of a following stanza. But then we are devastated to reach l. 3030 and the second break in the sense, of which we have had previous warning, and which marks the loss of another 100 lines.

*   *   *   *   *   *

This loss is more serious than the last. When we resume, the Bad Angel is apparently quarrelling with the Good Angel over possession either of the body or of the Soul. But what has happened in the meantime is more difficult to guess here. How was Mankind's body disposed of? This we cannot know. Who else spoke? Who else, among those we have not known how to dispose of, was given his 'exit' here? It seems wiser to accept the mystery, and pick up after it as best we can.

The quarrel over the possession of the Soul proceeds, perhaps with some appeals to the audience. The Good Angel gradually relinquishes, for, as he explains to the Soul, 'Covetyse he was thy foe'—confirming perhaps by the past tense that Covetyse has now gone. The Soul bewails his body's evil. But the Bad Angel asserts that 'in high hell shall be thine house'. 'We shall to hell', he says, and then: 'Now dagge we hence a doggë's trot' (l. 3100). Do they then set out over the grass to the Devil's empty scaffold? I think they do, for at the end the metre quickens to a 'curtain' and the Bad Angel, as he beats the Soul, is given a special stanza—with a wave of the hand to the audience in his last two lines—

(l. 3122)   lo! synful tydynge,
              boy, on þi bak I brynge.
              spedely þou sprynge;
              þi placebo I schal synge;
                to deuelys delle
                I schal þee bere to helle.
              I wyl not dwelle:
              haue good day! I goo to helle.

              (Lo! Sinful tiding,
              Boy, on thy back I bring!
              Speedily thou spring!
              Thy *placebo* I shall sing.
                To devil's dell
                I shall thee bear to hell.
              I will not dwell.
              Have Good-Day! I go to hell!)

They go into the Devil's scaffold and then there is silence and an empty Place.

The Epilogue: 'Set him here by my knee'

We have still some 520 lines of the script. The playwright uses them in a great final scene somewhat in the nature of an Epilogue. No character save one (the Soul, and he does not speak) appears who has appeared before.

We suppose this finale begins with the procession of four ladies from the Pavilion, through the entrance into the Place. We are told something about them in one of the legends on the Plan.

The Four Daughters shall be clad in mantles; Mercy in white,

Righteousness altogether in red, Truth in sad green, and Peace all in black; and they shall play in the Place altogether till they bring up the Soul.

—a nice piece of significant early costume-direction, ending with that particular instruction that these four figures shall perform in the plain itself till such moment as they have to take the Soul up to God. Note that we have specifically only *four* figures mentioned here. The edited version and other authorities are inclined to see five characters introduced at this point in the lines, perhaps because one of the four, *Justicia*, is sometimes called Righteousness and sometimes Justice. But Pity in her second stanza specifically says: 'my sisters Rightwiseness, Peace and Truth . . .'. And both the legend just quoted and the List of Characters are unmistakable; there are *four* Daughters of God, called Mercy, Righteousness, Truth and Peace, and no more.

Each speaks two stanzas of introduction. A dispute arises about whether the Soul should be saved or damned, and in her last stanza Peace proposes that the other three should go with her 'to yon high place', where they shall 'inform the High Godhead, and pray him to deem this case' (l. 3218). She points then to God's Scaffold on the East, which has remained silent all this while.

That scaffold now must open, and God is revealed; the next speech proves this, for Peace begins: 'Hail, God Almighty' (l. 3230), and at l. 3246 God responds to the greeting with his first speech. But a curious distraction is thrust upon us at the end of Peace's speech, and before the greetings to God, for after l. 3229 there comes stage direction No. 30, '*Then they shall ascend together to* The Father *and* Truth *shall say*;'. Thus we are offered a flat and inescapable contradiction; on the one hand we have 'The Four Daughters shall play in the Place altogether till they bring up the Soul' (which is a way of stating that they shall *not* ascend until l. 3594), and on the other hand we have the above direction which states that they *shall* ascend at l. 3229.

There is another difficulty; the next stage direction we are to encounter is No. 31—and that, instead of being a direction to go *down* again as we would expect, is another direction to ascend— '*Then they shall all ascend together to the* Bad Angel . . .'. There is no direction to descend between the two.

Again, we have this consideration; what next follows in the script, after the greeting to God, is a very long and slow scene after the fashion of a legal disputation as, before God's throne, two of the Four Daughters, Truth and Justice, plead for the condemnation of Mankind's Soul, and one, Mercy, pleads for his forgiveness. Truth speaks for five uninterrupted stanzas; Mercy then speaks for the same space. Justice (also called Righteousness) follows with an equally long exposition. Following on this, Mercy speaks again for two stanzas; Truth for one; and in conclusion Peace has no less than six stanzas, the longest unbroken speech in the play. The whole scene lasts over 300 lines—possibly between a quarter of an hour and twenty minutes. Now, can we suppose that the above remarkable scene (with its absolutely essential message for the audience, and where the whole kernel of the belief at the back of the play is presented), demanding so much eloquence and therefore so much freedom for action, could be effectively spoken up on a single high scaffold, cramped by a throne and five people, at an extremity of the audience on one edge of the arena?

If it were so played, it would have been ineffectual theatrically, its dialectic would have been lost on the audience, and the whole climax of the play would have been ruined by the people breaking up and starting to go home.

I believe, then, that this grave and important scene seems likeliest to have been presented as the instruction on the Plan directs— that is, with the Four Daughters playing in the Place altogether, and with God the Father listening to them from his throne on his scaffold—and not as the direction in the lines implies; that is, with the Four Daughters ascending to the scaffold and holding their disputation around God's throne.

With this conclusion reached we would do well briefly to run through the business again up to this point to avoid confusion. We watch the Four Daughters make their entrance in the Place; we come to Peace's final suggestion—'Go we to yon high place'— and we note that it suggests that they are some little distance as yet from God's scaffold; it is not 'go we up'.

Next the scaffold on the East opens, and the Four Ladies go over the grass towards it, but pause in a group a short distance away from it. Thus the whole intention of stage direction No. 30 is fulfilled except the one word *ascend*. The Latin here is pretty certainly corrupt; *ascendet* seems unmistakably written in the original, and quite free from any abbreviation. But a verb *cannot* be in the singular, as this one is, when the subject is in the plural, and the subject is *omnes*—'all' the four together. If the number is corrupt, then the word itself may be corrupt and may not have been anything to do with 'ascend' before the scribe copied it.

Proceeding then with the picture we have begun; the Four Daughters have paused on the greensward of the Place itself at a respectful distance from God's scaffold, and they greet him.

God now answers their greeting, and answers them in terms *which are meaningless* unless the above picture is true. For he says 'Come forth and stand ye me near' (l. 3249). He would not say this if they were crowded round him on his scaffold. Surely he is summoning them from their respectful distance, and intimating to them that he is prepared to hear what they have to say, but he does not say 'Come up', nor 'Stand at my side' (as he later does to Mankind's Soul); he simply bids them come forward and stand nearer to him. The great disputation scene now begins, and instead of the Four being crowded round the scaffold, we suppose them at ease in the lane before it, and free to stride as they dispute and take in any hearers they wish in their harangues. The show, from this point, will run easily.

In addition to all the above arguments, we see that the development of the action from this point on, if we accept stage direction No. 30 as an ascent, is a muddle; and on the other hand that if we ignore the direction and follow the legend on the Plan, the action is clear and neat; and this is a practical test that takes a lot of upsetting. It is perhaps worth adding, from ordinary stage experience, that a plan is usually made *after* a play has been written, and therefore any notes on a plan are likely to be added after taking into account any notes that were in the script itself. That is to say, it is logical to suppose that a stage direction on a plan countermands or supersedes any contrary stage direction in the script for which the plan was made.

At the end of the long disputation scene God, having heard the arguments for and against, determines to give his judgement 'not after deserving' but mixed with 'all peace, some truth and some right, and most, of my mercy'. He says:

(l. 3577)   goo to ȝone fende,
                         & fro hym take Mankynde!
                         brynge hym to me!
                         & set hym here be my kne,
                         In heuene to be. . . .

> (Go to yon fiend,
> And from him take Mankind,
> And bring him to me
> And set him here by my knee
> In heaven to be. . . .)

Truth accepts God's judgement, and his order to fetch the Soul 'from yon ghost grill'; and it is immediately after this (at l. 3586) that we have the stage direction No. 31 which, as we have indicated, runs—'*Then they shall all ascend together to the* Bad Angel *and* (Peace) *shall say;'* . . . . Thus it is clear that the Four Daughters, after an obeisance to God, return to the centre and then swing right and approach the Northern scaffold.

What follows is strangely abrupt and brusque. No flashing battle now—not even a battle of words! Only the Daughters speak. Peace begins: 'Ah! thou foul wight! Let go that soul so tight!' and Justice-Righteousness proceeds: 'Go thou to hell, thou devil bold as a bell!' and whether she beats him after the example of the Evils before, so that he runs crying down the steps and through the Place and out to the Pavilion to change, or how the encounter ended we do not know. We have, very simply, at l. 3594 the last stage direction of the play (No. 32)—'*Then they shall ascend to the throne*'. So the Daughters go down again to the Place with the Soul, take him back with them to the East and there we reach the moment of the play referred to in the legend on the Plan—the moment when 'they bring up the Soul'. Now, therefore, they are at last free to leave the grass before God's scaffold and ascend its steps and stand beside his throne.

I may perhaps be permitted to add a reason why, after having condemned the idea of a scene in which the Four Daughters were crowded beside God on a scaffold, I have just accepted two scenes on scaffolds, both including the Four Daughters as well as two other players. The reason is, of course, clear in the former example of the scene with the Bad Angel, for the passage is only eight lines long, and is a scene of action and imprecation that could carry all over the arena even if it were played on a scaffold.

The latter scene is the last scene of the play. The Daughters take the Soul up to the Eastern scaffold, and God says to him: 'Come, sit at my right hand. . . .' Now, though there are six characters together here, I think they may very well be up on the scaffold, for all the action is over, and a 'tableau' is possibly forming. One voice only comes now, quietly from the East across the whole Place, and we trust that the player may, at this peak moment, hold the audience in suspended silence, while the last words come out, giving comfort to the redeemed Soul of Man. There are four stanzas. They conclude the performance. With a partly-to-be-forgiven technical digression we find ourselves prompted to ask, how will this accomplished playwright end his play? He has shown a sense for many things of the theatre that we have learned from experience are elements of technique; what now will he do for a 'curtain'?

Perhaps God is standing now. At any rate he ends:

(l. 3644) all men example here-at may take,
    to mayntein þe goode, & mendyn here mys:
      þus endyth oure gamys!
     To saue ȝou fro synnynge,
     Evyr at þe begynnynge
     Thynke on ȝoure last endynge!
      Te, Deum, laudamus!

   (All men example hereat may take—
    To maintain the good and mend their ways.
     So endeth our games.
    To save you from sinning,
    Ever at the beginning
    Think on your last ending!
     Te, Deum, laudamus!)

In fact, therefore, what happens is a strangely unexpected thing. God's great role is laid aside, and the Poor Player speaks: 'So endeth' (he says) '*our* games.' We players have finished. He adds a three-line tag, and then still in the dress of God but with the voice of a plain, human actor, he pronounces the three familiar church-words of praise to God.

So he hands the play down to earth again, and presumably the last scaffold-curtain closes; and the people turn to go home.

APPENDICES

ON THE USE OF THE 'PLACE' AND THE *PLATEA* IN MEDIEVAL THEATRE GENERALLY

APPENDIX I

'PLACE' AND *PLATEA* IN MEDIEVAL THEATRE

Place and Platea *in other Medieval Plays* * *Recent Opinions on the* Platea * *Winding-up of the Inquiry: Origin and Definition of the Place*

IN the preceding study the Place has taken on some considerable importance as a basis of the medieval theatre. But we have dealt with only one medieval play. What is there to be found about the Place in the stage directions of other British medieval plays beside *The Castle of Perseverance*? How frequently, in other words, was this technique which I have called the theatre in the round, but which is more exactly the theatre of Place and Scaffolds, used in the Middle Ages?

It is significant that we can add to the four references to Place in the *Castle* Plan, and the three references to *placea* in the *Castle* stage directions, the following:

  33 uses of Place in other English plays,
  4 uses of *placea* in other English plays,
  13 uses of *platea* in Cornish plays,
  9 uses of *placea* in Cornish plays,
  1 use of Place in a Cornish play,
  2 uses of Plain (in the sense of Place) in a Cornish play.

Uses of 'Place' in English Plays

(The following examples are numbered in sequence for reference, following the seven examples in *The Castle*, beginning with No. 8.)

Mary Magdalene: see E.E.T.S., extra series, No. LXX.

8. (l. 563) Here xal satan go hom to his stage, and mari xal entyr In-to þe place alone ...

9. (l. 587) Her entyr Symont [Simon] in-to ȝe place. ...

10. (l. 1445) Her goth þe shep [ship] owt of þe place.

11. (l. 1923) Here goth the shep owȝt ofe the place. ...

The N-Town Cycle, also called *Ludus Coventriae*, but not necessarily connected with Coventry; see E.E.T.S., extra series, No. CXX.

12. (p. 233, l. 80) here comyth þe masangere to cayphas and in þe mene tyme rewfyn and lyon schewyn hem in þe place in ray tabardys . . . (Here cometh the Messenger to Caiaphas, and in the meantime Rufyne and Leon show themselves in the place in striped tabards.)

13. (p. 235, l. 124) here þe buschopys [bishops] with here clerkys and þe Pharaseus mett and [?*for* at] þe myd place and þer xal be a lytil oratory with stolys and cusshonys clenly be-seyn lych as it were a cownsel hous.

14. (p. 238, l. 221) here cryst rydyth out of þe place And he wyl. (i.e. 'if he will', or 'if the actor so please'.)

15. (p. 251, l. 589). here judas rysyth prevely [privily] and goth in þe place. . . .

16. (p. 254, l. 669) Here The Buschopys partyn in þe pLace And eche of hem takyn here leve. . . .

17. (p. 264, l. 972) here jhesus with his dyscipulis goth in-to þe place . . .

18. (p. 267, l. 1040) here þe jewys lede cryst outh of þe place with gret cry and noyse some drawyng cryst forward and some bakwarde and so ledyng forth with here weponys A-lofte and lytys brennyng. . . .

19. (p. 271, l. 1) What tyme þat processyon is enteryd in to þe place and þe herowdys takyn his schaffalde. and pylat and annas and cayphas here schaffaldys Also þan come þer An exposytour in doctorys wede. . . .

20 and 21. (p. 273, l. 69) here xal A massanger com in-to þe place rennyng and criying Tydyngys tydyngys. and so rownd Abowth þe place. (. . . running, and crying 'Tidings! tidings!' . . .)

22. (p. 280, l. 244) here þei ledyn jhesu A-bowt þe place. tyl þei come to þe halle.

23 and 24. (p. 287, l. 465) here enteryth Satan in to þe place in þe most orryble wyse. and qwyl þat he pleyth þei xal . . . ledyn hym [Jesus] A-bowth þe place and þan to pylat be þe tyme þat hese wyf hath pleyd.

25. (p. 295, l. 697) . . . and þer þei metyn with symonem. in þe place. . . .

26. (p. 314, l. 1226) here þe knytys gon out of þe place.

Herod's Killing of the Children (Digby Plays, E.E.T.S., extra series, No. LXX).

27. (l. 232) here the knyghtes and watkyn walke a-bought the place tyll Mary and Ioseph be conveid in-to Egipt.

28. (l. 280) Here mary and Ioseph shall go out of þe place. . . .

The Conversion of St. Paul (Digby Plays).

29 and 30. (l. 140) Her sale rydyth forth with hys seruantes a-bowt the place, [&] owt of the pl[ace].

31. (l. 210) Here the knyghtes lede forth sale in-to a place, and cryst apperyth to annanie, sayng:
(This curious use of 'a' instead of 'the' may be a mistake of the scribe's, or of course it may imply that this is merely an ordinary use of the word 'place'.)

The Croxton *Play of the Sacrament* (Non-Cycle Mystery Plays, E.E.T.S., extra series, No. CIV).

32. (l. 444) Here shall þe lechys man [i.e. the doctor's servant] come into þe place saying:
(This most interesting play—the first example of the English horror-thriller, with many trick effects—is a first-rate example of the Place-and-scaffold technique of presentation, and of its problems.)

The Norwich *Creation of Eve* (Non-Cycle Mystery Plays).

33. (l. 88) *Adam and Eve walk* 'together about the place wryngyng ther handes.'
(A curious play in two versions; of which one specifically refers to a 'Pageant' while the other seems certainly to be 'stationary'.)

The Coventry *Shearmen and Taylors Play* (*Two Coventry Corpus Christi Plays*, E.E.T.S., extra series, No. LXXXVII).

34. (l. 331) There the sheppardis syngith ageyne and goth forthe of the place, and the ij profettis cumyth in and seyth thus:
(Again a play offering puzzling problems of staging, which appear to me insoluble unless descents from the scaffold (or scaffolds) into the Place are admitted.)

Skelton's *Magnyfycence* (*c.* 1516) (E.E.T.S., extra series, No. XCVIII).

35. (l. 824) And so they go out of the place.

36. (l. 828) *Courtly Abusion* alone in the place.

37. (l. 1326) *Crafty Conveyaunce* alone in the place.

38. (l. 1456) *Magnyfycence* alone in the place.

38a. (l. 1725) Here *Mesure* goth out of the place.

39. (l. 1796) Here goth *Cloked Colusyon* awaye, and leueth *Magnyfycence* alone in the place.
(Note the reference to this play on p. 227 below.)

Uses of 'Placea' *in English Plays*

Mary Magdalene.

40. (l. 1716) Ett tunc navis venit In placea*m*, et navta *dicit*:

41. (l. 1879) et tunc navis venit ad-circa placea*m*: rex *dicit*:

The N-Town Cycle.

42. (p. 116, l. 22) et sic transient circa placea*m*.

Here we are offered the extra problem of Latin with abbreviations. The translation of medieval Latin stage directions is not (as we have seen) a simple matter; but granted the above are correct records of the originals, then we may render the three last examples in English as:

(40) And then the ship comes into the place, and the sailor says:

(41) And then the ship comes round the place; the King says:

(42) And thus they shall go across round the place.

Whatever the details of translation, the main meaning here appears clear; in the first two examples, a ship comes into the Place and sails round that Place, and in the third, two characters, namely Joseph and Mary in *The Visit to Elizabeth*, are to 'go across round the Place', if I may so phrase it. The action is important; they do not simply go directly across the Place to reach Elizabeth's house, which is 'hens I trowe myles two and ffyfty', for not only have they to signify a long journey, but also to leave time for a speech of twenty lines by Contemplation in the nature of an explanation. Thus they cross *round* the Place, presumably travelling by the more or less hidden outer rim.

One other reference may be added under this heading, though the word in the text is abbreviated to only three letters and thus might belong to either the *placea* group or the *platea* group, but since it is in an English play I shall include it here:

The Pride of Life (Non-Cycle Mystery Plays).

43. (l. 470) et eat pla.

The direction comes after a speech ending 'Lorde, to wende I am prest; Lo, now I am gone.' and thus it presumably signifies '*et eat in placeam*'—'and he shall go [down] into the place'. The character here is a Messenger, and immediately after this stage direction his speech continues but is now addressed not to his lord but to the audience: 'Peace and listen to my saw, both young and old. . . .' (We are left, alas, only a fragment of this play.)

We next turn to a number of Latin references in a group of plays belonging to Great Britain like the above but written in Cornish with stage directions in Latin; the variant of the word here used is *platea*. There are five such plays; three forming a trilogy, one a later modification of a part of that trilogy and one a curious play in two parts dealing with the life of St. Meriasek. We take first the trilogy—the *Ordinale*.

Uses of 'Platea' *in Cornish Plays*

Origo Mundi, Ordinale I (Edwin Norris trans. *The Ancient Cornish Drama*, 1859). See also Appendix 2.

44. (l. 466) Tunc cum istis quatuor ritis iat ad altare spaciando in platea et dicit Caym. [Norris translates this as:—]
('Then with those four rites (?) let him go to the altar, walking on the stage; and Cain says:')

45. (l. 498) Hic venient omnes in platea[*m*?]
('Here all shall come upon the stage.')

46. (l. 1156) Et tunc veniet Deus pater ad Noe et stans in platea et dicit:
('Then God the Father shall come to Noah; and, standing on the stage, says:')

47. (l. 1533) Moyses ambulat in platea.
('Moses walks on the stage.')

48. (l. 2332) deus sit in platea.
('Let God be on the stage.')

Passio, Ordinale 2.

49. (l. 562) hic pompabit annas pro platea.
('Here Annas shall walk about in front of the stage.')

50. (l. 1086) hic venient princeps annas et tortores ambulantes in platea.
('Here prince Annas and the executioners shall come walking on the stage.')

51. (l. 1476) et tunc ducent Jhesum in angulo s. in platea inter eos.
('And then he [*sic*] shall lead Jesus into a corner, viz. on the stage among them.')

52. (l. 1628) et tunc ipsi transeant cum jhu et parumper spaciabunt in platea dummodo nuncius eat post doctores. . . .
('And then they shall pass with Jesus, and shall walk about a little on the stage while the messenger goes after the doctors.')

53. (l. 1640) nunc episcopus et princeps et milites omnes transient cum ihu et spaciabunt in platea.
('Now the bishop, and the prince, and all the soldiers shall pass with Jesus, and walk about on the stage.')

'PLACE' AND *PLATEA* IN MEDIEVAL THEATRE

Resureccio, Ordinale 3.

54. (l. 154) hic venit spiritus cum omnibus in platea[*m?*]
('Here the Spirit, with all, comes on the stage.')

55. (l. 1230) cleophas et socius ambulant in platea.
('Cleophas and his companion walk on the stage.')

56. (l. 1638) et tunc nuncius et iet et spaciabit in platea parumper et ei obuiabit uernona.
('And then the messenger shall go and walk about on the stage a little; and Veronica shall meet him.')

We may pause profitably here to glance at Edwin Norris's translations. He explains in his notes that his interest is chiefly with the Cornish text and its rendering into modern English; he modestly takes care to make clear that his purpose is not to explain the performance but only to render the dialogue literally and faithfully. He implies that there is much that he does not understand in the problems of the staging and that he has not considered it his business to delve into that side of it; and so far as possible he has refrained from readings which are tendentious, which exploit a theory, or which seek to amplify the directions so as to bring them in line with a modern reader's understanding of present-day techniques. He thus gives us what some editors do not—a rendering clear of any 'suggestions' meant to aid our understanding; for this we salute him; but he does unintentionally offer us one obstacle in that throughout he tends to translate *platea* as 'a stage'. I believe the whole presentation of this great tripartite play is made immensely more understandable if we read *platea* as 'Place' in the way that we have used the word in reference to *The Castle*. (see Appendix 2)

The tendency of editors to render *platea* as 'stage' is very common. I think it is not a true rendering. The difficulty that arises is that to an ordinary reader (and I think he is perfectly correct) a stage is a *raised* thing, an elevated platform. But can we possibly accept such an interpretation when we find directions like *descendit in placeam*? Is this to mean 'He goes *down* into a raised stage'! Clearly we cannot accept such a thing.

Whitley Stokes in his translation of the other great Cornish play, *The Life of St. Meriasek*, generally takes a more cautious and, I believe, a safer way, though he is not fully consistent. Here are the references in the two sections of *St. Meriasek*:

Uses of 'Placea' in a Cornish Play

The Life of St. Meriasek (*Beunans Meriasek*, trans. Whitley Stokes, 1872).

57. (l. 271) descendunt omnes in placeam.
('All go down into the open space.')

58. (l. 455) surrexit circa placeam.
('He rose (and walked) round the open space.')

59. (l. 525) descendit episcopus kernov in placeam.
('The Bishop of Kernou goes down into the open space.')

60. (l. 1287) trancit calo et tortores expectant in placea.
('The drudge goes off and the torturers wait in the open.')

61. (l. 1652) tranceunt tortores et mulieres expectant in placea.
('The torturers go off and the women wait in the open.')

62. (l. 1935) expectant in placea.
('They wait in the open space.')

63. (l. 2697) ad decanum in colegia in placea.
('To the dean in the college on the stage.')

64. (l. 2703) *Here the dean is directed to reply* in placea ('on the stage').

65. (l. 4030) descendit petrus [solus ad syluestrem in placea ('Peter descends [alone to Silvester in the open space.' *The words after the square bracket are in a later hand.*)

Here, then, we have a mixture of interpretations. The majority read *platea* as 'open space' non-committally. But in two examples, Nos. (63) and (64), the old reading of 'stage' is used, not, I think, correctly.

One further reference is of interest to add to the above, as follows:

Use of 'Place' in a Cornish Play

It may seem strange in view of what we have said in the foregoing to read the above sub-title; and more strange to find that the reference is in the play just discussed above. But *St. Meriasek* is one of those plays whose stage directions are mixed, some Latin and some English; and it is an argument for the importance and widespread understanding of the significance of the word that we find:

66. (l. 3941) her y dragon aredy in ye place.

Uses of 'plain' in Cornish Plays

The Creation of the World by William Jordan (*Gwreans an Bys*, trans. Whitley Stokes, 1864).

67. (l. 325) . . . spirytis on cordis runing into ye playne.

68. (l. 495) Let the serpent wait in the plain.

The word 'plain' is used also in the dialogue in *St. Meriasek* under its Cornish form *plen*. For example, when a Messenger is pointing out to the Emperor Teudar the arrival of Meriasek on his territory, and Teudar descends from his scaffold to accost him, the Messenger says:

(l. 819)   Surely I see him,
                           Lord royal,
                                There in the plain.

The Cornish words of the last line are *enos in plen*.

We may now withdraw somewhat from this close study and take a general survey of this remarkable total of sixty-nine instances. To begin with, the fundamental fact is that they are there to be found—the idea of *platea* or of Place was so commonly recognized that we can, even at first-seeking, collect together this impressive array of examples. The Place was an acknowledged thing in medieval stage practice, and acknowledged widely in various parts of Great Britain. We offer a few comments on the above quotations which help to extend our understanding of the Place.

Throughout we are confirmed in our belief that it was somewhere into which you could *descend*; it was *not* a raised space, and a direction to *ascend* into the Place never occurs in the whole literature. We therefore must repeat that we cannot accept the reading 'stage' in so far as the idea of a *raised* stage is implied.

Its area could be pretty extensive, for one could manœuvre a property ship within it, ride horses across it and bring processions into it (see examples 10, 11, 29, 40, 41, 14, 19).

It was somewhere into which, when one character had left it to go back to his raised scaffold, another character could enter apparently *not* from a scaffold; therefore it presumably had its own entrance or entrances (see ex. 12, 32).

It was somewhere into which, while one character was conducting business with another, there could come a totally unconnected group of characters who were concerned with some simultaneous or later action (see ex. 23, 24, 27).

Its centre point was a place of meeting for characters coming from various directions (ex. 13, 56).

It could act as a sort of withdrawing place where a player could walk 'privily' out of some other action (ex. 15).

It was somewhere into which a player could come running and shouting, and around which he could continue to run and shout (ex. 20).

It was somewhere where a piece of scenery in the form of a house or castle or chapel could be built, with certain observances (ex. 13, 63).

It was somewhere where an actor could stroll (see *spaciando*, ex. 44, 52, 53), and walk abroad (see *ambulat*, ex. 47).

Apart from the plays which give us examples of the use of the Place and call it by that word or a variant of that word, there are some which, though not employing the actual word in any form, yet undoubtedly use the system of the Place; example may be found in Lindsay's *Ane Satyre of the Threi Estaits*, where the name given to it is 'the green'.

On the other hand there is at least one play that uses the word 'place' but offers very little evidence of circular staging. Here it may be we have a survival of the use of the word when the system had given way to something else; the play is Skelton's *Magnyfycence* (c. 1516), a study of the presentation of which appears in my *Staging of Plays before Shakespeare*.

Recent Opinions on the 'Platea'

Important as we find the use of the Place to be in medieval theatre, it is somewhat difficult to discover a clear definition of the term or to learn how it came into existence. Let us ask first what the dictionaries have to tell us about it and then what explanations of it are given by modern writers on the medieval theatre.

References to dictionaries are not fruitful. Dictionaries of classical Latin only give *platea* as a public square or a courtyard in a house. Dictionaries of later Latin, and medieval word books, give as far as I have been able to find no specific meaning in a theatrical sense. Nor have I had success in finding any theatrical use of either *platea* or Place entered in *The Oxford English Dictionary*. Webster's *New International Dictionary* does, however, break the silence; surprisingly enough, it enters not only *platea* but *place*, both theatrically. Under *platea* we read: 'On the English medieval stage, a level space between stations.' If we ask what a *station* is, we find it is a place 'at which one scene in a series of mystery plays was performed'. The definition under *place* is possibly less to our purpose because it is somewhat non-committal and may refer to a later usage. It is: 'In early English drama, the locality in which the action proceeds.'

We may now take another step and ask what is said about the *platea* by the accepted authorities on the medieval stage.

I may take as representative of these authorities, Sir Edmund Chambers, Professor Allardyce Nicoll and Professor Gustave Cohen. We shall find that all three appear to accept in some degree the meaning *stage* among the equivalents of the word *platea*. Of this meaning we have so far been unable to discover any example in use. It will be necessary to decide therefore whether this further meaning is supported or not by the evidence available, and we must consider what these authorities say with particular care.

When we come to examine their references, we shall see that each of them quotes especially the usage of the word *platea* in one particular play, an Anglo-Norman Mystery Play in French (of between 1146 and 1174) known as *Le Jeu d'Adam*, and none of them mentions any earlier use than this. Perhaps, then, we are here getting near the origin of its use.

Before we read their remarks, we may list the uses of the word in this French play as we have listed those in the British plays above. As far as I can ascertain there are only three such uses:

Uses of 'Platea' in a French Play

Le Jeu d'Adam (Paul Studer ed. *Le Mystère d'Adam*, Manchester University Press, 1928).

69. (l. 112) Interea demones discurrant per plateas.
(In the mean time let the demons run about through the places.)

70. (l. 172) Tunc recedat diabolus et ibit ad alios demones et faciet discursum per plateam; et facta aliquantula mora hylaris et gaudens redibit. . . .
(Then let the Devil go away, and he shall go to the other demons and shall make an excursion through the place; after a short time he shall come back cheerful and rejoicing. . . .)

71. (l. 590) Et facta aliquantula mora exibunt diaboli discurrentes per plateas.
(After a short time the devils shall go out running through the places.)

It will be useful to consider the comments made by our authorities on these directions in particular, before going into their general deductions. Thus Chambers (*The Mediaeval Stage*, ii. 80) says of ex. 69: 'Meanwhile the demons are to run about the stage (per plateas).' A few lines later, he says, presumably referring to ex. 70: 'The *diabolus* thinks he is prevailing upon Adam. He joins the other demons and make sallies about the *plateae*. Then he returns *hylaris et gaudens* to the charge.' (Presumably 'make' is a misprint for 'makes'.) But Chambers does not unfortunately offer a full translation of *et faciet discursum per plateam* in this reference; he merely says 'and make sallies about the *plateae*', leaving *plateam* in Latin but now putting it in the plural—*plateae*, 'the places'. It is clear that he might be justified in this rather surprising usage because in the other two references (69 and 71) we in fact find (if the editing is correct) the plural used—*per plateas*. Here then we are faced with an unexpected development: What can 'Places' mean?

Turning now to Nicoll, we find that in *Masks Mimes and Miracles*, p. 195, he says (a little incorrectly)—'In the Anglo-Norman *Adam* "demons enter and run about the place [*per plateam*]." ' And he adds a footnote concerning the word *platea*, saying—'Often in this text it is referred to in the plural; cf. *per plateas* on pp. 7, 29.' The page-reference is to Studer's edition. One queries his 'often' since there appear to be only two such plural uses.

Cohen, in *Le Théâtre en France au Moyen Age*, p. 26, says of the above incident in *Adam*—'les démons circulent sur le devant de la scène (*per plateas*, littéralement "sur les places publiques") sur le "plateau" ', which seems at first to increase the puzzle.

It is not easy, therefore, even to understand the opinions on the word, let alone the word itself. But it appears that Chambers thinks of *platea* as 'stage', Nicoll as 'place', and Cohen as 'le devant de la scène . . . sur le "plateau" ' which I take to be renderable in English as 'the front of the acting-area . . . on the "platform" '—*but* he states also that *per plateas* literally means 'on the public squares' (if I may so render the modern French *places*).

So much for this rather knotty beginning. Now let us study Chambers's remarks about the *platea* in fuller detail. He renders the action mentioned in *discurrant per plateas* as running 'about the stage'. If, however, we turn to his p. 85 we shall find a considerable qualification of this, for he there says: 'I have spoken of a stage, but I am not sure that there was any stage in the sense of a platform. There is certainly no such scaffold in Fouquet's miniature, and the *plateae* of . . . the *Adam* are probably only the open spaces kept free for the actors between the *sedes*. In the *Adam* the devils are able to make sallies from the *plateae* amongst the spectators.' I submit that we have no evidence whatever of such an action in the *Adam*; what we do read is that the devils run *through* the plateae, not *from* the plateae. But our main point about this passage is that Chambers here says the *plateae* are probably open spaces kept free for the actors between the *sedes*, the *sedes* being the scaffolds. And with this, so far, our own study is in general agreement. But the confusion of 'stage' and *platea* is not cleared away by Chambers's qualification; other writers fall into it, and Chambers himself is not able to keep free, as we shall see at the end of the next quotation.

He refers further to the *platea* and the *sedes* on p. 135 in dealing with the Cornish *Ordinale* plays, about which he says: 'Within a circular area is arranged a ring of eight spots which probably represent structures elevated above the general surface of the "playne". . . . From the stage directions it would appear that the raised portions were called *pulpita* or *tenti*, and by Jordan at a later date "rooms"; that the "playne" was the *platea*; and that the action went on partly on the *pulpita*, partly on the *platea* between them. Except that it is circular instead of oblong, the scheme corresponds exactly to that of the continental plays shown in an earlier chapter to have been determined by the conditions within a church'—and he refers in a footnote to his p. 83, where, however, is no reference to staging outside churches; then he goes on—'Those plays also had their *platea*; and their *domus, loca,* or *sedes* answer to the *pulpita* and *tenti* of Cornwall. Judging by the somewhat scanty indications available, the disposition of other English "standing" plays must have been on very similar lines. . . .'

(All this is in full agreement with the reading of our own evidence, but now comes the recurrence of the confusion:)

'. . . In some cases there is evidence that the level *platea* was replaced by a raised "platform", "scaffold", or "stage". Thus Chaucer's "joly Absolon" played Herod "on a scaffold hye". ' Then there is inserted a footnote which reads—'C.T. 3384 (*Miller's Tale*). This "scaffold" may have been merely a throne or *sedes* for Herod. But plays on platforms or scaffolds are found at Chelmsford, Kingston, Reading, Dublin.'

This passage runs so contrary to what we have come to expect that we read it a second time. But the statement remains: 'in some cases there is evidence that the level *platea* was *replaced by a raised platform* . . .'. We eagerly read on to find this evidence, but we are disappointed. Of course Herod played 'on a scaffold hye'! Of course there might have been scaffolds at Chelmsford, Kingston, Reading and Dublin—and at Lincoln for *The Castle,* and at scores of other places! World and Flesh in *The Castle* played on high scaffolds like Herod, yet that *does not mean that there was no Place below the scaffolds,* nor that the *platea* was 're-placed by a raised platform'! On the other hand, there is evidence, which is very well known, to the effect that another Herod who played similarly on a raised stage also descended from it and played on the ground below—and that evidence is the stage direction from the Coventry *Shearmen and Taylors Play,* l. 783, 'Here Erode ragis in the pagond and in the strete also'.

I would emphasize that so far as we have gone the Place and the scaffolds have always been entirely distinct. To accept what Chambers says is equivalent either to denying his own statement that the 'action went on partly on the *pulpita,* partly on the *platea*', or to claiming that the *platea* and the *pulpita* were the same thing—which is the same as saying that the Place became the Scaffolds.

If it can ever be shown that this latter is correct (and I believe it can-not) I think that the identification of the two had certainly not taken place at the time of *The Castle of Perseverance,* and that it is of immense importance to our understanding to keep them distinct in our minds for the period we are studying. We shall go on to see to what length Nicoll presses the idea, but for the moment it is useful to conclude our study of Chambers's remarks by saying that there is in our authorities a very marked hesitation to distinguish finally between two elements of medieval staging which our study of *The Castle* has taught us should be unequivocally separated—(*a*) the *platea* or Place or 'playne' and (*b*) the *mansions, sedes, tenti, pulpita, domus*, houses or Scaffolds.

We now turn to take up Nicoll's remarks enlarging upon the *platea*. The full context of the note on *Le Jeu d'Adam* that we quoted above is as follows:

'The use of the *platea* is of very ancient origin. In the Anglo-Norman *Adam* "demons enter and run about the place [*per plateam*]". There is no need here to quote other and later examples; the use of this "place" was constant in the religious theatre, and, as will be seen, it was employed later by secular players both in Italy and England. Where the scenes were set in order in one space the *platea* was a roped-in portion of the playing-ground; where the "pageants" were scattered, as at Coventry, it was simply the street—"Here Erode [Herod] ragis in the pagond and in the strete also".'

So far, then, in Nicoll's view the *platea* may be either a 'roped-in portion of the playing-ground' or 'simply the street'.

In his *The Development of the Theatre*, however (1st ed., p. 72), is a statement which again instances for us this confusion of *platea* with scaffold; he says that with the passing away of the miracle cycles, the interludes needed simpler settings: 'The setting of these plays, we must presume, was merely a raised daïs, probably backed by a curtain. . . . The *platea*, in other words, exists without the *mansions*.' This seems to me to be very much the same thing as saying, with Chambers, that the *platea* was replaced by a platform or 'raised daïs'.

In his *The English Theatre* Nicoll states it finally (p. 11): 'The [medieval] stage itself seems to have taken a variety of different forms, all dependent upon one common idea. This common idea was the presentation of a piece of unlocalized ground with the accompaniment of several localized positions. . . . The unlocalized space was known technically as the *platea*, anglicized as "place" or (in Cornwall) as "plain". This "place", forming the main "stage" and roughly corresponding to the acting ground in the cathedral nave, might be merely the street itself, the village green, the centre of the round amphitheatrical structure; on the other hand, it might be, and often was, a raised platform. . . . ' We especially note this categoric final sentence.

Again (p. 35): 'As has been seen already, there were two main methods of presenting a play in mediæval times. Both of these demanded the presence of an open unlocalized *platea*, but whereas one had no background save a possible curtain, the other employed a series of mansions or pageants for certain localized scenes. . . .'

This 'unlocalized *platea*' Nicoll later sees develop into the 'large platform stage' of the Elizabethans 'constituting the equivalent of the old *platea* and of the front portion of the acting space in the Teatro Olimpico' (see pp. 40, 41 and 46), and in some sense into the Elizabethan upper stage ('treating it as a kind of upper *platea*', p. 42), and he even recalls its quality of 'unlocalization' in the conventions of the Restoration fore-stage, see p. 84.

Nicoll's view would seem to be that, although the flat *platea* might in earlier periods have been used in conjunction with adjacent raised scaffold-stages, yet later these disappeared, leaving the *platea* which 'might be, and often was, a raised platform'!

It seems that we may be here faced with that sort of misconception that comes from arguing backwards. The platform of the Elizabethan playhouse is frequently called an 'unlocalized' stage (I have myself discussed what I have termed its 'placelessness' in *The Open Stage*). The idea developed by Nicoll is apparently that since the Elizabethan stage could represent one place in one scene and another place in the next scene without any change of 'scenery', then the Elizabethan platform was 'unlocalized', and since the medieval Place was also 'unlocalized' (or so it is said), then the argument follows that the Elizabethan platform must be descended from the medieval Place!

Last we return to Cohen's reference to the use of the *platea* in *Le Jeu d'Adam*. His chief contribution to our study is to equate *platea* with a town place or square—'(*per plateas*, littéralement "sur les places publiques")'—and with this we reach as nearly as we may perhaps to the origin of *platea*; though he appears to throw away this valuable suggestion in a parenthesis, instead of making it a principal idea. If Cohen is correct, we may say (and this leads on also from our other authorities) that for an early medieval performance there were two essentials; the flat surface of the existing ground, grass or pavement, and a raised addition either already existing (as for instance at the head of a flight of church steps) or expressly built (as a wooden platform or scaffold, or a group of these). The former, Cohen suggests, is what we should imagine when we picture the presentation of *Le Jeu d'Adam*. The latter we well know from our study of *The Castle*.

Thus, in *Le Jeu* we are to understand a performance outside a church with part of the action presented on the flat space at the top of the entrance steps, and part down below in the square at the foot of the steps. The square is *la place*; this, latinized, is *platea*, and the related technique of presentation, developed into a regular system, leads to the prepared or enclosed Place with scaffolds round it, when the requirements of professional players begin to exert their influence.

One thing about this identification of the Place with a 'public place', whether street, square or stretch of grass, is that it is already implied that the audience would be in the Place—it was in fact their own ground. There is some psychological value in such an idea in the theatre, the idea of taking the play to the people out of the church and performing it in their own world. Such a mental approach may make for immediacy in the presentation, for a sort of particular truth, an intimate contact.

(I wonder if the plays left the churches, not because they became so popular that the churches could not hold them and therefore they bounded spontaneously into the wider world, as is generally suggested, but because so few people came to them in their liturgical form that the presenters decided to move them to the threshold of the church—and eventually out into the streets of the town, Salvation-army-like?)

If now such 'Places' were public squares or streets, they may well have been thronged for a play, and if such a play had in its technique the descent of players from their elevation, and their moving across the square, one can well see how the need for marshal-men would surely arise, and thus how stytelers would become important—as well as how one would not want too many of them, cluttering the Place and blunting the immediacy of the show's contact.

One final point about the problem of *plateae* in the plural; it is perhaps worth noticing that examples 69 and 71, in which this plural form is found, both deal with the excursions into the Place of several demons; whereas in example 70, where the singular is used, we have unmistakably the excursion into the Place of one figure alone—the Devil himself. Thus it is understandable that a scattered crowd of demons might, and would, run in *several places* at once, while the Devil on his own could do no more than make his progress through *the Place* singly.

There is one other stage direction in *Le Jeu d'Adam* which I think offers some confirmation of the identification of *platea* with 'public square'. At l. 204 the Devil—'ibit usque ad portas inferni, et colloquium habebit cum aliis demoniis. Post ea vero faciet discursum per populum . . .' ('—shall go up to Hell-gates and shall have speech with other demons. Afterwards, however, he shall make an excursion through the crowd. . . .'). This at least confirms that an actor might go among the audience, and I think that *per plateam* and *per populum* mean the same thing.

To summarize: Cohen contributes an idea concerning the origin of the word as the public place where the show was performed. Chambers identifies scaffolds and *sedes*, but stumbles perhaps involuntarily into suggesting that the *platea* developed into a *sedes*. Nicoll accepts this suggestion and goes much farther, apparently seeing the *platea*, after becoming a *sedes*, suffer a development into a raised stage which ends in the conventions of the fore-stage of the Restoration.

To Nicoll's suggestion about the later development of the term, we have an alternative to offer before winding up our review. As it seems to me, he tends to give us to understand that the *platea* developed into the *stage* of the earliest forebears of our modern playhouse. There is reason to believe, however, that the *platea* did not develop into the stage but into a very different part of the modern playhouse. It was a part such that it did not lose its identity as the place before and below the stage into which a descent from that stage could conceivably be made. In proof I can offer an example of the word *platea* actually surviving in normal, common use in the eighteenth-century playhouse.

To explain the matter—I had by chance, just before finishing this present book, to examine some theatrical plans in the Royal Library of Malta. There, under reference, *Cabreo osia Descrizione della Fondazione Manoel*, 1732 (Register or Description of the Manoel Foundation), I found a set relating to the Manoel Theatre in Valletta as it was built in 1731. Written clearly upon the space which we today should call the pit and stalls was the following legend, of which the central word is of prime importance:

'Banchi della Platea in Anfiteatro'

or 'Benches of the Pit arranged in an amphitheatre'. *The Italian word which is used to refer to the Pit is 'platea'*, and here in fact is the part of a modern playhouse which *does* lie in much the same relation to the raised stage as the Place lay in relation to the medieval scaffolds. Now at length, as I believe, we have uncovered the true descendant of the medieval Place or *platea*; namely, not the stage but the ground-floor of the auditorium, called in Italy the *platea* even to this day—for the word continued in use after 1731 up to the present time with exactly the same meaning, as the following references in Italian dictionaries show. (I am much indebted to Doctor G. Aquilecchia of University College, London, for his assistance here.)

In Tommaseo and Bellini's *Dizionario della Lingua Italiana*, 1861, ed. 1929, the word *platea* is given, under meaning 4, as: 'Also the name given to the lower part of a theatre where the spectators are.' (*Così dicesi anche la Parte più bassa d'un teatro, dove stanno gli spettatori.*) Among the examples cited is one from Tommaso Crudeli (1703–45): 'Love, that is not limited to the low platea . . .' (which the humbler folk frequent). (*Amor che non si ferma Nella bassa platea, . . .*)

Again, the remark—'The boxes and the pit are shouting to you' (*A te gridano i palchi e la platea*) exemplifies the two typical parts of a theatre (beside the *galleria* above), disposed round the sides and on the floor.

Bringing the term up to the present day, we have Cappuccini and Migliorini's *Vocabolario della Lingua Italiana*, 1951, where *platea* is defined as 'The floor of the theatre, where the rows of seats and stalls for the spectators are', and the expression 'the acclamation of the pit' (*gli applausi della platea*) is a further example of the slightly derogatory sense with which the 'low' *platea* is associated, for it may suggest a somewhat meretricious fame.

(It may be added that *platea* is used today in the Catalan language with the same theatrical meaning, and that in Portuguese the parallel word is *plateia*.)

Thus the word *platea* survives today with a meaning that is almost exactly comparable with the theatrical *platea* of the Middle Ages.

To recapitulate: the *platea* developed not into the stage of our modern theatre, but into the pit-and-stalls of our modern theatre. And in doing so it kept the essential relation to the raised stage that it had in the beginning—namely the space below and before that stage.

Winding up of the Inquiry: Origin and Definition of Place

We seem now, as far as our information goes, to be able to offer an origin for the term *platea* in that it was a latinization for acting direction purposes of the French term *la place* meaning the public square or place (as in the Place de la Concorde, or in our Waterloo Place; compare the Italian *piazza* and the German *Platz*). It was the public place upon which the stage was erected and down to which the actors might descend from that stage (or stages); across which they could walk along lanes cleared through the crowd of people; and which, if several lanes were left from several stages, might well be alluded to in the plural—hence *per plateam*, 'through the Place', and also *per plateas*, 'through the Places, or various lanes in the Place'.

Finally we may ourselves try to frame a definition of this term: the Place (also *platea*, *placea* and plain) is the area on which the audience stood before a raised stage or stages (*c.* 1146 to *c.* 1516 (?)). In Italy *platea* retains this sense today (save that the audience in a modern theatre now generally sit).

If this is true, then it must surely be an instance of over-determination to talk of an 'unlocalized' *platea*. How could the ground on which the audience stood be localized! This would be too sophisticated an idea for a direct medieval theatre-man. To him the Place was simply the ground before the stage, the 'here'. The actors might descend to it as part of their technique whenever necessary, and use it on occasion for considerable passages of action—why not? But they themselves remained actors performing the action of their drama, and it was the *action* not the *place* that told the story. They never pretended they were in an imagined locality relevant to that action, when in fact it was clear for all to see that they were not—that they were *here*. The actors and the action together were the vehicle of the drama; the Place was the vehicle of that action, but never of the drama.

Hence it was that lines and acting were enough scenery for the Elizabethans.

235

It was not until the Italian Renaissance that the place of a performance could become attired in costume like an actor and take a part in the drama—and scenery was born. But to distinguish the existence of any such thing as an 'unlocalized scene' in the Middle Ages is to think backwards with a Renaissance approach towards a time before such a distinction could ever have been conceived.

APPENDIX 2

PLACE, SCAFFOLDS AND COSTUMES IN THE *ORDINALIA*

The Presentation of the Garden of Paradise ∗ Other Problems in the Origo *or First Day's Presentation ∗ Summaries of the* Passio *on the Second Day and of the* Resurrexio *on the Third Day ∗ A Note on the Players' Costumes*

THE ambitious range of spectacle presented in the *Ordinalia* surpasses anything to be found in any pageant-wagon presentation, which is not surprising seeing the boundless possibilities of the circular Place. This Place is 'placeless'; or rather, can represent the World or any part of it on land or sea as and when required—almost like a blank cinema screen. But the scaffolds do refer, at least temporarily, to places or to the people who dwell in those places. They are well named *domus* or 'houses' From such origins one can well see how the Tudor Interlude tradition and, later, the Elizabethan playhouse tradition developed.

It seems best to describe the *Origo* performance by means of small sketches of certain episodes in action, so making an addition to the treatment in *The Castle* where the concern was with verbal description rather than with the visual presentation of action. Only a very summary selection will be possible in the space of this Appendix, but behind it lies the idea of outlining how a practical production might be worked out today.

I allow myself to assume the existence of certain anonymous, and possibly black-cloaked, attendants like Japanese *kōken*, basing on the conveyour' mentioned in Jordan's *Creation of the World* (see Whitley Stokes' translation, *Gwreans an Bys*, 1864, at l. 339: '*Adam and Eva aparlet in whytt lether in a place apoynted by the conveyour & not to be sene tyll they be called . . .*' and on the 'Ordinary' mentioned by Carew (see above p. 87) when he says 'The players . . . are prompted by one called the Ordinary, who followeth at their back with the booke in his hand.') Also the construction of light properties, the existence of 'stytelers' to control the movements of the spectators, and particularly the literal interpretation of certain significant lines in the script.

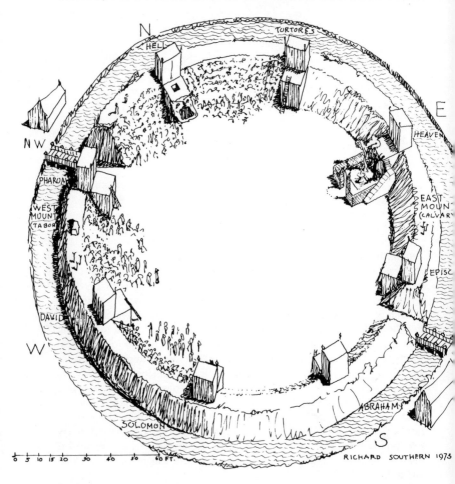

FIG. 23. Axonometric plan showing conjectural layout of scaffolds for *The Creation of the World* on the first day's performance, some of the audience indicated on the left half of the figure.

The Presentation of Paradise Garden

To begin with the question raised in the Preface, the manner of representing Paradise. There are certain data·in the script. It was at ground level in the Place, but fenced off from it by some means that included a practicable gate. It seems likely that it would be near Heaven for the convenience of the early action. It must contain at least one tree, and Seth says later when he looks in on it through the closed gate that he can see fruit, fair flowers and a fountain. It may or may not be relevant to add that William Jordan, re-writing his version of the drama in or before 1611 says, '*Let Paradyce be fynelye made wyth ii fayre trees in yt And an appell vpon the tree & som other frute one the other*' and '*A fowntaine in Paradice & fyne flowers in yt painted*' (Stokes, ll. 350 and 354). How much this might apply to a performance two hundred years before Jordan's version is not, of course, certain, but it may not be irrelevant.

In order to place Paradise, I take the plan of the first day's play (reproduced in Fig. A on p. xiv) and suppose it developed and set up in a Round about 120 ft. in diameter after the manner of the system revealed in *The Castle* (see Fig. 23, p. 238). This figure is drawn in axonometric projection (not perspective), on a true plan, and the scale can therefore be used to measure any part. Heaven is at the East and Hell at the North in the traditional positions. Two entrance bridges are shown across the ditch at Northwest and Southeast respectively. Hell is provided with a 'hell-mouth'. A portion of the 'Hill' is reserved at two points for presenting scenes on Mounts—on the East, between the Heaven and Episcopus scaffolds, for Mt. Calvary; and on the West, between the David and Pharoah scaffolds, for Mt. Tabor. There are two dressing-tents or Pavilions outside the Round.

The experiment is tried, in view of the frequent use of the direction *pompabit*, 'he shall "pomp" ', to allow a small projection of the scaffold-floors in front of the curtain of the booths that back them, for particular actors to 'pomp' upon.

The enclosure of Paradise is set before the foot of the Heaven scaffold, and is based partly on the enclosure before the temple in the plans for the Lucerne Mystery of 1583, and partly on contemporary manuscripts depicting Paradise. It is bounded by a lattice fence that allows some vision of the interior, and has a double gate that can be opened and closed.

Access from scaffolds to Place is generally by ladder as in the Fouquet miniature but (again following Fouquet) Heaven is provided instead with a ramp for more dignified, and occasionally processional, descents. Since the Garden takes up all the front of the Heaven scaffold, this ramp leads down at first sideways to a small landing, and then forward to the Place beside the Garden wall.

Other Problems in the Origo or first day's presentation

It is convenient to break the first day's performance into eight episodes.

FIG. 24. Movements at the opening of *The Creation*.

Episode 1, the Creation, ll. 1–416. See Fig. 24. God opens, speaking from A, and describes the first days of creation, referring at l. 10 to heaven being 'filled with bright angels', thus it might be that certain angels appear behind him here on the Heaven scaffold. At l. 48, the fifth day of creation is reached and thereafter comes the following direction: '*Hic descendit Deus de pulpito* [. . .]'—*Here God comes down from the upper stage,* [. . .] Thus Norris. But I would rather see *de pulpito* as 'from his scaffold', for the original meaning of 'pulpit' according to the *O.E.D.* is 'A scaffold, stage, or platform for public representations . . .'. He has still to announce the work of the sixth day, which he does in ll. 49–56. These lines he might well speak as he pauses at the landing B in Fig. 24 before proceeding down the ramp to the Place.

I suppose God to be followed here by perhaps two angels, and then by two cloaked figures shortly to be revealed as Adam and Eve, and finally by two other cloaked figures acting as Attendants. There are no details about the creation of Adam beyond the direction '*Hic faciat Adam*'—*Here let him make Adam,* thus one must invent. It is however clear that Adam is not created in Paradise for, afterwards, they (God and Adam) are directed to go to Paradise: '[*ient ad paradisum*]'. Curiously, this direction (in square brackets and therefore by the later hand) is not translated by Norris. The implication is that he considers it to be incorrect. Here is an interesting point. He notes on his p. xi that 'The stage directions of the subsequent possessor are printed between brackets . . . , and where they are obviously wrong, no trans-lation is given.' This clearly implies that he considered the present direction to be 'obviously wrong'—in the belief, I suppose, that Adam must have been created in Paradise and therefore could not have 'gone to' it after his creation. But to create Adam *in* Paradise would be to present a highly significant piece of business in such a way that it could hardly be seen, for Paradise is walled in (albeit with only a lattice fence). Much more effective would be for God to pause at the head of his procession near the point C in the Figure, and for the cloaked Adam to walk from his place to before God's feet, lie down and then, at the command 'Adam, stand up in glory' (l. 65), shed his cloak and rise— either 'naked' or 'aparlet in whytt lether' as Jordan had it. The Atten-dants would remove the cloak.

It is only thereafter that God takes Adam *ad paradisum* (l. 92) that is to say 'to', or rather 'towards', Paradise—say to point D, but still not *into* Paradise for Eve has yet to be created, and this action is as significant as Adam's creation was. The direction is clear. Adam lies down again; '*Et Adam dormiet. hic facit deus euam et ducet eam ad Adam* [. . .]'— *And Adam shall sleep: here God makes Eve, and shall lead her to Adam*, note 'shall lead her to'. Thus Eve was created some distance from Adam (probably, as he was, at C) and was thereafter led to him where he lay outside Paradise at D. Presumably God simply bent over the sleeping Adam as he said 'Forthwith from one of thy ribs, / I make thee an equal' (l. 99).

Eve has a single stanza of acknowledgement, and then there comes another later-added direction, omitted again by Norris in the translation —presumably because it also seemed to him to be wrong—it is '[*eva exit*]'. Adam, however, has still to name all the animals, and there follow nearly 150 lines of dialogue before Eve is concerned again. And when she is, she is clearly *in* Paradise, for the Serpent is speaking to her from the tree. Thus the implication is that this direction is correct, and that Eve does 'exit', and exits by going through the gate into the Paradise enclosure.

During the temptation of Eve in Paradise, Adam is still outside and unaware, until Eve offers him the apple through the gate. He tastes it, drops the core on the threshold, sees he is naked, and only then comes the direction: '[*Adam abscondit se in paradiso*]'—[*Adam hides himself in*

FIG. 25. Seth looks three times into Paradise.

Paradise.] (l. 256). Thereafter comes the descent of the Angel (l. 342) at God's order for the expulsion and—'[*hic adam et eva recedunt de paradiso*]'— [*Here Adam and Eve depart from Paradise.*] and the gate is closed.

▪ Episode 2 is the story of Cain and Abel (252 lines). It involves no new problem. Abel presumably mounts the west Hill for his sacrifice and Cain kills him as he descends again. Lucifer sends his devils to take Abel to Hell.

Episode 3 (already described in the Foreword) now follows for 245 lines. In it the dying Adam sends his third son, Seth, to seek for mercy. Supposing Adam to go to point F in Fig. 25, Seth can then leave him to go to take his three glimpses through the gate of the barred Eden, with the Angel, or 'Cherubyn' as the script has it, standing aloft at B to question him and order him to take three pips from the apple core at the gate (l. 823)—with Seth part-returning each time to report what he sees, both to Adam and to the Angel (see the arrow at E). I am supposing that no notice need be taken of Norris's translation of *iterum vadit in sup:* as 'again he goes up', but that the Latin can legitimately read as 'again he goes and for the last time', and it is entirely effective that way,

242

and there will be no cause to visualize the Garden as on a raised scaffold.

We would then have in this Episode 3 confirmation that the *Origo* script expands our knowledge of Round technique with the almost certain evidence (which *The Castle* does not directly offer) that 'scenic elements' could be built in the Place not only in the centre but before one of the peripheral scaffolds.

The Episode closes with Seth's return to his father with the news that he shall receive mercy at the last, in token of which Seth puts the three apple pips in Adam's mouth as he is dying. A particular problem now arises; how could burials be effected in a Round performance? The means might be very simple here. Seth might perhaps mime digging a grave for he says 'In the earth I will dig / A hole, that he may be covered in it;' '[*seth facit sepulcrum et sepellitur adam*]'—[*Seth makes a grave and buries Adam.*] (ll. 865–6). But supposing the digging is only mimed, how is the body actually disposed of? Simply by dragging it into the concealment of the lower curtain of the nearest scaffold. Specific evidence for this convention is offered later at David's death when a Counsellor '*sepelliret ipsum et portabit corpus sub aliquo tento . . .*' —*shall bury him, and carry the body under some tent, . . .* (see l. 2370).

FIG. 26. Preparing to build the Ark.

243

A suitable scaffold for Adam would be the *Episcopus* scaffold since the seeds in Adam's mouth eventually spring up into 'rods' upon the immediately adjacent Mt. Calvary, where Moses is later to gather them in Episode 6 and take them to Mt. Tabor opposite, just before he dies.

Episode 4, Noah and the ark, (ll. 917–1258). The problems here are: how was the ark built, and how was the flood represented? Of the method of building the ark there is no evidence except vivid exclamations from Noah demanding his axe and auger and hammer (ll. 1001–2), and his complaint a few lines later that he is 'weary of cutting oak sticks'. But the lines imply that the ark is actually built. A possible way would be for Shem, Ham and Japhet to enter from the Northwest Entrance each 'running' a canvassed wooden framework like a modern flat, or like a Tudor 'frame', as suggested in Fig. 26, and to set these up with the addition of three poles and an awning as in Fig. 27. In this Figure the business of driving the animals into the ark is suggested as being mimed to the accompaniment of the lines. The flood is sufficiently suggested by the lines themselves when Shem announces 'I will now cover / The top of the ark with a cloth, / . . . That the rain may not come in.' (ll. 1073–76). And by the subsequent vivid stanza from Japhet

FIG. 27. Driving animals into the finished Ark.

describing the downpour. After the rain the ship is uncovered—'*Et tunc discooperiant nauem . . .*'—*And then let them uncover the ship: . . .*

There is nothing unduly difficult in the next Episode of Abraham and Isaac (135 lines). Abraham leads Isaac from his scaffold (shown in Fig. 23) to 'the mountain'—possibly the clear space on the Hill at the west side—and Gabriel must descend in good time to cross the Place and arrest the sword and prevent the sacrifice: '*hic descendit gabriel et veniet ad abraham et tenet gladium ejus*'—*Here Gabriel comes down, and shall come to Abraham; and he holds his sword.* (l. 1364)

Episode 6 (503 Lines), concerning Moses, begins with two small conjuring tricks in the Place representing the appearance of the burning bush, and Moses' staff turned into a snake. But the outstanding interest is how could the crossing of the Red Sea and the drowning of the Egyptians be presented in a Round? Again, the solution might be surprisingly simple; the lines carry almost the whole effect. After argument at Pharoah's scaffold (glimpsed at the top left corner of Fig. 28) between him and Moses and Aaron, Moses calls to the Children of Israel 'Let us go hence to the Red Sea' (l. 1622) and mounts a horse to lead them with their burdens from, probably, the Northwest Entrance

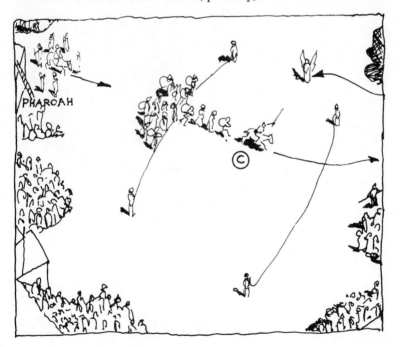

FIG. 28. The Israelites cross the Red Sea.

out into the Place. Then '[*hic descendit Gabriell*]'—[*Here Gabriel comes down.*] He watches the Exodus. An Israelite cries 'We shall never be able to cross / This sea, . . .' (l. 1648) and they pause at a shore created by those words (or, if more were needed, at a ribbon laid down by a couple of Assistants, see Fig. 28). At Gabriel's command, Moses '[*percutit mare*]', that is [*He smites the sea.*] (l. 1674), and cries 'Open wide a path for us'. They cross as in Fig. 28. Pharoah's army follows: 'I will follow them, / To put them to death, . . .' etc. Then he recreates the whole calamity by means of his lines—'Oh, sad, alas! alas! / The great sea is fallen upon us, / We shall be quite drowned.' (l. 1699–1701). One might be forgiven for wondering if the effect were strengthened by the insurge of four Attendants from the Southeast Entrance, sweeping a red sea-cloth with them to encircle and submerge the Egyptians before leading them back to the Northwest Entrance, and out? (see Fig. 29.) For an instance of such a 'red' sea refer to Illustration 106 in Mitchell's *Medieval Manuscript Painting*.

Episode 7 concerning David is the longest, taking 1,047 lines. It can be divided into three parts; David and the 'Rods' (205 lines), David and Bathsheba (789 lines), and David building the Temple (53 lines). The

FIG. 29. The Egyptians about to be overwhelmed in the Red Sea.

FIG. 30. The movements in the David and Bathsheba Episode.

part concerning David and Bathsheba is the longest passage in the whole play, and it contains the character study of a woman intent upon achieving a certain destiny that is unique in early drama.

In the first part David brings down the Rods from Mt. Tabor and takes them across to his own scaffold, at H in Fig. 30. While he sleeps they replant themselves magically and unite into one tree (presumably the Attendants remove them and replace them with a tall timber). This tree is eventually to supply the wood of The Cross.

The Bathsheba scene is remarkable enough as an early study of eternal-triangle psychology to justify particular notes on the succession of movements implied in the script. At l. 2104 David is at his scaffold at H, remarking the miracle of the Tree. When he turns away his eye is caught and this direction immediately follows —'*Et dicit rex David ad bersabe [abluendo vestem in rivilo]*'—*And king David says to Bathsheba [washing her dress in the stream]*. Thus Bathsheba must have entered, presumably from the Southeast Entrance, I, and proceeded possibly to point J where if the Red Sea ribbon were left in place she might kneel and treat it as the river bank. David seeing her advances, perhaps to K. What he says is; 'Damsel, on thy gentleness, / Shew me how to love

247

thee; / For never have I seen / A woman who pleases me better,' (ll. 2105–8). They might now close together at L. Her reply is: '. . . It would be a pleasure / With me, to do the will of thy mind, / . . . If the villain knew, / Immediately I should be killed.' (The 'villain' is her husband Uriah.) Immediately now follows the direction: '[bersabe transeat domum cum rege dd]'—[Let Bathsheba go home with king David.] They go then together from L towards M (see the arrow). David says: 'Bathsheba, flower of all the world, / Certainly, for thy love, / Sir Uriah shall be put to death; / . . .' Bathsheba says: 'I cannot deny thee, / . . . kill all, / Else he will spit at me / If he shall hear of our sport.' And David replies: 'My dear beloved heart, / God made a rose, flower of her sex, / ' and adds 'He shall be, without fail, / Dead for thy love.'

 She now possibly falls back a little, maybe towards the Solomon scaffold, while David advances to his own scaffold to call up to Uriah, who enters through the curtain and receives his marching-orders to ride to battle immediately (ll. 2140 ff.), only asking to speak to his faithful wife before he gets armed to go (ll. 2171 ff.) David now probably withdraws contentedly towards C after having summoned his Butler and a Messenger to help in preparing Uriah. Uriah calls to Bathsheba who advances from the Solomon scaffold to M to listen, and—'[dicit ad barsabe]'—[He speaks to Bathsheba.]: '. . . Need is to me to labour / At a battle . . .' (l. 2176–7) '[hic paratur et armatur hurias]'—[Here Uriah is prepared and armed.] Bathsheba, sure of her ground, replies: 'Do not you go, on my soul, / . . . My heart is separating / When I hear you talk so. / If you go away . . . / Never will I taste bread.' The Messenger goes now presumably to the Northwest Entrance to fetch horses. Uriah descends saying 'It is necessary . . .'. Bathsheba mounts David's scaffold while Uriah meets the horses below in the Place. Perhaps she waves goodbye to him before she disappears; '[ascendit ea et vadit]'—[She goes up, and exit.] She has a stanza of farewell to him as he begins to mount—and immediately upon this the first sense of coming retribution is felt: '[hic descendit gabriel]'—[Here Gabriel comes down.] He must descend from the Heaven scaffold opposite, and he can then wait and significantly mark the progress of the horses and riders round the Place as they go clockwise to the Southwest Entrance; 'Et tunc equitabunt extra ludum'—And then they shall ride out of the stage. (Thus Norris; I would prefer simply the literal 'ride out of the action', or the 'play'.)

 After a pause—possibly quite dramatic—the Messenger re-enters: 'et postea venit nuncius et dicit ad Dd regem'—And afterwards the messenger comes, and says to David the king:—that Uriah is killed in action. 'Tunc veniet angelus ad regem dauid et querat questionem . . .'— Then the angel shall come to king David, and ask him a question;—the all-seeing figure therefore walks now straight across the Place from the foot of Heaven to David's scaffold (see the arrow in Fig. 30), and there he pronounces what is to be David's doom. David sits in remorse under the Tree and begins to write the Psalter (l. 2254).

In the beginning of the third section of this Episode a Counsellor tells David his best way of atonement would be to build a Temple. David calls Masons to set to work 'in the midst of the town' (l. 2282) thus, one supposes, in or about the centre of the Place (C in Fig. 31). There is no evidence of how the temple was built. A particular problem is the mention of scaffolding (l. 2322). Is the translation right here? Supposing it is, then eight posts could be wheeled in on a truck (there is evidence for a truck, see l. 2318), and eight post-holes could have been previously made in the green to drop the 12 ft. poles into, and four 10 ft. and six 6 ft. crosspieces lashed between them on prepared stops 7 ft. up, and planks laid on the ends (see Fig. 31) for the temple pieces to be eventually set up inside. It is all a question of how much time was thought to be allowable for such a piece of business treated as a light-hearted interlude—perhaps, given six men with two ladders and two pullies, thirty-five seconds?

But at the height of the bustle of erecting the scaffolding, God suddenly intervenes with a most fateful dozen lines; '[*deus sit in platea*]' —not, as Norris says, [*Let God be on the stage*], but 'Let God be in the Place', that is to say, let him descend into the midst of the workmen (D in Fig. 31). And there among them he says, 'David, thou shalt not make me a house, . . . Solomon, thy son . . . shall . . . build it, . . .' David forbears, transfers his crown to his son, and dies. And is buried *sub aliquo tento* (see above, p. 243), probably under Solomon's scaffold glimpsed at the centre-bottom of Fig. 31. Thus David is, as in the Bible narrative, barred from building the Temple as punishment for his affair with Bathsheba. The Temple is built instead by the second child of that affair.

Episode 8, Solomon, (ll. 2371–845). The problem of the building of the actual Temple inside the scaffolding is a very considerable one. There is little doubt from the lines that Solomon first descends from his scaffold (l. 2388), then takes his place on David's scaffold (l. 2394) and sends a messenger to re-start the building (l. 2418). The Masons next have a scene wherein they describe their building to Solomon (l. 2492 *et seq.*). Solomon then descends about l. 2482 and goes to inspect the progress of the work. Something must therefore have gone on during this passage to suggest building in the centre of the Place. A brief provisional reply as to 'what?' would be that the Masons bring in on a truck something like six columns, two major arch-pieces, and four minor arch-pieces, and set them up within the scaffolding so as to be ready to look like what is shown later in Fig. 32 for the Second Day's

Performance, *The Passion*. But they do not at first complete this; the roof tree is lacking (see l. 2492 *et seq.*). They try to provide it by cutting down the Mystic Tree at H. But it proves eternally and magically to be the wrong dimension (ll. 2492–581), and Solomon tells them to leave it on the Temple floor (l. 2554) and find another timber. With this they eventually finish the building.

Now, at l. 2599, begins the passage which explains the existence of the 'Episcopus' scaffold. Solomon decides to create the first Bishop of the new Temple, and he actually invests him:—'[*hic consultor induit vestimentum clic*]'—[*Here the counsellor puts on the clerical dress*]—and gives him his mitre—'[*hic dat metram episcopo*]'—[*Here he gives the mitre to the bishop*]. And all this is done while the Counsellor is on the Episcopus scaffold, for at l. 2622 '[*hic descendit episcopus et transeat ad templum*]'—[*Here the bishop goes down, and may cross over to the temple*], (or, 'and let him cross to the temple').

Now a most remarkable and astonishingly brutal interlude takes place. It is heralded by the longest direction in the play (l. 2628)—'*Et tunc orent et murmurabunt quasi dicendo orationes et veniet maximilla in*

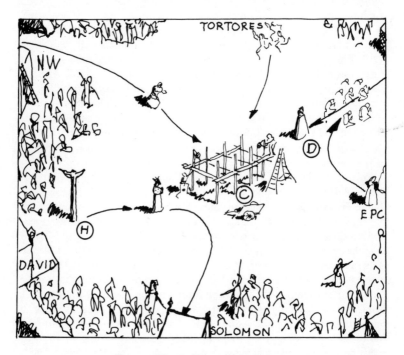

FIG. 31. The building of the Temple.

templo et sedet super stuppam [*scuppam* in the manuscript] *et vestes ejus concremantur a stuppa* [*scuppa*] *et ipsa clamat dicens'*. Norris is here inconsistent either in printing his translation in square brackets or in omitting the square brackets from the Latin; he gives—[*And then they shall pray, and speak low, as if saying prayers; and Maximilla shall come into the temple, and she sits upon a stove; and her clothes are set on fire by the stove; and she cries out, saying*—]. I imagine her entering from the Northwest Entrance and running across to the Temple in the centre (see the arrow in Fig. 31) while the Bishop and his procession are praying towards the Heaven scaffold near D. I suppose the *scuppa* or *stuppa* (or whatever the original word was) to have had something to do with the Mystic Tree; a 'stove' seems impossible. However that may be, the result is she exclaims in the name of Jesus Christ (l. 2635) and is hauled away on a charge of 'making a god' to herself (l. 2650) since no such name (then) existed, and she is brutally, and at great length, beaten to death by the *tortores*, and thus becomes the first martyr.

A final phantasy about disposing of the Mystic Tree by using it as a bridge over the Water of Cedron (l. 2818) ends the first day's play, the *Origo*.

Summaries of the Passio domini nostri *on the second day*, and of the Resurrexio domini nostri *on the third day*

At this point I may claim that something of the usage of the medieval Place and of the passages into and across it as elements of presenting the drama has—however inadequately—been offered for the reader's guidance. The actions in the second and third days' performances, the *Passio* and the *Resurrexio*, are far simpler and depend much more upon the dialogue; thus I may present them more briefly, and with the help of only one general diagram—except for the final harlequinade.

Suppose the arrangement of the Round for *The Passion* to be as in Fig. 32 with the re-assigning of the scaffolds as shown, according to a second diagram in the original manuscript, also the removal of the Garden and its substitution by the Table of the Last Supper at G, the addition of another smaller table for Simon the Leper's house before Herod's scaffold, a small 'dock' at F, the Scourging Pillar near the Northwest Entrance, three holes in the ground ready for the erection of the Crosses, and finally the completion of the Temple by the addition of a light turret, or pinnacle, approached by a step ladder—then the action might proceed in this way:

Jesus opens at A in Fig. 32, preaching to the Disciples from Mt. Quarentana. He descends, is tempted by Satan to turn stones into bread at B (l. 60), and again to cast himself from the pinnacle of the Temple, C

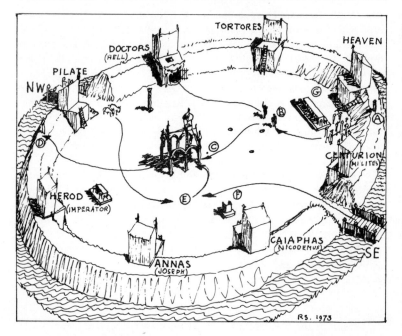

FIG. 32. The arrangement of scaffolds, etc., for *The Passion* (the second day's play). The smaller names in brackets indicate the allocation of the scaffolds for *The Resurrection* (the third day's play).

(l. 100), and finally to accept the (real) world as displayed to him from D (l. 130). After, two disciples are sent 'to a village to seek for an ass and foal' ('*et tunc mittens duos discipulos ad castellum ad quaerendum asinum et pullum*'—l. 172). These they bring, and Jesus mounts and rides to E. Next, '*Tunc veniunt pueri ebreorum et deferant palmas et flores contra ihesum . . .*' (*Then the Hebrew children come, and let them carry palms and flowers to meet Jesus . . .*' l. 228). They could well run in in a crowd from the Southeast Entrance to E.

Jesus then rides on to the Temple to accost the traders. Caiaphas intervenes and then Pilate, (each descending from his scaffold). Jesus goes to Simon's house to eat, and meets Martha and Mary (see the table before Herod's scaffold). Annas and Caiaphas plot with Judas. The Lord's Supper follows at G, (ll. 616–930). Judas betrays Jesus. Jesus watches and prays on the Mount of Olives, A, (l. 1010). Peter denies Jesus (ll. 1234 *et seq.*). Jesus is tried at F and beaten, is tested by the Doctors (ll. 1646 *et seq.*), and is brought before Pilate (ll. 1816 *et seq.*). Then after elaboration of further episodes the three crosses are made and set up (see the three holes between B and C) and a particularly brutal nailing follows. (The centre cross is brought in from Cedron.) After, the Centurion descends from his scaffold to go to the foot of the cross.

A problem is created by three directions immediately following the death of Jesus and referring to the darkening of the sun, the shaking of the earth, and the opening of graves. But these supernatural events I take to have been represented simply by the vividness (and at this point possibly by the sheer hypnotism) of the lines.

Finally Joseph of Arimathea and Nicodemus take down the body of Jesus and bury it in a special sepulchre, '[*paratur sepulcrum et lapis superponitur*]'—[*A sepulchre is prepared, and a stone put upon it.*]

Day Three, *The Resurrection*, is even more confined to dialogue, and contains little that need be enlarged upon in the brief space available here (except the extraordinary final Episode, see below). Some scaffolds are re-assigned according to the smaller names in brackets in Fig. 32, the rest are unchanged. Tables, scourging pillar and dock would be removed, and possibly the Temple replaced by a simple skeleton house. A boat would replace the ass and foal inside the Northwest Entrance ready for the penultimate Episode, The Death of Pilate.

At the opening of this episode Pilate, in the protection of the robe taken from Jesus before the crucifixion, is led before the *imperator*, Tiberius Caesar, who on the advice of Veronica takes away that robe (l. 1957), and Pilate is dismissed to be condemned to 'The cruelest death that is' (l. 2033). The Emperor discusses with Veronica what this death should be but then hears that Pilate has already stabbed himself (l. 2065). So Caesar commands his Gaoler—'thou and thy boy, / Take *him* by the two feet, / And put him in deep ground.' And now the fun starts (I use this word deliberately and in the bitterer Johnsonian sense).

There follow three lines from the Gaoler's Servant and then a most remarkable direction: 'Master, I will do it indeed; / Vengeance take him, amen, / And a bad end.' '*et tunc proicietur extra terram*'—*And then he shall be thrown out of the earth.* (ll. 2084-6). (Notice; no square brackets and thus, presumably, an original direction not an embellishment by any later hand.) It seems impossible. But the Servant confirms, exclaiming to the Gaoler '. . . Out of the earth he has jumped . . .' (l. 2090). The Gaoler, understandably, is incredulous:—'Forth he could not surely move himself . . .' (l. 2098), but he concludes, 'Let us put him in the earth again . . .' (l. 2110), '*et tunc ponent eum in terra et proicietur iterato sursum*'—*And then they shall put him in the ground, and he shall be thrown up again.* And they go to report this miracle to Caesar.

One may be tempted either to disbelief, or to propose some elaborate

FIG. 33(a). The 'burial' of Pilate.

catapult hidden in a hollow in the Place. But a remarkable other possibility is suggested by the words of the Servant's report. He says, 'When we put him in the grave, / Soon come devils / Upon us fallen; / And throw him forth upwards . . .' (ll. 2123–6). From this a picture emerges (Fig. 33a). Before the burial, four Devils may have run out from Hell and spread a cloth and waited at its corners. The Gaolers mime digging a grave upon this cloth, then stand back. The Devils in delight toss a dummy in the blanket (Fig. 33b). But this is only the beginning.

The (somewhat unchristian) Veronica hears of all this, but is equal to the emergency; she advises Caesar to have the body shut in an iron box and thrown into 'the water of Tiber' (l. 2136). This, Caesar orders his 'tortores' to effect. They obviously do so for the Secundus Tortor says, 'Behold the body put into the box; / Carry it immediately / To the corner of the water' (ll. 2183–5), and another confirms—'There in the water to the bottom / Certainly thou shalt go; . . .' '*et tunc proicietur corpus in aquam*'—*And then the body shall be thrown into the water.* (l. 2200).

What water? Like all such references in performances in Rounds it turns one's mind to the Ditch outside the Hill. But this is scarcely visible to the audience inside the Round. And yet, of course, to carry the box *out of sight* (e.g. through the Northwest Entrance) and to follow with an immense audible splash would be a completely possible and dramatic effect.

What comes next is certainly unexpected, indeed it seems scarcely possible if the foregoing were not true. It is that a fresh character, *Viator* (a traveller or wayfarer) suddenly announces: I will 'go to wash my hands / Immediately / . . . here in the water,' (l. 2202–4)! Wonders increase with the ensuing direction—'*et lauabit manus et statim morietur*' —*And he shall wash his hands, and shall die immediately* (l. 2206). This

FIG. 33(b). The 'burial' of Pilate.

might be a brilliant bit of nonsense. What is a *Viator*—a wayfarer? Is it a visitor, or member of the audience? It would be effective if such a man (planted of course) could rise from his seat, vanish through the North-west Entrance, with his typical purpose expressed, and fade to silence as he goes. Then scream, come rushing back, finish his speech, and die. The 'tortores' might then simply drag out his body. But even more is to come.

A Messenger begs Caesar to have the poisonous body dredged up and taken out of the country (l. 2218). Caesar is baffled, but the re-sourceful Veronica rises to the occasion again—'Take him in a boat to the sea' (l. 2233). So Caesar orders the 'tortores' 'To draw Pilate up, / Out of the water. / Put him in a boat into the sea' (l. 2254-6). They obey, casting in two grappling-irons, and call out (so that the audience may be under no delusion): 'See the hateful carcase / Coming up' (ll. 2278-9).

Then they actually bring in the (dripping?) box and put it 'into a boat'; not only this but they 'draw . . . her sail up' (p. 2291) and 'push her out' (l. 2295). There must have been a boat waiting by the North-west Entrance. Now what can possibly happen?

The lines seem unmistakable. The Fourth Tortor cries 'I hear an ugly noise / On a rock in the sea meeting him. / .·. . many devils / Forth have carried him' (ll. 2296-300),—and the First Tortor adds; '. . . devils have sucked *him* / To the deep; / They are crying loudly. / Let us come away, for fear of witchcraft, . . .' (ll. 2301-5).

Next, in case there should be any doubt, Lucifer speaks: 'My devils, come . . . / To carry . . . The body of Pilate . . .' (ll. 2307-10) Beelzebub and Satan reply and describe in detail what has happened to the boat—they must, it seems, have seized a rope and dragged it across the grass to the Hell scaffold. Satan cries '. . . thou, great cursed body / To hell, with thy soul, / By us shall be dragged; . . ', (ll. 2347–9), and Beelzebub responds, 'Now every one put his hand / To drag him in the same boat . . .' (ll. 2351–2). A fourth Devil, Tulfric. proposes a song with the others and—'*et sic finitur mors pilati*'—*And so ends the death of Pilate* (l. 2360).

Immediately then follows the direction '*et incipit ascensio Xti in celum . . .*'—*And the Ascension of Christ to heaven begins . . .* It consists of 269 dignified lines, with a quiet transition of Jesus in a red robe from the Place up the Mount of Olives, and eventually into the Heaven scaffold among white angels.

The Emperor has the final sixteen lines ending, 'Now let all go to the side of home. / Now minstrels, pipe diligently, / That we may go to dance.'

A Note on the Players' Costumes

One other consideration to conclude: what might these players have looked like in their costumes? I am privileged to add certain notes from Iris Brooke who originally prepared designs for the dressing of the whole *Ordinalia*. (In order to help students, the bulk of the authority for these designs has been restricted to information in two inexpensive reference books that should be readily obtainable. These and other sources will be quoted in a brief iconography.)

Towards the close of the fourteenth century, when the *Ordinalia* was first performed, the church had a well-established pictorial tradition of biblical history—stained-glass windows, wall-paintings, sculptures and many exquisite illuminated manuscripts clearly show that there existed

FIG. 34. Costumes for (*a*) God, full papal vestments; (*b*) The 'Cherubyn', armour and tunic; (*c*) and (*d*) Eve and Adam, leather fleshings(?); (*e*) A Devil.

FIG. 35. Costumes for (*a*) David, standard king's dress; (*b*) Bathsheba, kirtle; (*c*) Uriah, full armour; (*d*) Soldier, armour and tabard; (*e*) Moses, Jewish hat, robe and chest-belt with bells.

an easily recognizable convention for characters and their costumes. For example the magnificent windows at Chartres cathedral (12th. c.) show that kings—even Pharoah—all wore crowns (cf. Fig. 36*c*), and that Aaron was dressed as a Hebrew priest in *ephod* and *hoshen* (that is, overrobe and breast-piece with twelve jewels representing the Twelve Tribes, cf. Fig. 35*e*). The Christian vestments of alb, chasuble, dalmatic and cope were reserved for God and the angels, Figs. 34*a* and 36*d*. Wigs and beards, wings and white leather 'fleshings' (Fig. 34, *c* and *d*) are mentioned in early records; also 'shining armour' for the archangel Michael, and 'a hideous mask with horns and huge teeth' (Fig. 34*e*) for Lucifer in *The Presentation of the Virgin* at Avignon in the fourteenth century.

Cornwall might seem remote from the centres of fashion, but it was easily accessible from the Continent, and merchandise from both France and Spain found its way into the grander homes and the monasteries that governed the lives of the majority. Thus it would seem not improbable that these performances could have borrowed suitable garments when they needed them.

Fashion contributed possibilities in its 'disguisings'. It helped in facilitating quick changes of character (and even of sex, since many young men wore their hair long as they do today). The basic male costume (Fig. 37*a*) consisted of waist-high hose, often particoloured, with a tightly fitting and very short tunic, and a hood which had at least two separate uses—first, to keep shoulders and head warm (Fig.

FIG. 36. Costumes for (*a*) Pilate, full houpeland; (*b*) Pilate's Wife, cotehardie over kirtle; (*c*) Herod, king's dress over armour; (*d*) Angel, in chasuble; (*e*) Lucifer, disguised as friar.

37*b*) and second, to make an ornamental headdress by wearing the face-opening on the head and arranging the gorget to hang over one side or to stand up in a sort of glorified cock's comb, held in place by winding the liripipe around the head (Fig. 37*e*). Over the basic garments could be worn a tabard (Fig. 37*b*)—originally a sleeveless open-sided covering for armour which early in the fourteenth century had influenced both men's and women's dress—it was an easy, often very decorative, over-dress made simply from a straight length of material uncut save for a hole for the head in the centre. Tabards could be worn short and loose with some heraldic motif or household badge—or they could be knee-length and belted. A variant of this simple garment was made from two half-circles joined along the straight edges but leaving a centre opening wide enough to put over the head, resulting in a full, flowing garment that might be belted at waist or hip (Fig. 37*c*).

Dignity was emphasized by impressive hats, flowing robes, trailing sleeves, contrasting linings, and dagging or jagging of almost any edge of the fabric (Fig. 36*a*). Wealth was displayed in collars, shoulder-pieces or belts hung with bells (e.g. Fig. 35*e*) and embellished with precious stones, possibly also by the long, pointed toes of aristocratic footgear.

For women, the basic kirtle or underdress was as tightly fitting as possible from shoulder to hip, but flared out in increasing folds to the ankle (Fig. 35*b*). Tabards, cotehardies (sleeveless cutaway overdresses, Fig. 36*b*) and high-waisted houpelands were all diverting alterations to

FIG. 37. Opportunities for dress variation. (*a*) Standard male dress, but with parti-coloured tunic and hose and thrown-back hood; (*b*) Same, varied by raising hood and adding tabard; (*c*) Same, with short circular cape and gorget worn under cape (e.g. for a messenger); (*d*) Same, with plain hood and mid-length tabard made from two half circles; (*e*) Same, with houpeland and hood arranged as chaperon.

the basic kirtle. The great majority of pictured female elegance shows that the neckline was very low-cut, the hair worn long either loose or plaited and often held by a fillet or coronet. The older women, and the working women, still wore a wimple or veil over their heads. (The fanciful headdresses—hennins, horned, heart-shaped, etc.—so familiar to us from the fifteenth century when every vestige of hair was hidden or plucked from the forehead, did not appear until the last decade of the fourteenth century).

More details of such matters can be found in the following brief iconography.

Iconography

1. The Wilton Diptych (*c.* 1377), National Gallery, London.
2. The Nine Heroes Tapestries (*c.* 1385), Metropolitan Museum (The Cloisters), New York.
3. *Troilus and Creseyde* frontispiece (*c.* 1400), Corpus Christi College, Cambridge.
4. *Le Térence des Ducs* (1405), Bibliothèque de l'Arsenal, Paris.
5. *Les tres riches heures du Duc de Berry* (1413–16), Musée Condé, Chantilly.
6. The Arnolfini Marriage, Jan Van Eyck (1434), National Gallery, London.

7. Les chasses à Chantilly (manuscript).
   also
8. Sabrina Mitchell, *Medieval Manuscript Painting*, 1964.
9. Souchal, Carli and Gudiol, *Gothic Painting*, 1965.
   (Both the above obtainable in The Contact History of Art series, pub. Wiedenfeld and Nicolson, London.)
10. Iris Brooke, *Medieval Theatre Costume*, 1967, A. & C. Black, London.
11. Iris Brooke, *Western European Costume*, Part I, 1963, Theatre Arts Books, New York.

INDEX

(In the foregoing book the word 'Place' in the theatrical sense—or its equivalents *placea* and *platea*—and the related words 'Hill' and 'Ditch', being so essential to the subject of the study, are referred to, directly or indirectly, on almost every page; but in the Index these five words are listed only as far as concerns the main references.)